Representing Men

Representing Men

Cultural Production and Producers in the Men's Magazine Market

Ben Crewe

Oxford • New York

First published in 2003 by
Berg
Editorial offices:
1st Floor, Angel Court, 81 St Clements Street, Oxford, OX4 1AW, UK
838 Broadway, Third Floor, New York, NY 10003–4812, USA

Berg is the imprint of Oxford International Publishers Ltd.

Library of Congress Cataloguing-in-Publication Data
A catalogue record for this book is available from the Library of Congress.

British Library Cataloguing-in-Publication Data
A catalogue record for this book is available from the British Library.

ISBN   1 85973 736 6 (Cloth)
       1 85973 741 2 (Paper)

Typesetting by Avocet Typeset, Chilton, Aylesbury, Bucks.
Printed in the United Kingdom by Biddles Ltd, Guildford and Kings Lynn

www.bergpublishers.com

Contents

Illustrations

Acknowledgements

I owe a great deal to many people and institutions. This book was made possible by a three-year funding award from the Economic and Social Research Council and by the practitioners who gave up their time to be interviewed. I am very grateful for all the help that they offered and for the enthusiasm they expressed for the research. I hope that they enjoy it.

The Department of Sociology at the University of Essex provided a stimulating and appreciative environment in which to develop the research, and a number of valuable friendships. These are amongst the many relationships that helped me complete the study fairly smoothly, and have provided huge amounts of pleasure, comfort and conversation over a much longer period. Friends from Colchester, Cambridge and elsewhere have made my life extremely rich; I am lucky to have them and hold them in great esteem. Particular thanks must go to those people with whom I lived during the course of the research – Ruwan Fernando, Rachel McLachlan, Madeline Moncrieff, Sue Randall and Sam Wallace – and to Anna Raphael, whose enormous affection and support I shall not forget.

The comments of Mike Roper, Frank Mort and one anonymous reviewer proved extremely stimulating and encouraging, whilst the guidance of Sean Nixon was exemplary throughout. I am indebted to him both intellectually and personally. I would also like to thank Kathleen May and Berg Publishers for taking on the book at a time when many other publishers are reluctant to promote monographs of this kind.

Most of all, I want to thank my grandmas, mum, dad, Deborah, John and Daniel.

Introduction

When *loaded* was launched in April 1994 there was no fanfare reception in the publishing trade press and no protracted debate over the likely success of this new kind of men's magazine. Details of IPC's forthcoming product, a 'cross between *Viz*, *The Face* and *i-D*', covering music, affordable fashion, sport, sex and comedy, had been announced in *Media Week* (28.1.94: 1) and *Press Gazette* in January 1994 (31.1.94: 7), but there was little subsequent discussion of its significance and barely any comment when it arrived on the news-stands in the spring. A short report in the *Guardian* represented Fleet Street's only interest in IPC's endeavour (11.4.94: G2, 16). Only three and a half years later, in August 1997, the *Independent* was devoting its main editorial column, as well as a half-page news story, to events in the men's magazine market (15.8.97: 1, 13). The coverage marked a significant moment in British media history. *FHM* had overtaken the women's magazine *Cosmopolitan* to become the UK's most popular monthly lifestyle title, selling over 500,000 copies per issue. At its peak the following year, *FHM*'s sales reached over 775,000, more than ten times those of five years earlier, whilst overall monthly sales of men's lifestyle magazines topped 2.3 million. Indeed, circulation figures represented average monthly sales over six-month periods, and *FHM* alone was rumoured to have sold over 1 million copies of certain issues during 1998 (see Figure 1). Its achievement was especially remarkable because, whilst general interest magazines for women had flourished throughout the twentieth century and *Cosmopolitan* had been on British news-stands for twenty-five years, the equivalent sector for men had only been resuscitated in the late 1980s after twenty years of being known as the 'graveyard' of magazine publishing (*Campaign Report*, 11.4.97: 4–5).

The initial renaissance of the men's magazine market through the style press and the figure of the 'new man' has been well documented in existing work (Mort 1996; Nixon, 1993; 1996). However, it was in the period following the phase covered by such accounts that the market entered a new paradigm, with 1994 the watershed year and *loaded* pivotal in its transition. Just as *The Face* had transformed the idea of what a popular magazine should look like in the 1980s, *loaded*'s rapid market penetration redefined what advertisers, distributors, retailers, consumers and the publishing community at large understood as 'the

Figure 1 Cover of *FHM*, November 1998, courtesy of *FHM*/Emap.

general interest men's magazine'. Significantly, it was against the existing titles, *Arena*, *GQ* and *Esquire*, that *loaded* appeared to define itself, with the 'new lad' replacing the 'new man' as the imagined consumer of a new generation of magazines. By the end of the decade, promoted through the broadsheet press and the advertising industry, this representation had eclipsed the new man throughout consumer culture as the dominant emblem of contemporary masculinity. As the influence of *loaded* extended beyond its own marketplace into wider commercial culture and public consciousness, the new lad became the new 'truth' about men.

The new lad label had first appeared within men's style titles in the early 1990s as they described their own editorial shifts away from the dominant codings of the market's early years. The transition was marked in both *GQ* and *Arena* in 1991 by an increase in sexualized imagery and examinations of women, and a more 'assertive articulation of the post-permissive masculine heterosexual scripts' already identifiable in both publications (Nixon 1996: 203). Within the industry, Sean O'Hagan's article in *Arena*'s 1991 Spring–Summer issue was one of the earliest and most influential attempts to identify this new male species. Seeking to lay bare the 'myth' of the 'sensitive, caring, emotionally balanced, non-sexist, non-aggressive New Man', O'Hagan depicted his emerging successor as 'a New Man who can't quite shake off his outmoded, but snug-fitting laddishness' (1991: 22). Informed by post-feminist discourse, intelligent, articulate and in tune with contemporary culture, new lads were 'not quite as boorish/tribal/drunken or loud as their prehistoric predecessors' but had neither the will nor the nerve to embrace the new man's more stringent behavioural demands (O'Hagan 1991: 24). They could defend their ideological shortcomings in socio-political terms (though they actually somewhat relished them), and 'tell you how misogynist the new David Lynch film is' (O'Hagan 1991: 24), but might well do so primarily as seduction strategies. Indeed, one of the new lad's defining characteristics was this very ability to switch from old lad to new man as appropriate, albeit never quite descending to the sexist depths of the 'utterly unreconstitutable' male (O'Hagan 1991: 24).

Other early sketches of the new lad portrayed a similar figure. A feature in the *Independent on Sunday* by Alex Kershaw described him as 'a twentysomething, well educated urban male with cosmopolitan tastes ... something of a sophisti-cate, but never pseudo or pretentious' (14.4.91: 19). His icons included 'Pat Nevin, the art-collecting Everton footballer, Roddy Frame, sensitive lead-singer with Aztec Camera, Terry Christian, the cocky Mancunian presenter of *The Word* and Gary Oldman, the film star', but not Gazza: 'too northern and too thick' (Kershaw 1991: 19). His value system was a conscience-free, pragmatic hedo-nism rather than the liberalism of the thirtysomething generation. He was cultured, style-conscious and interested in art: redolent of the sharpness of the mod, and with many of his working-class overtones. Accordingly, he was keen on both the tribal and physical aspects of sport, particularly football, without being a lout. 'If anything, they're hooligan intellectuals', declared one new lad exemplar. Another, the comedian David Baddiel, outlined the new lad's post-feminist position on the opposite sex: 'he finds pornography funny. Of course he's aware of all the arguments about pornography. But he's capable of treating women as sex-objects without being sexist' (Kershaw 1991: 19).

Three years on, *loaded*'s launch team enlisted the new lad label, but also rearticulated some of his primary characteristics. Having informed the press that the magazine would target 'the irreverent sensibilities of the new lad' (*Guardian*, 11.4.94: G2, 16), editor James Brown reiterated the tone of his title by stamping 'superlads' upon the cover of the first issue. Addressing men who 'have accepted what we are and have given up trying to improve ourselves' (Brown, in the *Independent*, 8.9.94: 26), *loaded* seemed to be targeting a male public fairly similar to O'Hagan and Kershaw's conceptions. However, the magazine's rendition of the new lad script was different in several ways from the model of the early 1990s: younger, louder, more hedonistic, not necessarily well educated, well groomed or cosmopolitan, and more likely to mock than celebrate 'sophistication' and earnest sensitivity. Whereas O'Hagan's new lad was knowing and somewhat manipulative in his chameleon posturings, *loaded*'s was presented as unrestrained and without pretence. And whilst O'Hagan's portrait was of an urban intelligentsia distinct from the mass male population, IPC's was of the 'man-on-the-street': the '98% of the male population' for whom the existing publications were 'totally unreal' (*Press Gazette*, 28.3.94: 9).

This characterization was certainly useful in giving colour to *loaded*'s representation of its imagined audience. However, it was the national press, rather than the magazine's producers, which sought to interrogate 'the meaning of new laddism'. Articles about shifts in men's lifestyles and attitudes had proliferated in broadsheet features sections for some time, as growing paginations, changes in taste cultures and the quest for younger consumers and lucrative advertising markets demanded new editorial formats (Tunstall 1996; Curran and Seaton 1997). With the evident success of the mass-market titles, the new lad now became the primary focus of such discussions. Such articles could be divided into three main categories. First, an abundance of pieces that concentrated on explaining the popularity and significance of individual magazines and of the sector as a whole. Second, those that used the market's development as a springboard for broader contemplations on contemporary gender relations. Thus, for example, Suzanne Moore and Ruth Picardie questioned the value of 'laddism' in the light of changing family structures and labour markets (*Independent*, 22.11.96: 21; *Independent on Sunday*, 19.5.96: Features 2–3), whilst Susan Faludi, whose treatise on modern masculinity was given three consecutive days of coverage in the *Guardian* in September 1999, presented men's magazines as indicative of men's increasing integration into 'ornamental culture'.

A third set of articles referenced the men's press and the new lad as signifiers for contemporary masculinity in reports on issues ranging from educational underachievement to male suicide and misogyny. Most notably, in April 1998, the *Independent*'s main story related 'Blair's plan to rescue the lost generation of boys' (27.4.98: 1). The article described the Labour Party's concern about teenage boys involved in crime and drugs whom it had dubbed 'the Loaded

Generation'. Several months later, framed by the launch of *Front*, a ministerial speech calling for men to drop their 'beer, sex and football image' provoked further broadsheet attention (*Observer*, 18.10.98: 12; *The Times*, 10.10.98: 20). The *Leading Lads* report (Katz 1999) on British teenage boys, released in early 1999, likewise drew upon a vocabulary rooted in the men's press. The *Observer* suggested that young men were 'caught in no man's land between Nineties New Man and New Lad' and were 'increasingly turning to laddishness for comfort' (14.3.99: 14). When additional research recorded an increase in young male suicide, 'Lads' culture' was explicitly implicated, both by the *Observer* and the chief executive of the Samaritans (*Observer*, 17.10.99: 13). That the government and one of the country's most established charities were invoking the new lad and the men's press to discuss contemporary masculinity was a telling indication of the currency that both had achieved by the end of the decade. Laddism had become the dominant label for any expression of masculinity that was hedo-nistic, 'ironically' regressive or assertively heterosexual, from the author Arthur Koestler's aggressive womanizing to the Labour Party's 'obsession' with football (*Guardian*, 22.10.98: 6–7; *New Statesman*, 7.8.98: 8).

While the 'new lad' entered public discourse as a written shorthand for these scripts via the broadsheet press, it was through another institutional regime, the advertising industry, that it became embedded as a visual idiom for the condition of modern masculinity. Efforts by advertising agencies and commentators to coin a new way of appealing to the young male consumer featured repeatedly in the industry trade press in the early 1990s. In a number of agency reports, the most celebrated masculine coding of the late 1980s, the new man, was attacked as a defunct and unrealistic portrayal of modern masculinity, out of touch with the 'man-on-the-street'. Grey's 1990 study, 'About men', suggested that new man portrayals had become too 'feminine' and 'soft': 'paying lip service to the more feminine qualities the male has embraced when underneath men are still male chauvinists' (*Campaign*, 16.3.90: 35). Burkitt Weinreich Bryant's 'Man or caveman' report in 1992 echoed such conclusions, suggesting that new man imagery was 'fine if you're offering women a fantasy 90s Prince Charming', but a transparent stereotype to most men (*Campaign*, 7.2.92: 14).

Although displaying command of the cultural zeitgeist was the prime purpose of such reports, notable within them, and the commentary on their assertions, was the absence of a coherent suggestion of what a more suitable representation might be. Grey's vice-chairman, Scott Sherrard, charged that the industry had 'swung hysterically between being too hard and too soft' in its male imagery, and called for a middle course between these extremes (*Campaign*, 16.3.90: 35). Neil Saunders, the author of 'About men', observed that: 'Today's ads contain all sorts of ambiguities and definitions of men because agencies themselves have not decided what men are – macho or sensitive. They don't know the answer'

(*Campaign*, 15.6.90: 39). Three years later, Publicis' 'Rebels without claws' reiterated these sentiments, claiming that young men were still wavering between the 'new man myth' and the 'real man tradition' (*Marketing*, 2.12.93: 22). Matthew Batstone's feature for *Marketing* summed up industry frustration: 'What appears to be happening is that the conventional stereotype of men has died, but nothing has emerged to replace it … marketers have run out of shorthand ways to talk about men' (*Marketing*, 20.10.94: 20–21).

It was the dramatic growth of the men's press that presented an unexpected solution to such uncertainties, offering a clear identity through which to approach young men and capture the changes that agencies had only nebulously grasped. From 1994, advertising campaigns across a range of media drew on the new lad codings projected in the men's press: unashamedly heterosexual, irreverent, often self-mocking, laced with innuendo, culturally referential and generally 'blokeish'. One of the most successful campaigns of this type was WCRS's work for Worthington beer in 1995. When WCRS inherited the Worthington account, the product was struggling with a double-digit sales decline and an outdated image that stood in contrast to the regenerated brand personalities of its competitors. As Charles Vallance, account director at WCRS, recalled, in order to prevent a long-term slump into anonymity, 'It needed its own vocabulary, its own anecdotes, its own identity within beer drinking culture' (Vallance 1997: 1–2).

WCRS looked to focus group research to find an appropriate identity for the Worthington brand. Amongst a sample of target consumers, it found a consistent mood of 'Positive Retrenchment': a belief that the economy was resurgent, that there was 'a greater sense of honesty and realism in society', and that the pressures of the previous decade had been replaced by a 'more tolerant, relaxed and less divisive' culture (Vallance 1997: 3). WCRS believed that this resettlement would have implications for the nature of male sociability and men's attitudes towards what they considered an essentially male product. Indeed, respondents reported feeling less obliged to live up to external expectations of male behaviour, citing the new man as an example of a false ideal being imposed upon them by others. Reacting against such 'gender rules', the target group endorsed a return to more traditional male values, 'a recognition and a celebration of the differences between the sexes, the failings and limitations of both' (Vallance 1997: 3).

Vallance's team believed it had latched onto 'the beginnings of a major social trend … [a] new (or re-discovered) male identity', which it labelled 'blokeishness' (Vallance 1997: 3). What also emerged from the research was men's increasing self-awareness and their grasp of gender stereotypes and emotional display. With *loaded* identified as a similar indication of male self-consciousness, this knowingness became an important component of the Worthington campaign. The advertisements were designed to ride upon a wave of 'blokeish pub culture', drawing on 'mischievously chauvinist ads' from the 1980s but without their brand of anti-female humour (Vallance 1997: 4). Comedian Harry Enfield was chosen as the ideal personality to fit the adverts' values of 'blokeish, funny, knowing, guilt-free political incorrectness' (Vallance 1997: 4). Dressing Enfield in women's clothing, and parodying a well-known pet food campaign, WCRS's effort was widely praised within the industry and lauded as the impetus behind the long-term reversal of Worthington's sales decline.

The same tone, clearly drawn from the men's magazine market, was employed in a host of campaigns during the following few years. Press work for football goods producer Umbro pictured a young fan lying on his bed underneath a poster of a topless model covered only by a football top placed over her body. With him smirking knowingly at the camera, the tag line read 'Who says girls look better with their kit off?' For their Nissan Almera television ads, in a genre conventionally themed through 'performance' and 'escape', TBWA spoofed the 1970s police-action series *The Professionals*, describing the result as 'fun, nostalgic laddishness'. An acclaimed campaign for Supernoodles featured a man yielding to his girlfriend's pleas for a portion of his meal only after having spotted their dog, out of her sight, lick the plate. Some 'laddish' adverts were rather more heavy-handed, resulting in several censures from the Advertising Standards Authority about distasteful language and imagery. Amongst those deemed to have breached acceptable boundaries were Atlantic 252's 'Long-wave radio has the biggest hits' advert, and Club 18–30's 'Beaver Espana' campaign (*Campaign*, 1.11.96: 7).

There were certainly differences between the tones and target markets of those campaigns bracketed together as 'New Lad ads' (*Campaign*, 11.10.96: 40). However, as in the press, the term had become a sweeping descriptor for modes of representation that both mocked and celebrated traditional stereotypes of the male role. Quickly and deeply engrained in advertising vernacular, it provided an easily recognized language amongst industry agents and seemed to offer a realistic and effective means of addressing the young, male public. Indeed, the realism of the approach was deemed to be a significant part of its appeal. Vallance's belief that men had become more aware of gender stereotypes and representational conventions was repeated throughout industry assessments of male markets. In such circumstances, 'inclusive' or 'complicit' codings, which acknowledged the hyperbole of traditional marketing approaches and recognized a more critical, less idealised consumer, were considered more effective than the highly aspirational appeals that had characterized the 1980s (*Campaign*, 1.11.96: 27). Many adverts, such as those for Umbro and Supernoodles, were thus designed to speak to the viewer who recognized that he was fulfilling a male cliché.

The spread of new lad formats was equally striking elsewhere in commercial culture. Television programmes such as *Men Behaving Badly*, *TFI Friday*, *Fantasy Football League* and *They Think It's All Over* typified screen versions of the new lad script, whilst the books of Nick Hornby (in particular, the football themed autobiography *Fever Pitch* and the music-oriented novel *High Fidelity*), Mike Gayle (*My Legendary Girlfriend*; *Turning Thirty*; *Mr Commitment*) and Tony Parsons (*Man and Boy*) exemplified a lucrative new publishing canon, labelled 'lad lit'. Meanwhile, the appeal of the new lad address was such that, by the end of the decade, the *Daily Star* tabloid appeared increasingly like a newsprint version of a 'lads magazine', a congruence that was almost cemented in 1999 when *TFI Friday* host Chris Evans tried to take over the title with plans to install at its helm the former *FHM* editor Mike Soutar.

Whether the new lad was a genuinely 'realistic' characterization of modern masculinity is not the main concern of this book. Undoubtedly though, and despite the frequent misuse of the label, the dramatic ascendance of mass market magazines and the codings that they fostered registered important elements of lived masculinity amongst a significant population of men beyond consumer publishing. The broader impact of the market should also now be apparent. The aim of this book is to examine the market's development during the 1990s though an empirical investigation of its production conditions and producers, based largely upon interviews with publishing practitioners and analysis of the industry trade press (see appendix and bibliography for further details).

There are important precursors here, both in the magazines that preceded the emergence of the mass-market titles and the studies that have explored them. In this respect, the works of Frank Mort (1996) and Sean Nixon (1993, 1996) have been crucial in framing the conceptual approach and empirical substance of this book. In its broad perspective, my study emulates their departure from established modes of cultural analysis that have focussed upon the political-economic determinants, textual meanings or consumption of cultural forms. The latter phases of the 'cultural circuit' have been the focus of most research into girls' and women's magazines. Thus, a number of accounts have examined the representations of femininity that such products have promoted (McRobbie 1978; Tuchman et al. 1978; Winship 1980, 1983, 1987; Ballaster et al. 1991; Jackson 1996), and the often active, escapist and self-supporting ways in which they are consumed (Frazer 1987; Radway 1988; Hermes 1995). However, such studies have often divorced production contexts altogether from discussions of content and consumption, or have subsumed them into overarching logics of capitalist or patriarchal reproduction. In noting that representations need to resonate with fantasies that readers would 'already recognize and be embroiled in, "outside" the magazine context' (1983: 45), and in outlining how publishing companies construct titles in response to wider social and cultural shifts, both through research (as in Ernest Dichter's assessment of *Woman's Own* in 1963) and intuition (for example, editors at *She* who sought primarily to please themselves and then hoped to find readers who would share their values), Winship (1987) has been almost alone amongst scholars of women's magazines in touching upon the mechanisms through which producers necessarily engage with the lived cultures of consumers (see also McRobbie 1994, 1999a). And yet this point is crucial, for while magazine culture appears particularly agile in responding to shifting cultural currents (Thornton 1995) – albeit within certain parameters of profitability – we have little understanding of how this process occurs.

This dialectic and the practitioners at the heart of it are central to the interests of and influences upon this book. In focussing on the professional knowledges and practices of commercial producers, and the institutional cultures and contexts in which they operate, Mort and Nixon, amongst others, have not only helped to excavate a rather concealed area of the cultural circuit and challenged political-economic approaches to commercial production. They have also looked at the means by which lived identities are assessed, refashioned and re-presented by cultural intermediaries within commercial institutions in what is a two-way dialogue between consumer capitalism and popular experience. Structural factors and economic imperatives are by no means elided here, but the influence, authority and informal knowledges of specific individuals are also foregrounded as key determinants of cultural markets.

This book's primary argument draws heavily on this approach, contending that the cultural resources and identities of certain key practitioners within the men's press need to be taken into account in order fully to understand the formation of individual titles and the sector as a whole during the 1990s. Although, as I outline in due course, this is suggested in the work of Mort and Nixon, my research elucidates their claims through a more direct inquiry than has been previously undertaken. I establish the analysis in Part II, where I attend to the processes, practices and structures of magazine publishing. Here, the chapters are organized to emphasise the relationships between different determinants, practitioners and knowledges in the formation of magazines and markets, both during launches and in their subsequent and ongoing elaboration. This sensitivity to the temporal is also important in the sense that this account examines a particular magazine market, at a particular stage, and during a particular time period. Although my findings will have relevance beyond these spheres, they must be seen in the context from which they were ascertained.

In Chapter 2, then, I provide some of this context by scrutinizing the launches of the sector's most successful and influential products, and summarizing the resulting shifts in the men's lifestyle press over the decade. The aim is partly to describe in more detail the transitions I have already outlined. It is also to explore how individual magazines, potential audiences and the market as a whole were discursively conceptualized at this time by industry personnel. One issue that begins to be addressed is why the publishing community, for all its claims to be in intimate contact with wider culture, was taken by surprise by *loaded*'s success and the subsequent transformation of the sector. I identify the relationship between formal and informal knowledges and the pivotal role of editorial personnel in the perception and formation of new products as particularly relevant. These issues receive further attention in Chapter 3, where launch logics and anatomies in the 1990s men's press are examined at a more general level. Here, I distinguish between the different stages of launch developments, the roles and expertise of editors and publishers in these processes, and some of the institutional and economic factors that structured them.

Chapter 4 expands on these concerns, situating editorial and publishing practices and personnel within a broader context, and outlining the structural conditions and dynamics of the industry. Here, I continue to analyse the relationship between competing imperatives in the market, mainly those relating to editorial and advertising interests, and their effects upon magazine forms at different publishing companies. This does not represent a capitulation to the terms of political economy, but an attempt to map in more detail than has previously been offered the conflicts, coalitions and connections between 'commercial' and 'creative' practitioners, and the interaction of the 'economic' and the 'cultural' in the determination of magazine forms. The power of individual editors to negotiate autonomy and to assert authority in defining their magazines is a key concern here, and is related to factors such as market conditions and the scarcity of knowledge about readers.

It is by detailing in Part II the strategies by which editorial personnel assessed and understood their audiences, and by deconstructing the nature of editorial knowledge and expertise, that an in-depth examination of the backgrounds, affiliations and ambitions of some specific editors is justified. Men's lifestyle journalism in the 1990s is marked out as a job in which personal and professional knowledges were relatively indivisible, such that personal identities and forms of cultural and social capital were key elements in the employability of editorial practitioners. In the first chapter of Part III, I suggest that there were significant implications here for the occupational self-understandings of *loaded*'s editorial co-founders that coalesced around issues of class and gender. Indeed, masculinity is implicated throughout this Part of the book, as I focus on the connections between the masculine subjectivities and journalistic identities of the editors of *loaded*, *Esquire* and *Arena* and the scripts produced in their titles. With *loaded* the most formative magazine in the transformation of the men's press, its selection for detailed attention in Part III is clearly appropriate. As upmarket titles associated with an earlier moment in the market, the choices of *Esquire* and *Arena* are also germane.

Indeed, it is important to understand the new lad as part of a longer history of the commercial representation of masculinity that has been particularly intensive in the post-war years, and especially in the last two decades. In attempting to integrate men into spheres traditionally associated with women, consumer industries have offered an increasingly diverse range of identities to men, in which consumption practices have often been more significant than conventional tropes of masculinity relating to work, class and provision. The new lad may, in this respect, seem somewhat anachronistic. Whilst, as Nixon points out, its emergence did not, in fact, 'mark a complete reversal of the shifts associated with the "new man"' (Nixon 1996: 5), to many commentators, the new lad appeared far more rooted in working-class culture and considerably less progressive in its sexual politics than its predecessor. A typical interpretation bemoaned a 'hedonistic, hard-drinking he-man … interested only in football, booze, bonking and babes' (*Independent*, 8.9.94: 26). My analysis does not attempt a formal semiotic reading of the new lad. However, by addressing the production determinants and producers responsible for its formation, it does suggest the need to understand this representation of gender as rather more complex than certain accounts (Edwards 1997; Whelehan 2000) have claimed it to be. It is by comparing branches of the men's press identified with the new man and the new lad that I draw attention to certain similarities and distinctions (or continuities and discontinuities) between different editors and magazines, and the social, educational and professional experiences in which these differences were based. The stratified and dynamic nature of cultures of masculinity is not only intrinsically significant here; it is also relevant in relation to the commercial importance of established magazines adjusting to perceptions of shifting and differentiated readership structures. Accommodations made by the first generation of men's magazines during the late 1990s are thus assessed in Part III, in relation to market instability, brand histories and the resources, interests and identifications of their editors.

The book draws upon significant academic fields on masculinity and magazine culture. However, as I have suggested, it has been primarily informed by a growing literature in an emerging area of cultural analysis, one that pays particular attention to the role of cultural intermediaries in the passage of cultural forms, or the 'circuit of culture' (Hall 1980; du Gay 1997). It is these spheres that I shall now address, outlining some of the theoretical, conceptual and empirical works that have situated this study.

Part I
Magazines, Masculinity and Cultural Analysis

Literature Review and Conceptual Orientation

Political Economy and Productionist Paradigms

My focus in this book upon cultural producers and cultures of production in men's magazine publishing has been stimulated by a growing interest in cultural intermediaries and media institutions that I shall outline shortly. The emerging paradigm of cultural economy (du Gay 1997; du Gay and Pryke 2002) in which this work is located has been developed as a challenge to traditional productionist approaches to commercial culture, yet it retains many of the concerns of political economy and other established branches of media sociology. Many of these – questions about producer–consumer relationships, the interaction of the commercial and the creative, professional knowledges and practices, the perception of media audiences, and occupational autonomy and constraint – are revisited in this book.

Underpinning the foundational claims of media 'political economy' is classical Marxist theory, in particular, a portion of *The German Ideology* of 1845 which states that control of 'the means of mental production' and thus 'the production and distribution of the ideas of the age' lies in the hands of 'the class which has the means of material production' (Marx and Engels 1938: 64). At its most vulgar and determinist, the passage could be taken to indicate that the media are simply ideological tools of the ruling classes (Murdock and Golding 1977; Garnham 1979). However, from their earliest articles, political economists rejected this crude version of materialism, insisting that economic relations were determinate in Raymond Williams' sense of 'setting limits, exerting pressures and closing off options' (Williams 1973: 4, in Murdock and Golding 1977: 16).

Regarding the economic as '*ultimately* the most powerful of the many levers operating in cultural production' (Murdock and Golding 1977: 20), political economists have made patterns of ownership and capital accumulation the privileged objects of their analysis. Empirical work has outlined how the economic dynamics of production, such as the need to maximize audiences and advertising revenues, and tendencies towards concentration, monopolization and conglomeration, have material effects on media output and wider public discourse, systematically promoting the values of the powerful and marginalizing those of the economically subordinate (Murdock and Golding 1977, 1991; Garnham

1980; Murdock 1982). Thus, for example, Murdock and Golding (1977) reasoned that newspapers serving working-class readerships would prove unviable even at circulations significantly higher than those serving middle-class constituencies because their audiences appealed much less to advertisers.

As even committed proponents have recognized, and as critics have emphasized, illustrating precisely how economic determinants are converted into media messages is not possible through a narrow political economy alone (Murdock and Golding 1977; Garnham 1990). Unless media institutions are to be presented as unmediated mechanisms of ruling-class control, and their practitioners merely as ciphers for ruling-class ideology, their internal social structures, ideologies, interests and practices would also need to be investigated. In recent work, whilst reiterating their belief in the primacy of economic forces, political economists have recognized that previous work has suffered from a degree of determinism, and that the precise relationship between the economic and the symbolic, and the practices and motivations of cultural workers, demand renewed attention (Murdock 1982, 1997; Garnham 1990; McGuigan 1992; Ferguson and Golding 1997).

Traditions of such studies do exist. First, in the ethnographic, but ultimately limited, sociologies of American media workplaces and newsroom 'gatekeepers' (prototypically, White 1950; see Schudson 1991 for a critical appraisal); and, second, in UK studies of media professionals that have highlighted the complex interplay of autonomy and constraint, and 'cultural' and 'commercial' goals. Thus, Tunstall's (1971) study of specialist journalists revealed the different balances of revenue (advertising and audience) and non-revenue (policy, influence, prestige etc.) goals that were germane to different news fields (see also Schlesinger 1978). Meanwhile, Elliott (1977) noted the significance of notions of 'professionalism' in enabling media workers to deal with their daily role dilemmas and conflicts, and to steer between the rocks of 'art' and 'commerce'. Thus, 'professionalism' was invoked strategically to negotiate autonomy from executive control or to justify peer group judgement criteria above those relating to purely commercial ends. As Tunstall's study also illustrated, these means of accommodation meant that overt conflict with owners was a rare occurrence.

The observation that professionalism was used as a guiding mechanism for production decisions, in which the judgements and tastes of producing agents were, in effect, transposed onto those of the audience, was significant here. Schlesinger (1978) proposed that professionalism was the missing link between communicators and the effectively abstract recipients that they often knew little about and whose feedback they generally ignored. Professionalism, then, was the condensed definition of implicit occupational knowledge about how to communicate, whilst the real audiences that journalists had in mind were often each other, superiors, sources and highly interested readers.

The assessment of consumers and markets by the institutions of media production is an area that has also been addressed in the 'production-of-culture' paradigm that has developed in the US, relatively independently of British media enquiry (see Gans 1972; Peterson 1976; Crane 1992, 1994). This perspective has aimed to identify laws of symbol production using oligopoly models from economic theory (Peterson and Berger 1975), according to which organizations produce relatively homogeneous products and innovate little unless threatened by competition. Cultural products are seen to reflect not the values of a single, class producer, as in political economy, but as being primarily dependent on the size and financial power of production companies and the nature of their markets. Producers are thus forced to be responsive to consumers when sectors are turbulent, and are better able to represent public tastes when audiences form as observable groups, as in the popular music industry (Crane 1992). In other markets, uncertainty about consumers (Gitlin's 'problem of knowing' (1983)) demands alternative strategies. If production costs per unit are low, firms may overproduce, accepting that many products will fail for others to succeed (Hirsch 1972; also Garnham 1987: 31). Other techniques that might be used to mitigate the uncertainties of production include the deployment of successful past formulae, recognized 'stars', psychological knowledge and intermediary contacts (Elliott 1977).

Recent research within productionist paradigms confirms that, to guide their production practices, media industries and practitioners rely on rules, precedents and axioms about audiences and commodities (Gitlin 1983; Turow 1991; Ettema and Whitney 1994). Yet, despite enormous advances in audience research techniques, cultural producers often remain unclear about how to conceptualize consumers, and cynical about attempts to survey them (Gitlin 1983). Such scepticism may be justified, not just because rules of thumb ('science fiction doesn't work on television') and empirical data are so often proved wrong. More importantly, knowledge about an audience can be seen as 'institutionally effective' data (Ettema and Whitney 1994: 5): a discursive construct measured within a body of institutional knowledge to 'serve particular purposes and reflect particular interests' (Ettema and Whitney 1994: 10; Peterson 1994). The point, then, is that there is always some discrepancy between actual consumers and the form in which they are imagined or measured as a 'market' (Turow 1991; Peterson 1994). Such incongruities are highlighted when, in their revelation of 'new' consumer segmentations that demand new product conventions, innovative measurement techniques effectively reconstruct the markets they have been employed ostensibly to 'gauge' (Gitlin 1983; Peterson 1994).

Some analysts have regarded attempts by media institutions to measure their audiences with ever-greater accuracy as somewhat sinister. Ang (1991) contends that audience appraisal techniques are designed only to meet the 'vested interests' of media producers, and elsewhere echoes a Marxist argument that audiences are merely commodities sold by producers to advertisers. Here, consumer sovereignty is seen to exist only insofar as consumer interests overlap with those of advertisers (Smythe 1977, cited in Garnham 1979 and Turow 1991; Harms and Kellner 1991). What is missing from such analysis is the sense that, in allowing cultural producers to respond to audience preferences, market research might actually empower consumers. It is an emerging model of cultural analysis that does assume a more sensitive dialectic between cultural production and consumption which I now want to outline.

Post-Fordism and 'Cultural Economy'

It is in providing a more 'joined up' guide to cultural analysis that the 'circuit of culture' (du Gay et al. 1997) is proving an increasingly popular heuristic amongst researchers of commercial culture. Represented as a circular system without an apex or endpoint, the model indicates that the full analysis of cultural forms must take into account each 'moment' in a circuit of production, regulation, represen-tation, consumption and identity. Each moment is connected to every other via two-way arrows to imply codependence at every level and to avoid suggesting the guaranteed primacy of any one stage in determining the outcome or shape of any other. The aim here is to indicate that each field exerts some influence on every other, and to suggest the investigation of the relationships between how cultural forms are constructed, represented and distributed by producers, their formal, textual properties and their use and interpretation by consumers (du Gay et al. 1997; see also Johnson 1986; Thompson 1988). Jackson et al. (2000) have likewise recommended tracing commercial chains 'not in linear terms of encoding/decoding, but in terms of circuits of exchange, with permeable bound-aries that are subject to all manner of creative leakages', whilst, in consumption studies, Fine and Leopold (1993: 22) have argued for the need to look concretely at how the character of consumption in any one sector is affected by a distinct system of provision in which production, distribution and consumption processes are 'not independent of each other, nor is there a rigid one-way line of determi-nation between them' (see also Miller 1995).

The treatment of power and determination in such models could be seen as a little vague or 'capillary'. However, there are considerable gains in assuming that the connections between different determining factors are contingent and multiple rather than necessary and one-directional, and in presenting such rela-tionships as open to empirical investigation. Furthermore, the cultural circuit avoids a simplistic understanding of power in the cultural field as residing at the top end of a linear 'chain' of production–text–consumption – which is how it is, in effect, postulated in mass communications, Frankfurt School and political-economic paradigms. This is not just to appreciate the complex and active nature of consumer practices, and that cultural circuits are thus 'leaky' (Glennie and Thrift 1993; Jackson 2000). More significantly, to imagine consumers at the end point of a production chain is to misrepresent the reality of the production process in most commercial markets. Consumers have an effect in the cultural field not just as interpreters and meaning-makers of pre-produced artefacts. They also play a critical role in the production process itself, as imagined audiences in the minds of programme-makers, editors and similar practitioners, or through direct feedback via focus groups and consumer questionnaires. Invoked and incorporated into decision-making processes, cultural consumers are thereby comprehensively integrated into the production dynamic.[1]

The concerns of previous research fields with these 'imaginary feedback loops' (Gans 1972) and the ongoing dynamic between producers and consumers are much better served by this conceptualization of the cultural field than their own more mechanical, uni-linear and determinist assumptions. This is particularly the case in a post-Fordist culture of flexible specialization where manufacturers are increasingly able and commercially required to respond rapidly to changes in consumer demand. There are technological, economic and cultural dimensions to this tighter, more integrated system of production, distribution and retail: the enabling technologies of 'just-in-time' computer-aided production techniques, and point-of-sale electronics that provide retailers with immediate purchase data that can be fed into stock and manufacturing orders (du Gay 1993; Nixon 1996); increasingly powerful retail conglomerates who have wrested control away from manufacturers in certain commercial sectors (du Gay 1993; Glucksmann 1998); more intense supply side competition in many markets (Lury 1994); rising consumer literacy; and the perception of increasingly unpredictable and fragmented consumer markets (Nixon 1996). In such circumstances, marketing-led procedures have become crucial in battles amongst cultural producers for competitive advantage. As their preferences are monitored with increasing interest, consumers are drawn ever more closely into decision-making in the sphere of production.

Cultural intermediaries – by which I mean those practitioners who mediate the spheres of cultural production and consumption – are central in such articulations and in post-Fordist commercial dynamics as a whole (although the degree to which they represent a new, expanding and increasingly influential strata is debatable – see McFall 2000; Featherstone 1991; Lash and Urry 1994). As advertising planners, image-makers, market researchers, retail psychologists and lifestyle designers, they are pivotal in assessing consumers, conveying their values to cultural producers, and re-representing consumers back to themselves through the symbolic work that they perform in aligning products – via appropriate meanings, images and 'retail relationships' – to consumer lifestyles (Lash and Urry 1994).

In such brokering positions, cultural intermediaries also demand attention because, by assessing market potential ('Will advertisers back it? Is there an audience for it?') and mobilizing consumer representations ('our reader is *middle-youth*'), they bring into relief the mutual constitution of the 'cultural' and the 'economic' that is a central assumption of 'cultural economy'. Whilst political economy regards economic determinants as unproblematically 'objective' and abstract phenomena that bring cultural meanings into effect, cultural economy sees them as always, inherently cultural (Nixon 1993, 1996; Lash and Urry 1994; Mort 1996; du Gay 1997; Jackson et al. 2000). Thus, economic processes and practices do not unfurl through an effortless logic or 'rational calculus' (Jackson et al. 2000: 1). To be effective, they must be imagined and given meaning by those people involved in them. As Don Slater (2002: 59) summarizes, 'in practice, social actors cannot actually define a market or a competitor, let alone act in relation to them, except through extensive forms of cultural knowledge'. The economy itself has to be conceptualized by governments, businesses and individuals in order to be intervened in and managed (du Gay 1997; du Gay and Pryke 2002). Likewise, Nixon (1993, 1996) shows that in the UK men's magazine market in the late 1980s, 'economic' practices and production decisions had discursive conditions of existence in the sense that they only came into force through professional languages and understandings of target markets that were evidently cultural.

Cultural economy holds no foundational preconceptions about the relative determining power of culture and economy. Treating questions of causation in this way does not mean evacuating such issues from the research agenda, nor does it preclude one from making strong assertions about the power of economic forces (du Gay and Pryke 2002). In fact, it engenders a commitment to subjecting commercial dynamics to empirical scrutiny such that the economy–culture dialectic can be more richly delineated (Mort 1996; Jackson et al. 2000). This does, of course, imply the existence of some distinction between culture and economy that compromises an attempt to fully transcend the established dualism (see du Gay and Pryke 2002: 8–12). However, it also reflects an important difference between the ambitions of cultural economy and those of the other research paradigms I have so far reviewed. In looking for general, rather than abstract laws of cultural production, both political-economic and production-of-culture approaches subordinate individual intentions and influences, and interpersonal relationships and resources, to economic, social and organizational structures. Cultural products are seen almost entirely as the outcomes of coherent – rather than complex and often conflictual – group processes, organizational 'needs', market arrangements and material forces. A cultural economic focus on the micro-practices of commercial culture emphasizes the agency and creativity that occurs within, and itself reconfigures, these structural constraints and imperatives. Its concern with the cultural dimensions of commercial provision highlights the specificity of occupational languages and institutional conventions, as they develop historically and often incoherently. Change and anomaly are much better explained through such close scrutiny. Equally, seeing cultural markets, forms and representations as intrinsically interesting encourages the gendered, ethnic and sexualized characteristics of commercial production to be brought fully to the fore. As relatively powerful agents in this field (du Gay 1993; Nixon 1996, 1997; McRobbie 1998, 1999a), cultural intermediaries are not, of course, neutral conduits here. Rather, they have values, interests and identifications that operate in distinctive and formative ways in defining the cultural goods they are involved in producing.

Cultural Work, Production and Producers

One of the most influential commentaries on cultural practitioners remains Pierre Bourdieu's discussion of the 'new petite bourgeoisie' in *Distinction* (1984). Bourdieu locates the new petite bourgeoisie within a lower middle-class that includes shopkeepers, craftsmen, junior executives and office workers, and that sits alongside the new bourgeoisie in an emerging middle-class.

> The new petite bourgeoisie comes into its own in all the occupations involving presentation and representation (sales, marketing, advertising, public relations, fashion, decoration and so forth) and in all the institutions providing symbolic goods and services. These include the various jobs in … cultural production and organization (youth workers, play leaders, tutors and monitors, radio and tv producers and presenters, magazine journalists). (1984: 359)

The class backgrounds of members of the new petite bourgeoisie are diverse. Some derive from high social origins, but have not acquired the academic qualifications expected of them and seek refuge in occupations where their inherited cultural capital – an ease with culture and concepts – and connections can be most profitably employed (Bourdieu 1984: 357–62). Others have been promoted from lower social class backgrounds, those who Lury (1996: 101) suggests have benefited most from the expansion of further education in the post-war decades. For both sub-fractions, cultural occupations are attractive in demanding little in the way of formal qualifications, but, rather, non-certified, unofficial knowledges that are more populist and eclectic – 'jazz, cinema, strip cartoons … jeans, rock' (Bourdieu 1984: 360) – than the elite culture of the traditional bourgeoisie.

Bourdieu is also decisive in positioning the new petite bourgeoisie as the 'vanguard' promoter and beneficiary of the 'new economy' that values individualism, consumerism and a 'morality of pleasure as duty' over the sobriety and asceticism of an older economic system (1984: 367). The new petite bourgeoisie is presented as the 'natural ally, both economically and politically', of the new bourgeoisie, recognizing in its commercial partner its 'probable destination [and] human ideal (the 'dynamic' executive)' (Bourdieu 1984: 365–6). Accompanying such commitments, the new petite bourgeoisie is at the forefront of a range of new lifestyle practices. These include 'the search for self-expression ... a cult for personal health and psychological therapy' (Bourdieu 1984: 367), and new forms of childrearing, exercise and sexual expression in which 'liberation', pleasure, creativity and communication are emphasized over conventional values of discipline, responsibility and solitude. Such practices are transformed into expertise and occupations whose countercultural spirit reflects the new petite bourgeoisie's self-image as 'unclassifiable ... "marginal", anything rather than categorised or assigned to a class' (Bourdieu 1984: 370).

Despite doubts about the generalizability of Bourdieu's findings (Lamont 1992; Peterson and Simkus 1992), some authors have adopted his stencil of this culturally eclectic, hedonistic, consumerist and highly self-reflexive class fraction to make claims about the role of the new middle-class in promoting an increasingly dominant postmodernist sensibility (Featherstone 1991; Lash and Urry 1987). This is seen to entail the collapse of traditional taste boundaries, the aestheticization of everyday life, and the growing popularity of practices such as 'travelling-the-world' (Munt 1994), vegetarian cuisine and body maintenance techniques (Featherstone 1991). Savage et al.'s (1992) empirical work confirms the existence of a 'postmodern' lifestyle amongst certain private sector workers, with young, male, London-based advertising executives most likely to fit the template, in which high art and opera are consumed along with clubbing and stock car racing, and health and fitness are taken seriously alongside a hedonistic consumer ethic (1992: 108). However, the mechanisms through which such values and interests might be hegemonized through the working practices of these professionals are not investigated. Indeed, studies that take as their *starting* point the attitudes, affiliations and work practices of cultural intermediaries, rather than postmodern culture itself, are scarce. One consequence is that cultural workers are often portrayed as a relatively homogeneous stratum, a depiction that I seek to challenge in this book.

There are some precedents to Bourdieu's work, though limited and partial ones, in British media sociology's concern with the occupational structures and dynamics of media institutions. These were found consistently to draw their personnel from a broad range of middle-class backgrounds (Boyd-Barrett 1970), to demand little in the way of educational certification, to lack routinized and organized career paths, and to recruit and promote people according to factors such as reputation, track record and other 'personal' qualities rather than through formalized and universalistic criteria (Elliott 1977). What McRobbie (1998) has recently confirmed as the indeterminacy, fluidity, volatility and sheer 'messiness' of media careers are amongst those features that rather undermine any claims that media industries might have to be true 'professions' (Tunstall 1971: 69). Indeed, they point to some of the distinctive characteristics of work undertaken in a wider, expanding set of service and creative industries. Conventionally, work has been defined as something oppositional or supplementary to leisure and consumption. Industrialization is seen to have fragmented everyday life in a way that has differentiated work and non-work time into distinct domains, such that they are 'rarely engaged with at the same time' (Anderson 1961/1998: 22; see Wynne 1998; Clarke and Critcher 1985). What is striking, then, about work in cultural and creative realms is that it involves more than the provision of abstract labour or technical skill, instead demanding aptitudes and knowledge that would normally be associated with the spheres of consumption, leisure and the 'everyday' rather than work and production (du Gay 1993; Hochschild 1983). Although there are significant differences between the air hostess, marriage guidance counsellor, advertising creative, clothes shop assistant and hotel receptionist in terms of skill level, pay and conditions, each is asked to deploy some form of cultural or aesthetic capital (Bourdieu 1984), 'emotional labour' (Hochschild 1983) or 'personality' (albeit that this is often trained or scripted). As Bourdieu himself notes, this blurs normal boundaries between work and non-work: 'In place of abrupt, all-or-nothing breaks, between study and work, between work and retirement, there is an impalpable, infinitesimal slippage' (1984: 155–6). One question raised in this book is how such characteristics might have implications for the gender identities of the people who work in such occupations.

The realities of creative labour are certainly becoming clearer through a number of recent empirical studies. McRobbie's (1998) research on fashion designers reveals a set of predominantly female practitioners who see themselves as artists rather than 'dressmakers' and rationalize economic failure as creative success. Such values are encouraged by the institutions of fashion education, which nurture 'expressive individualism' (1998: 40) and defend their high-art credentials by detaching design from the 'debased' skills of manufacture and labour. McRobbie highlights how these characteristics are particularly problematic given the brittle nature of the industry's economic foundations. Most designers experience unemployment, low pay and long hours, yet their training and self-understandings render them unable or disinclined to work in more productive ways.

Even more recently, McRobbie (2002: 97) has labelled self-employed cultural work as 'permanently transitional', requiring 'risk-taking activity and high degrees of mobility' and relying on 'disembedded and highly individualized personnel'. Jackson et al. (2001) identify the same characteristics in men's magazine publishing – and I address these issues in coming chapters. They suggest that high staff turnover indicates the hard-nosed ambitions of certain personnel, but also a working world in which the shelf life of knowledge and expertise is highly transient. The industry's 'public front of playfulness', spontaneity and informality not only masks some of the realities of editorial work, and supports gendered connotations of hedonistic sociability, it also points to the 'willingness of magazine journalists ... temporarily to reinvent themselves' to suit the demands of the occupation (Jackson et al. 2001: 59).

The bigger picture, McRobbie argues, is a profoundly insecure and demanding occupational sphere, lacking loyalty, unions and social insurance, which presents itself, and has been portrayed through government discourse alike, as empowering, egalitarian and self-expressive when it may be quite the opposite. Thus, like other service sector workers addressed or 'subjectivized' by ideologies of creativity and entrepreneurship, cultural and creative workers may experience their labour as pleasurable and rewarding even when it is in many ways exploitative and disempowering (du Gay 1996). Certainly, as McRobbie (2002: 110) outlines, the few empirical accounts of contemporary creative workers confirm conditions of meagre rewards, frequent unemployment and 'enforced youthfulness'. However, she maintains that, rather than colluding in a form of self-regulation that services capitalist reorganization, fashion designers oppose the tenets of Thatcherite enterprise culture in their retention of notions of artistic commitment. By also suggesting that they are not 'artists' in the 'traditional and elitist sense' but 'very ordinary people' (1998: 149), like Featherstone (1991), she depicts creative professionals as more progressive than the new petite bourgeoisie described in *Distinction*. Likewise, McRobbie's (1999a) collected writings celebrate an entrepreneurial stratum of music producers and artists, often from socially, educationally and ethnically marginal backgrounds, whose works she welcomes as culturally and aesthetically innovative and radical.

One implication is that cultural producers and output may be progressive even when production cultures and conditions are quite deeply oppressive. What is less clear, as in Featherstone's work, is the crucial question of *how* the backgrounds and values of these personnel are transmitted into progressive forms of culture. Elsewhere, McRobbie (1994, 1999b) has rightly called for further investigation into the knowledge, debates and cultures that have created the new femininities emerging in girls' magazines, and demanded more research into how consumers are imagined and represented by editorial staff in their production decisions. In her own (1998) brief discussion of women's fashion magazines, she argues that editors are fairly active and prescriptive in setting the terms of their magazines. To do so, they deploy power and justify decisions through references to 'the reader' which are ways of 'controlling the flow of copy' (1998: 152). More specifically, through such strategies, editors on UK fashion titles have been able to sponsor individual designers and explicitly champion British design.

Marjorie Ferguson's (1983) analysis of women's magazines represents an earlier and important contribution to the analysis of editorial 'gatekeeping'. Ferguson highlights, first, how editorial power is enhanced by the 'special expertise' that the editor carries about the nature of the audience (1983: 128). Second, she notes that editors use 'all aspects' of 'experience' to write their magazines (Ferguson 1983: 129), with formal research playing only a post hoc role in editorial production – though the rational 'thinkers' amongst editors are more receptive to research findings than the intuitive 'feelers' (Ferguson 1983: 141). Third, Ferguson suggests that editors often have significant personal invest-ments in their titles, viewing their magazines as extensions of themselves. Despite such commitments, she claims, editors define professional success in economic terms (i.e. according to circulation and advertising revenues), with duties towards readers only secondary matters. Nonetheless, negotiations between the two markets that editors feel obliged to serve are clearly ongoing, subject to professional vetoes and claims of 'personal integrity'.

More recently, Conekin (2000) has argued that *Playboy* cannot be understood without a consideration of the biography and character of Hugh Hefner, its creator and editor (see also Osgerby 2001). Thus, the magazine's 'playboy' iden-tity and its format of 'beautiful women and conservative fashions' are traced to Hefner's own self-image, his obsession with sex which developed through reading the Kinsey Report whilst at university, and his brief employment at *Esquire* (Conekin 2000: 463). Though incisive and provocative, what is missing from Conekin's report is a sense of how Hefner's editorial ambitions were sustained, compromised and negotiated within the publishing system itself. It is these dynamics of cultural production that I seek to outline in this book, dynamics in which editorial practices, and the processes of consumer assessment that are central to the new commercial economy, are axiomatic.

Again, there is some work on which to build here. Concrete studies indicate that market research features increasingly as an intermediary tool in advertising, the music industry and magazine publishing (Negus 1992; Mort 1996; Nixon 1996; Nava 1997). However, it is also clear that the actual influence, role and status of research findings are not straightforward matters. By academic stan-dards, the quality of much research work is often poor, incorporating dubious methodology and analysis (Mort 1996; Nava 1997); and research reports in advertising may be used by agencies to impress clients rather than to inform campaigns (Nava 1997). When research is taken more seriously, it may still only function as a supplement to 'experience and gut feeling', and may be considered valuable only by certain personnel – although there may be elements of machismo and self-aggrandizement in disavowals of the utility of research

(Jackson et al. 2001). Negus (1992) notes that, in the music industry, marketing staff use research to refine intuitive judgements of how to develop and promote already established artists, whilst artist and repertoire staff see research as incapable of identifying and assessing potential new acts and products. Instead, they use a network of smaller record and production companies, regional contacts and talent spotters to keep in touch with new musical trends and artists, and apply 'intuition' alone to judge potential new artists – albeit that notions of 'gut feel' mask implicit criteria such as song quality, originality, image and live performance.

Nixon (1997) corroborates Negus' observations, showing that the value placed on research in the advertising industry varies across occupational divisions, with 'creative' practitioners particularly cynical about its utility (see also Lury 1994). Certainly then, as Negus proposes, there may be no consensus amongst commercial practitioners about how to imagine and create cultural artefacts. Products are the outcomes not, as Ryan and Peterson (1982) suggest, of united aims and interests but of differentiated and often conflicting goals, expertise and perceptions. Meanwhile – and this is fundamental to my research – informal knowledges and conventions, personal values and commitments, and professional cultures continue to inform cultural production processes despite the apparent growth and importance of formal, 'objective' research practices. Negus (2002), for example, argues that the predominance of a small, relatively elite, educated, middle-class white male cohort within the British music industry has had a significant impact in advancing the 'college-rock tradition' at the expense of other, often black, musical genres. The industry's masculine culture of production has, likewise, marginalized both female performers and personnel, pushing the latter into specific positions, such as secretarial or public relations work, that are themselves highly gendered (Negus 1992, 2002).

Equally, occupational divisions and personal philosophies inflected approaches towards the new representations of masculinity that emerged during the late 1980s. Mort (1996) illustrates how the post-libertarian values of advertising creatives informed support for imagery that linked masculine achievement and commercial culture, whilst also setting limits upon the gender self-consciousness that might have been implied in such campaigns (1996: 83–4, 118). When some industry insiders called for a return to more traditional masculine iconography, invoking established notions about the 'doubtful masculinity' of creative teams, their purportedly professional arguments barely camouflaged personal discomforts and ongoing turf battles between competing sets of industry practitioners (Mort 1996: 120).

The 'new man' imagery that prompted such concerns was significant, *inter alia*, in embodying the increasing importance of consumption as a source of identity for men and the expansion of products and identities made available for men through commercial culture. The notion that work-based identities are no longer the sole sources of male identification has become standard fare in recent masculinity literature. It is worth turning to this field, before returning to the new man whose development within magazine publishing forms the foundation for the events covered in this book.

Masculinity and the 'New Man'

A concern of much early masculinity scholarship was to highlight the range and diversity of male identities that exist both within society as a whole and in specific social settings. Materialist studies emphasized the significance of class as an axis of difference between men, relating distinctions between working-class and middle-class masculinities to different experiences of capitalist working practices (Tolson 1977; Willis 1977). Thus, Tolson described working-class masculinity as characterized by collective recognition and solidarity, physical toughness and presence, bravado, confrontation, anti-authority sentiment, and the avoidance of 'feelings'. He theorized an exaggerated, almost performed, masculinity at work, involving blatant machismo and chauvinism, and an authoritarian identity in the home, as forms of compensation for the humiliations of capitalist subordination faced in daily working life. In contrast, middle-class masculinity was seen to rest upon ideals such as moral dignity, emotional restraint, 'respectability' and individualized notions of self-discipline, ambition and competitiveness.

The interweaving of masculinity and class was most clearly illustrated in Paul Willis' (1977) ethnography of a group of working-class 'lads'. Most striking was how the lads associated different types of work with different genders such that they valorized their own identities and the futures that awaited them in explicitly masculine terms. Manual labour was 'suffused with masculine qualities and given sensual overtones ... difficult, uncomfortable or dangerous conditions are seen, not for themselves, but for their appropriateness to a masculine readiness and hardness' (Willis 1977: 150). Conversely, mental activity was derided not only because of its associations with the educational system, but also because it was regarded as 'effeminate' and outside the 'manly scope of action' (Willis 1977: 149; see also Cockburn 1983).

Subsequent research suggests that adherence to such values is not limited to working-class men. As Roper notes, it is not just shop floor workers but also middle-class managers who 'construct a masculine hierarchy in which physical labour is at the summit' and management is perceived as less heroic and manly (Roper 1994: 106). Managers struggle to prove their personal masculine status and that of their work, a task made particularly difficult if a lack of shop floor experience means that they have never held the status attached to manual labour.

Collinson and Hearn (1996) suggest, similarly, that whilst shop floor workers reject the idea of promotion because it would compromise their masculine self-images, office workers such as insurance salesmen are threatened by what they consider the unmasculine nature of their work. Bolstering their workplace reputations means concealing the interpersonal and nurturing skills that are crucial to their daily practices, and reconstituting their work as masculine through an imagery and vocabulary of heroism and danger. Work then, is not a 'neutral' practice, but something endowed with emotional meanings that are tied to understandings of class and masculinity. And in the hierarchical ranking of different masculine types, it is working-class masculinity that frequently sits at the zenith of the pyramid of credibility.

The relational and stratified nature of masculinities is evident here, as in the notion of 'hegemonic masculinity' that has become rather paradigmatic in sociological studies of gender. Connell's (1987, 1995) term denotes a cultural ideal of masculinity whose ascendancy over other gender formations (including black masculinities, homosexuality and femininity) is historically contingent rather than fixed. Connell is careful to distinguish between what men are actually like and the hegemonic ideals – 'embedded in the dynamics of institutions ... as much as in the personality of individuals' (see Carrigan et al. 1985) – that structure their practices. 'The public face of masculinity is not necessarily what powerful men are, but what sustains their power and what a large number of men are motivated to support ... Few men are Bogarts or Stallones, many collaborate in sustaining those images' (Connell 1987: 184–5). Hegemonic masculinity, then, is the common-sense understanding of legitimate maleness that regulates male behaviour despite its distance from the realities of male experience: the expectations to which men are made accountable. Thus, in schools where sporting prowess is the ultimate indicator of masculinity, even those boys who are scornful of the hegemonic ideal cannot just avoid it. They have to 'fight or negotiate their way out ... to establish some other claim to respect' (Connell 1995: 37).

The discrepancy here between the normative and the actual – what men would like to be, and what they are – is critical. As Dawson comments, 'masculine identities are lived out in the flesh but fashioned in the imagination', with cultural representations providing the 'repertoire of cultural forms' upon which fantasies are cast (Dawson 1991: 118). Psychoanalytic research has consistently revealed the tensions that exist between men's public roles and identities and their personal preoccupations and anxieties: the 'awkward hidden realities' of the unconscious that destabilize even the most apparently secure men (Segal 1990: 628). Although this book does not draw upon formal psychoanalytic concepts, it understands identity and subjectivity as things that are often experienced as conflictual, contradictory and ambivalent, shot through with aspirations, motivations and desires.

Foucault's concept of 'discourse' – a way of talking about a topic that simultaneously defines, constructs, makes intelligible, regulates and restricts what can be said and done in relation to that topic (Hall 1997: 44) – is a useful alternative here. Foucault identifies institutional and professional knowledges as key domains in the development of new discourse positions which 'establish the conditions for agency and identity' (Nixon 1996: 13): what it means to be a man, or Asian, or working-class. Meanwhile, he suggests that the existence of a multiplicity of discursive regimes (i.e. the family, the workplace, religion, advertising, magazine culture) and subject positions (the feckless father, the obedient worker, the good Christian, the hedonistic consumer, the new lad) means that individual men are addressed by a range of competing formations of masculinity, some of which may be more normalized than others though their recurrence across regimes and the structures of power that sustain them.

Although Foucault rejects notions of the unconscious (Hutton 1988), there is room in his conceptualization for a view of identification as potentially contradictory, and identity as therefore fractured and incoherent. However, there are well-known problems in the way that Foucault relates lived identities to the discursive formations that address them. In most of his work, the subject is obliterated, seen merely as the outcome of the interplay of discourses (Jefferson 1994). The offering in his later work of a more performative and creative subject swings too far towards a picture of identity construction as something unhindered by gender, class, ethnicity and other axes of constraint (Best and Kellner 1991; McNay 1992). Yet there are ways of integrating the individual and the social without abandoning the concept of discourse – and it is this that partly guides this book's analysis of men's magazine editors. Davies and Harré (1990) argue that discourses are constitutive of social life, but are also resistible by interpretive agents (see also Henriques et al. 1984; De Lauretis 1987). To position oneself within a discursive category depends on the recognition of that category as appropriate. This may involve a discourse being grasped 'indexically', based upon one's past experience of it, or 'typically', based upon a recognition of the culturally sanctioned meanings attached to it. Thus, both 'subjective history with its attendant emotions and beliefs' and 'a knowledge of social structures (including roles) with their attendant rights, obligations and expectations' determine whether subject positions are taken up and how they are negotiated (Davies and Harré 1990: 52). Contradictory positionings are generally avoided because individuals attempt to organize their identities as unitary and coherent. Meanwhile, since discourses offer preferred subject positions from which they make sense, their take-up will be mediated by structures such as ethnicity, class and gender. For example, it is more difficult, which is not to say impossible, for women to inhabit aggressive sexual drive discourses, involving wolf-whistling or bottom-pinching, than for men to do so (see Hollway 1984). In such ways, discourses tend to reproduce themselves but are also subject to change.

There are implications here for the impact of new identities on actual groups of men, though this is not an area that the book seeks directly to address. For masculine ideals to have effective power on actual men, they have to resonate in certain ways with actual or imagined identities. What is relevant for current purposes is that it is for this reason that publishing companies seek to 'keep in touch' with their audiences, and why the mechanisms that articulate the producers of representations like the 'new lad' with lived cultures of masculinity need to be explored. As I have also maintained, the emergence of such representations should be seen as the outcome of struggles between different personal, institutional and social interests, and the historically specific masculinities associated with them. Highlighting the range of masculinities in men's lifestyle publishing, at different moments in the market's formation and in the identities of its practitioners, is an important commitment here. There are significant variations between the male scripts portrayed in magazines such as *loaded*, *Men's Health*, *GQ* and *Esquire*, and one concern has been to trace these divergences to discourses of class, education, age, nation, sexuality and ethnicity. A sensitivity to the relational nature of masculinity has also directed my analysis, such that I have sought to examine how the masculine subjectivities of different editors and representations have formed in relation to each other and to broader hierarchies of masculine status.

The work-related identities of magazine editors are given a central place in this research, and this seems particularly appropriate in a sector that is explicitly concerned with the kinds of consumption practices that now appear to anchor masculine status as much as conventional discourses of production and provision. In their efforts to draw men into the world of goods, the commercial cultures in which magazines are imbricated have become increasingly important sites in the elaboration of these new masculinities (Mort 1996; Nixon 1996). Although it is important to recognize that such commercial explorations of masculinity are by no means new, the 1980s did mark a moment in which both the intensity and the terms of such scrutiny seemed to shift. Thus, the decade saw not only an explosion in the commercial interrogation of men's lifestyles, but also a context of investigation that was more self-conscious about male identity, cynical about the value of class categories of analysis, and influenced by homosexual and feminist culture than in previous years (Chapman and Rutherford 1988; Mort 1996).

It was in this context that the figure of the 'new man' emerged within commercial culture, in particular, within retailing, advertising, and the early formation of the UK men's magazine market. The common point of reference in discussions of the new man was the proliferation of imagery that represented men in ways that were more narcissistic, self-conscious, emotionally expressive, domesticated and 'feminine' than conventional iconography of patriarchal authority, action and machismo (Brannon 1976; Goffman 1979; Wernick 1987). Much attention focussed on the striking visibility of the male body, and its potential to undermine traditional conceptions of masculinity by encouraging men to take pleasure in themselves, and other men, as sexual objects (Chapman 1988; Mort 1988; Pumphrey 1989; Nixon 1992; Simpson 1994; see also Dyer 1983; Neale 1983). Optimistic readings suggested that men and women were now able 'to appear with equal plausibility, at either end of the objectified–objectifying sexual scale' (Wernick 1987: 293), and that the constant visual reassembly of masculinity through the marketplace would encourage men to question and reform self-identities that had previously appeared immutable (Mort 1988; see also Rutherford 1988). Nixon argued that new man imagery was most significant in that it represented a 'loosening of the binary opposition between gay and straight-identified men and extended the space available within the representational regimes of popular consumption for an ambivalent masculine identity' (Nixon 1996: 202). Across a range of commercial industries, then, forms of looking traditionally the sole preserve of the homosexual man were made available to the heterosexual viewer.

Sceptics claimed that the impact of new man imagery on mainstream visual and sartorial culture was limited (Edwards 1997; see also Spencer 1992), and that, where such imagery did exist, it surrendered its transgressive potential by concealing male nudity behind phallic symbolism (bottles of champagne, saxophones etc.) that expressed conventional qualities of control, action and power (Chapman 1988; Simpson 1994). Others noted that the increasing visual objectification of men may merely mean that gender equality has been 'won' along 'precisely the lines upon which it had already been lost' (McRobbie 1994). Ehrenreich (1983, 1989) located the new man as the latest manifestation of a number of post-war masculinities whose characteristics of emotional lability and self-indulgence were ideally suited to consumer society. In, likewise, linking the rise of the fashion-conscious male consumer to ideologies of individualistic materialism, Edwards (1997) rightly highlights his more socially divisive and exclusionary characteristics.

Applying the same perspective to the emergence of men's lifestyle magazines in the late 1980s, Edwards (1997) argues that their materialization reflected a number of connected developments, including the advancement of a stratum of affluent, professional and unattached men, and the period's encouragement of ideologies of aspirational individualism and self-awareness. It is not clear, however, how these or other shifts impacted on the thinking of those publishing institutions and personnel who would have effectuated and moulded the market's fabrication. Edwards deploys such a wide lens to try to understand what fuelled the market that the specific cultures and practices of production that form the bridge between broader social shifts and concrete commercial resolutions are elided. It is this decision-making sphere that this book explores empirically, building both conceptually and historically upon accounts of the sector's initial formation to which I now turn (Mort 1988, 1996; Nixon 1992, 1993, 1996).

The Early Years of the Men's Magazine Market

The first general-interest men's publication, *Gentleman's Magazine*, was launched in 1731, and men's titles were published with considerable success from the eighteenth century until the First World War. A revival in the interwar years saw the publication of pocket-sized products *Lilliput* and *Men Only*, the former blending humour, short stories, general features and discreetly airbrushed nude pictorials, and the latter promoting a heroic version of masculinity amongst style features and pictures of female nudes.[2] The most ambitious early post-war effort to regenerate the men's press was *Man about Town*, published in various forms from 1953 to 1968. The first attempt to launch a British version of *Esquire* was a less successful endeavour, lasting only from 1954 until 1957. Only two more ventures, the semi-pornographic *King* and *Club*, sought to break the mainstream men's market before it entered a sustained fallow period in the early 1970s (*Campaign Report*, 11.4.97: 4–5). Although Conekin (2000) is correct to claim that *Playboy* addressed men in self-consciously gendered terms throughout this period, and was more than merely a soft porn title, it was not perceived within the publishing industry as a general-interest title, and was far less culturally influential in the UK than the US.

Enthusiasm for the development of a general-interest men's magazine accelerated across the clothing industry and its subsidiary sectors from the early 1980s (Nixon 1993, 1996). Male markets were seen to be more fertile for commercial exploitation and creative innovation than the relatively saturated women's sectors. At the same time, companies such as Next were starting to open up the menswear middle-market using flexible production techniques and 'lifestyled' product collections. However, in the absence of suitable media outlets, promoting menswear, grooming products and other luxury items to appropriate male cohorts was difficult and expensive. While there existed a host of general lifestyle magazines aimed at women and young girls, men's titles focussed on specific areas such as sport, cars and pornography. These provided neither sufficiently glossy paper nor suitable editorial environments for advertisers' requirements, forcing them to spread their budgets across several unsatisfactory publications to try to reach desirable consumers (Nixon 1993).

Motivated by this enthusiasm for general-interest men's titles amongst the advertising and retail communities, magazine publishers were also encouraged by formal and informal assessments of shifts in male cultures. According to

Nixon, lifestyle and psychographic research conducted within advertising circles was influential in indicating the existence of a new set of 'avant-guardian' and 'innovating' men whose contemporary and self-conscious attitudes towards masculinity and consumption made them potentially receptive to the editorial and advertising appeals of glossy men's magazines (Nixon 1996: 101–2, 130–1). Developments in magazine culture, industry discourse and personal hunches also informed appraisals of the viability of men's lifestyle titles. Some practitioners, such as men's magazine missionary Paul Keers, regarded the success of American men's lifestyle magazines in isolating the 'male yuppie audience' as the key to establishing similar magazines in the UK (Nixon 1996). Other industry insiders were dubious that the 'more mature' American male, conscious of fashion and personal appearance and informed by the women's movement, had a British counterpart (Nixon 1996: 128; Mort 1996). Mobilizing standard stereotypes of the 'typical British man', such sceptics claimed that men's inter-ests were well served by other media (in particular, newspapers), that men had no psychological desire for the male 'clubbiness' offered by lifestyle magazines, and that British masculinity would be uncomfortable with the explicitly gendered address that a men's title would need to evoke (Nixon 1996).

The failure of *The Hit*, launched by IPC in 1985 for the late-teenage male market, only fuelled such assertions. The product was given considerable backing by IPC and attracted strong support from advertising agencies. Consumers proved less sympathetic, apparently reluctant to induct themselves in the magazine's self-consciously male community, with its supposed implications of personal weakness and effeminacy (Mort 1996: 21). In the light of this miscar-riage and the confused inertia of the major publishing houses, it was the pros-pering style press, *The Face*, *Blitz* and *i-D*, that became highly influential in setting the terms for the eventual formation of the men's magazine market (Nixon 1993, 1996). Each launched in 1980, these magazines were produced by independent publishing companies and written by a dedicated cognoscenti of producers immersed in the avant-garde cultures that they represented to readers (Mort 1996; Nixon 1993, 1996).

Amongst them, Wagadon's *The Face* was particularly influential in offering a clear indication to publishers and advertisers of how to appeal to the elusive male consumers that they craved. Advertisers flocked to *The Face*, perceiving it as the route to the wallets of an affluent, innovative and trendsetting elite, whilst using its distinctive visual imagery in their own campaigns. For the magazine houses, the title provided firm evidence that 'new men' were viable targets for a general-interest product. Meanwhile, *The Face*'s style-led journalism offered an editorial recipe through which to address male consumers that was an alternative to the formats suggested by the women's press. Indeed, it was using the leverage he established as an authority on the style-conscious young man that Nick Logan,

The Face's publisher-editor, launched *Arena* in November 1986 (Mort 1996). Although Emap's *Q*, a *de facto* men's lifestyle magazine masquerading as a monthly music title, had been released in September 1986, and Condé Nast had already announced plans for a dummy version for *Vogue Man*, *Arena* represented the first explicit news-stand version of a men's lifestyle magazine for almost twenty years (Nixon 1993, 1996; Mort 1996).

Significantly, the title was intended as the next destination for readers and writers alike who were outgrowing *The Face*. The style and subject matter of the younger title was thus critical in directing the tenor of the new one: an '"avant-garde metropolitanism" based around the modernity of urban consumption' (Nixon 1996: 164). Men's fashion and accessories featured heavily, along with reviews of consumer products and outlets (shops, bars, restaurants, clubs), detailed through a tone that marked out the magazine's readership as a discriminating, trendsetting, metropolitan elite. Areas such as sport and travel were examined through a journalistic idiom that highlighted the 'look' and subcultural positioning of the people, places and events concerned. Meanwhile, individuals in film, music, architecture, design, fashion and other media industries were selectively profiled in a manner that confirmed the magazine's celebration of stylish urban success and consumption.

Arena's first cover star, Hollywood actor Mickey Rourke, was fitting in other respects. As Mort noted, his roles tended to be versions of 'the complex man with the gun': tough but sensitive, violent but psychologically-developed characters (Berens, cited in Mort 1996: 80). Interviews with other male icons tended to examine their mental complexities whilst also celebrating their implicitly 'masculine' characteristics. Such competing scripts were typical of the magazine's early representations of appropriate masculinity, snaking between a new man identity clearly informed by the voice of second-wave feminism and a more traditional masculine standpoint. What was more distinctive was the tone of ironic self-consciousness that *Arena* often employed in discussing male rituals, roles and relationships. Received notions and expressions of masculinity, including the visual scrutiny of women, were thus subjected to critical deconstruction, even if they were not quite rejected as sources of pleasure and status (Nixon 1996).

Arena's first audited circulation of 65,000 matched its success in gaining support from advertisers. With the myth of the impossibility of the men's lifestyle magazine further exposed, and Wagadon taking a grip upon the market, Condé Nast stepped up its efforts to launch a title of its own. New impetus was provided by the arrival on the project of Stephen Quinn and Paul Keers as publisher and editor respectively. Following a period of research and development, *GQ* (*Gentleman's Quarterly*) was launched in 1988, pitched at the upmarket advertisers that were the mainstays of Condé Nast's other products.

The influence of *Arena* was apparent in *GQ*'s focus on menswear and style, and, more specifically, in the organization of its editorial sections (Nixon 1996: 159). Broadly speaking, as Mort (1996) highlights, the titles were linked by a veneration of style and consumer culture. Informed and self-conscious purchasing decisions were presented as crucial means to organize the expression of identity. Thus, dress, grooming and the selective consumption of brands, from beer to hi-fi equipment, were depicted as the primary identifiers of a new kind of liberated masculinity, an identity thereby rooted in the offerings of consumer society.

Nonetheless, *GQ*'s target reader was not *Arena*'s trendy young Londoner, but an older and more conservative audience, 'the professional who has achieved success with style' (Nixon 1993: 488). Central in *GQ*'s address was the identity of the modern young executive, a more mainstream figure than *Arena*'s style leader. *GQ*'s tone also diverged from that of *Arena* in relation to the portrayal of women, comprising a 'sexualized scrutiny of women and a sense of the incommensurability of the cultures of men and women' (Nixon 1996: 162). Furthermore, *GQ*'s editorial format drew upon the conventions of news journalism, with more heavyweight features and fewer aesthetic preoccupations than *Arena*. Its promotion of consumption was also informed by a more traditional coding, that of the deluxe and discerning wardrobe of the gentleman. As Nixon summarizes then, *GQ*'s overall identity was that of 'modern conservative metropolitanism', an updated version of 'the gentleman' (1996).

As this book demonstrates, these magazine identities would evolve over the course of the 1990s in accordance with developments in the market, shifts in the conception of 'the men's magazine reader' and changes in the editors employed to deliver appropriate audiences. Before embarking on the story of these events, I want to underline a number of points identified by Mort and Nixon that have informed my account.

A Cultural Economy of the Men's Press

It is crucial, first, to recognize the combination of informal and formal knowledges that underpinned the reformation of the men's press. Nixon (1993, 1996) suggests that the market was forged through shared understandings of new male consumers deriving from advertising industry research. Thus, it was through conceptions of the 'innovating' and 'avant-guardian' man that key publishing practitioners became convinced of the possibility of men's lifestyle magazines and it was through these conceptions that Wagadon's advertising manager sold back the ideas of *The Face* and *Arena* to advertising agents. It is in the sense that these representations of the target audience established the commercial relationships between publishing and advertising practitioners that the mutual constitution of 'the economic' and 'the cultural' in the development of the market is most clearly evidenced. Only through a specific vocabulary of style and masculinity were the 'economic' possibilities of the market animated.

The skill of Wagadon personnel in commanding authority over how to address the men's magazine audience is also significant. The initial tone of the men's press was determined by a small crew of journalists, publishers and designers who managed to monopolize the industry's understanding of the market and how to approach it. Mort's outline of a 'gallery of talented individualists' at Wagadon (1996: 34), led by Nick Logan, and including the writers Julie Burchill and Robert Elms, graphic designer Neville Brody and stylist Ray Petri, is fundamental here. The informal knowledges and personal commitments of this production cabal were essential in defining the market in a particular way. Burchill's crusade against liberal feminism and Elms' leftist style-politics were particularly influential in delimiting *The Face*'s editorial pitch (Mort 1996: 40–4). These were missions that were resonant with wider cultures whilst also reflective of the backgrounds, preoccupations and aspirations of their progenitors. For Burchill, this incorporated a working-class suburban upbringing, an ambitious individualism, a studied marginality and an assertive version of populist feminism (Mort 1996). For Elms, it involved a celebration of the hedonistic, collective masculinity of the proletarian hero. Logan's own input should not be underestimated. It was his commitment to values of creative independence that led him to leave Emap and establish a series of titles in keeping with his personal tastes and interests. Logan's concept for *The Face* was not based on an abstract notion or 'big philosophy' of the new man (Nixon 1993: 484), nor was the magazine driven by any formal editorial 'policy', but by a recollection of his own preferences from when he was a fashion-conscious, eighteen-year-old mod (Mort 1996; Nixon 1996).

The imprintation on magazine forms of the personal knowledges, resources and identifications of editorial practitioners that is suggested in Mort and Nixon's studies is the central concern of this book, and is the direct focus of Part III. Gender is a key sensitizing concept here, a concept that is marginalized in the work of Bourdieu (1984) and many accounts of cultural production, but whose specificity in localized environments needs to be studied empirically in order to map more fully the landscape of lived, and idealized, identity. Cultural economy encourages this kind of attention, not only to the details of gender, class and ethnicity that inflect commercial cultures, but also to the internal complexities of the processes of commercial production. Acknowledging the mutual interplay of 'cultural' and 'economic' determinants in these dynamics, and delineating the various forces, alliances and calculations involved in them, are important ambitions of this book.

The investigation of the new man as a consumer identity forged 'where the market meets popular experience and lifestyles on the ground' has also driven my interests (Mort 1988: 215). The articulation of cultural producers with consumers through the formal and informal knowledges of certain influential practitioners is a prime concern of much of the ensuing analysis. It is a key consideration of the chapter that follows, and that begins by charting the changes in the men's press that occurred in the years after the initial re-establishment that I have just outlined. The analysis of these developments gives context to the rest of the book, and forms the basis for its argument about the crucial role of editors in fashioning the UK men's press during the 1990s.

Notes

1. The *New Times* (1989) collection accented the political implications of this kind of reformulation of commercial culture. As Mort (1989) summarized, the Left's traditional condemnation of the marketplace was founded on a caricatured and outdated view of consumer industries that assumed that all power lay with the producers, and credited consumers with little agency and power both in their own decision-making and in the overall production cycle. Such a stance was not only naïve; it also divorced the Left from the mass of people for whom consumption practices were genuinely liberating, 'a source of power and pleasure' (Mort 1989: 161), and allowed the Right to monopolize the vocabulary of aspiration and consumer desire.
2. Many thanks to an anonymous reviewer for providing some basic information on these titles.

Part II
The Structure and Dynamics
of the UK Men's Press

–2–

Launches of the Mid-1990s

I suggested in the introduction that few publishing insiders anticipated *loaded*'s success. Summarizing his short review of its launch issue in advertising trade journal *Campaign*, Stefano Hatfield commented: 'I can imagine a real lad glancing at someone else's copy, but I can't see him going out to buy one' (*Campaign*, 22.4.94: 21). I begin this chapter by demonstrating that this dismissal represented a widespread industry view in the early 1990s that the quest for an audience for mainstream men's lifestyle magazines was futile. Publishing practitioners who had collectively identified the 'style conscious young man' (Nixon 1996: 128) as the object of their commercial concerns in the previous decade had formed no equivalent means of conceptualizing the untapped areas of the market. I show that this was the case until around 1994, by which time teams at four separate publishing companies were fleshing out target consumers for a range of forthcoming publications aimed at mass male publics.

The success of these titles, in particular *loaded*, and the subsequent growth of the market, surprised many of the people involved in its expansion and stunned the publishing community at large. Trade analysts wondered how industry common sense could have been so mistaken about the likely success of mainstream men's magazines, how IPC was persuaded to break the market mould, and what factors were significant in shaping the identity of its title and those of the publications that followed it into the sector. The chapter begins to address these questions by scrutinizing the launch anatomies of the market's most influential products, *loaded*, *FHM*, *Maxim* and *Men's Health*, elucidating the ways that editorial and publishing practitioners appraised and addressed the marketplace. Intuitive and informal knowledges feature significantly here, in particular, those held by editorial personnel. I suggest that the market's paradigmatic transformation was bound up with the decisive role of these practitioners and forms of assessment in fashioning the sector's new products, indicating some highly significant features of the production dynamics of the men's press. The expansion and reorientation of the market, precipitated by *loaded*'s emergence, confirms the cultural authority wielded by some specific editorial figures and by certain publications in shaping the UK men's lifestyle press in the 1990s.

The Early Nineties

A review of consumer magazine markets written for *Press Gazette*'s twenty-fifth anniversary in December 1990 (3.12.90: 18) by one of the elder statesmen of the publishing community was a telling indication of the standing of the men's sector in the eyes of most industry operators. Despite the breakthroughs of the previous five years, men's lifestyle magazines received no mention at all. The men's style press was widely considered only a niche market serving a minor audience at the margins of the male public body. Other trade press documentations of the state of men's publishing at the turn of the decade exhibited two connected tendencies. First, a palpable excitement about the prospect of future developments, displayed in breathless reports of circulation battles between the style press incumbents and announcements of potential new competition. Second, in apparent contradiction to such animated expectation, an entrenched scepticism about the likelihood of any significant extension of the market. Whilst advertisers supported publishers' hopes for more mainstream men's magazines, and both parties recognized the limited appeal of the current titles, the industry was overwhelmingly pessimistic that the mass male audience had similar thirsts. Without any firm conception of how the market's bare terrain could be successfully cultivated, and with the style titles gradually increasing their sales, industry practitioners were satisfied that the 'age of the male magazine' had effectively arrived (*Marketing*, 11.1.90: 3).

Esquire's launch in 1991, which I discuss further in Chapter 6, did little to destabilize this complacency. With a target demographic much like that of *GQ*, The National Magazine Company's (NatMags) product extended the reach of the men's press relatively little. Trade discussions centred on the magazine's American origins and the economic context in which it was being introduced, with little belief that it might introduce a wider audience to the market. Indeed, *GQ* and *Esquire* were happy to perch in the sector's high-ground during this period. Concerned to differentiate their products from pornographic magazines, the gay press and what they considered 'eighties' titles such as *The Face* and *Arena*, executives at Condé Nast and NatMags encouraged retailers to position their products next to current affairs publications such as *Newsweek*, *Time*, the *New Statesman and Society*, the *Spectator* and *The Economist*.[1]

Industry commentators recognized that the 'black hole' of British publishing remained unfilled. But whilst the existing publications were variously criticized as staid, patronizing, homogeneous, over-aspirational, unnervingly self-conscious and aimed more at advertisers than readers, it was assumed in publishing circles that the sector had been breached as best as could be expected given previous perceptions that it might be 'non-existent or at least impossible to penetrate' (*Campaign*, 11.2.94: 27). Thus, as *GQ* and *Esquire* gradually built circulations of 100,000 copies per issue, the general interest men's market was considered to have reached a state of stable maturity. Trade reviews of the sector, quoting relevant practitioners in publishing and advertising, rarely suggested that it might, in fact, be stagnating. The idea of titles aimed at the mass male public was raised only with a resigned sense of its implausibility.

A 'state of play' reflection in *Campaign* in April 1992 rehearsed the presiding discourses. Wagadon's Rod Sopp, who had himself challenged general scepticism a few years earlier in aiding the reconstruction of men's publishing, now doubted the viability of new magazines selling in significant numbers: 'There's not a market to launch into. The best way to do a launch is the Emap way – go into a nice, hard market and do something better than what's there. That won't work in the men's market. I don't think we'll see a situation where we have lots of men's magazines selling between 60,000 and 80,000' (*Campaign*, 3.4.92: 10).

David Dent, a media strategist at advertising agency HHCL, reiterated Sopp's pessimism: 'the mass generic male is not catered for and he probably wouldn't be interested ... I could never see a mass men's magazine with a sale of 300,000 to 400,000' (*Campaign*, 3.4.92: 10). Whilst the general interest men's market therefore continued to be occupied by smaller publishing interests – the upmarket specialists Condé Nast and NatMags and the 'independent' style-house Wagadon – until the mid-1990s, the industry's largest companies, Emap and IPC, whose structures I detail in Chapter 4, targeted the mainstream male public only through ostensibly specialist titles. Their successful launches in 1990 of music monthlies *Select* and *VOX* respectively, and the rising circulation of film title *Empire*, had confirmed that men would buy magazines covering interests beyond cars, flesh and fishing.[2] Moreover, in addressing music and film as parts of the overall lifestyles of their readers rather than as sole hobbies, these publications did represent a forward step in the forging of the men's lifestyle press (*Media Week*, 10.8.90: 16–18). Nevertheless, the announcement in the summer of 1992 of four forthcoming general sports titles emphasized publishers' continuing reluctance to offer men's magazines that proclaimed their lifestyle status explicitly (*Media Week*, 19.6.92: 8).

The launch of *Focus* a few months later in November 1992 therefore raised industry hopes that a more advanced formulation of the men's press might be imminent. Like NatMags, German publisher Gruner and Jahr (G&J) turned to an internationally proven formula to try to break into the UK men's market and build up an existing global portfolio. Across Europe, its popular science titles, such as *Ca M'interesse* in France, *Mui Interessante* in Spain and *PM* in Germany, sold in numbers way above the circulations of *Esquire* and *GQ*, drawing mixed-sex, family audiences. Observing that few successful magazines in the UK possessed consumer profiles of this sort, G&J decided to project *Focus* as a magazine aimed predominantly at ABC1, 18–35-year-old men, covering medicine, technology, sport, human interest, the body, nature and history (Stitt 1998; *Media Week*, 16.10.92: 10). UK managing director, Holger Wiemann, was confident of the momentousness of the occasion: 'We haven't just created a magazine, I think we're creating a market' (16.10.92: 10).

Advertisers responded tentatively but favourably to an additional vehicle through which to target young men, particularly because of the homogeneity of the *GQ* and *Esquire* audiences and increasing concerns about advert overpopulation in the existing publications (*Media Week*, 23.10.92: 8). Publishing insiders were more sceptical, specifically about the title's downmarket look and the lack of political and business coverage that would, in the eyes of the (clearly partisan) *Esquire* editor, make it 'escapist and marginal to what governs men's lives' (*Campaign*, 30.10.92: 15). Such reactions reproduced the prevailing feeling of uncertainty amongst publishing companies about how to approach the mass market, and the generalized doubt that there existed an interested male public beyond the upmarket titles. In fact, consumers were rather receptive, giving *Focus* a first audit of 92,000, well above its 80,000 guarantee to advertising clients. However, the magazine's inability to build upon this promising start soon bolstered conventional wisdoms. *Media Week*'s declaration in April 1993 that 'ABC1 men and the phrase "mass market" are likely to remain strangers for some time', and *Esquire* publisher John Wisbey's statement that 'the existing players are doing well to expand the market, but there's not room for anyone else just yet', represented the persistent public orthodoxies of the industry (16.4.93: 20). The following year, only two months before *loaded* entered the market, Wisbey was still dismissive: 'men's magazines are never going to be anything more than niche brands' (*Marketing*, 10.2.94: 20).

It would, nonetheless, be a mistake to see 1994 as the year zero of the men's press. Signs had emerged in the previous months that a new breed of men's magazine might be germinating. In July 1993, independent publisher C21 announced plans for *Phat!*, a magazine aimed at 'streetwise boys' aged between thirteen and sixteen covering urban, youth culture including films, women, computer games and television (*Media Week*, 2.7.93: 8).[3] Emap's revamp of unisex, youth-entertainment title *Sky* the following month signalled its mounting interest in the men's press, as it attempted to reposition the title in the men's style press rather than the teenage sector (*Media Week*, 6.8.93: 8). And, in November, youth lifestyle title *Zine*, a student magazine spin-off which claimed to have sold over 70,000 copies of its first three issues, revealed that it would publish monthly from February 1994 (*Media Week*, 26.11.93: 8). Meanwhile, in the existing men's market, growth rates had been encouraging for some time as the recession tailed off. At the start of 1994, sales had risen by 21 per cent over the previous year, and *GQ* could boast that it was not only finally in profit, but was the most popular men's style publication in Europe (*Campaign*, 4.2.94: 4; *Press Gazette*,

3.10.94: 8; *Marketing*, 10.2.94: 12). Perhaps most portentously, its inaugural use of a female cover star, Sharon Stone, in August 1993, coincided with a sales rise of 17 per cent that finally took the magazine past the circulation milestone of 100,000 monthly copy sales (*Media Week*, 13.8.93: 10).

Such developments hinted at what would happen in the following two years, as Emap, IPC and two smaller companies, Dennis Publishing and Rodale Press, executed their ambitions to seize market shares in the men's press equivalent to those they held in many other publishing sectors. But with newspaper review sections perceived as the biggest threat to the existing men's titles, and scepticism about mainstream men's magazines unmoved by rumours of a number of new projects, the forthcoming titles received little of the expectant coverage that the trade press had dedicated to *Esquire* and *Focus*. Few anticipated that their arrival would mark the sector's transition from a minority to a mass market. It is to the conditions of these launches that I shall now turn.

The Launch of *loaded*

> Heard the one about the two English blokes who went to Spain to watch a football match and came back with the most influential and controversial men's magazine in British history?
>
> It was 11.35pm on a balmy autumn evening in 1992. I was with my former Deputy Editor at NME, James Brown, in Barcelona, to see our beloved Leeds United defeat German Champions Stuttgart in the European Cup 3rd-round replay. After a sensational game we hit the bars and clubs of Barcelona's famous Ramblas district.
>
> We'd just emerged from a fancy nightclub full of very attractive and very accommodating Spanish nurses. We were delirious with the joys of life. ... I began a high-octane recounting of the night's amazing events. ... Suddenly James comes over all unusual, grabs me by the arm and fixes me in the eye with a strange, cold stare. 'Wait a minute,' he says, 'what you just said; there should be a magazine like this ... all about the best moments you ever had ... about having the best fucking time of your life'. (Southwell 1998: 1–2)

It was with this apocryphal tale that Tim Southwell, *loaded*'s co-founder and future editor, introduced his 1998 book on 'The Inside Story of loaded'. Often repeated by the magazine's producers, the story's suggestion of epiphanic creativity corresponded neatly with their view of the title as a revolutionary intervention. What it submerged, however, was the more complex publishing logic through which this European night out bore fruit. *loaded*'s materialization was the result of a specific set of market circumstances and several years of development.

Aware of the considerable advertising revenues that it was gifting to its publishing competitors, and relatively confident that the market was sufficiently solid to support new titles, IPC had been looking to break into the men's lifestyle press since the start of the 1990s. As early as 1991, the company had converted a number of concepts into dummy issues, but, lacking editorial clarity, none had progressed beyond rough cuts. Research into the existing sector did indicate that most men found the prevailing titles irrelevant and preferred the celebratory tone of women's glossies to the restrained pitch of the men's style press (*Marketing*, 21.9.95: 39–40). Such views were also held on a personal level by the development team working on early drafts of the new men's title. With neither the enthusiasm nor the expertise to produce a magazine founded on fashion and grooming content, their inspiration stemmed mainly from a sense of what it should *not* be, the kind of 'very aspirational, very glossy, very posh, quite unrealistic [and] not very interesting' products that editorial launch chief Alan Lewis bemoaned (Lewis 1998). Requiring a more positive and focussed conception, it was only when Lewis brought two of his former employees from IPC's music weekly, the *NME*, into the launch frame in 1993 that the magazine's editorial identity began to take shape.

James Brown and Tim Southwell shared their senior colleagues' sense of alienation from the style titles. 'Not one told me about my life. They never covered football or music or night-clubs, all of which were exploding across Britain. They were missing British culture' (Brown in the *Financial Times*, 4.9.99: 7). More precisely, they were ignoring the cultures that defined Brown and Southwell's lives and expressed their interests – to which I return in greater detail in Chapter 5. Brown recalled *loaded*'s editorial composition as expressing what would have come out 'if you'd picked me up and shook everything out of my head' (Brown 1999b). Indeed, his aim was simply 'to create a magazine that was for me and my friends, and an extension of my personality' (*Independent*, 8.6.98: 13). *loaded* was thus developed using himself and Southwell as the model readers.

Twelve focus group sessions organized towards the end of 1993 in London, Manchester and Birmingham were inconclusive. Opinions within individual groups tended to polarize, and overall outcomes were negative as often as they were positive. In the light of such indications, the future of the project was by no means clear. IPC persevered with only 50 per cent of concepts that reached this stage of development. However, three main factors secured the launch of *loaded*. The first was what Lewis called the 'bullish mood' of the company under a new managing director keen to protect IPC's position as the UK's largest publishing firm, and encouraged by the successful launch of *Vox* (Lewis 1999). Second, IPC's financial risk was relatively small. There seemed little to lose in testing the unchartered waters of the men's press, especially given the clear dissatisfaction amongst consumers with the existing offerings. *loaded*'s team was therefore given uncommon space and time to cultivate its ideas. Indeed, this latitude proved essential when the team's efforts received only lukewarm support in market testing, allowing Lewis to conceal the full truth of the findings from senior decision-making executives (Lewis 1998, 1999).

What proved decisive in guaranteeing *loaded*'s publication was the faith held by Lewis, Brown and Southwell that research results were misleading and the title would succeed. Rationalizing the situation, they concluded that the focus group participants had been 'the wrong people', and that the extremity of some reactions indicated that the magazine had struck some kind of significant chord. Lewis explained:

> Because the men's magazines that were around were pretty upmarket and aspirational for the intended *loaded* reader, they [the research participants] weren't reading men's magazines at all. Therefore, in some of the research groups they simply didn't get it at all, because it wasn't a vocabulary, it wasn't a language ... they simply weren't in the habit, they hadn't even thought of buying a magazine. [But] when you hit the right audience there was a very strong connection there. And we thought 'we know this audience is out there'. (Lewis 1999)

In effect, the development team pulled rank on what potential readers declared: 'I know the pure ethics of marketing are that you have to satisfy people's needs', proclaimed publishing director Robert Tame, 'but people didn't *know* that they wanted *loaded*' (Tame 1998)

Research practices did little to mediate Brown's editorial technique. Through several remodellings, the title remained rooted in music, sport and alternative comedy (although interview pieces became shorter and adventure-sports content was decreased) and retained what Lewis described as a 'sparky sense of humour, a sense of the absurd and obviously a determination to have a lot of attitude' (Lewis 1998). Brown believed that grooming was 'for horses' (Brown 1999b) and only reluctantly allowed fashion into the title at the behest of IPC advertising executives. Where his preferences were elsewhere overruled, it was Lewis rather than formal research that was decisive. There were no semi-naked women in Brown's original dummy, and trial readers maintained repeatedly that they had little appetite for such pictures. Lewis simply vetoed their assertions: 'the men that we spoke to were either deluding themselves or were not being totally honest' (Lewis 1999).

With the focus groups in this way disregarded, and no quantitative research as alternative support, it was 'gut faith' that underpinned the magazine's progression. As Southwell recalled, uncertainty was therefore a prime characteristic of the launch:

> We basically came to the conclusion that it was either going to be an almighty success, immediately, or it was going to be a complete flop. Because all it was was a little

fanzine, scrapbook of our ideas and doodlings at the time: just what we wanted to write about and what we wanted to put in, and it was no more than that. And we thought, if people pick up on it at all there's probably gonna be loads of them. But they might just think it's really crap. (Southwell 1999)

Brown's confidence was equally intuitive: 'I felt we were onto something, because it just really was a magazine that was like our lives' (*On the Ropes*, Radio Four, 16.7.02).

Industry insiders asked to assess *loaded*'s viability in the months before its emergence were customarily disregarding. IPC's pre-launch briefings signposted the company's intention to differentiate its product from the existing style titles, which publishing director Andy McDuff dismissed as 'too arty and fashion-victimish [or] bland and irrelevant' (*Press Gazette*, 31.1.94: 7). *loaded*, he declared, would be 'irreverent, controversial and dangerous' with a younger target readership, mainly single men in their late teens and early twenties, unencumbered by family and financial responsibilities, and into 'pub and club culture' (*Press Gazette*, 28.3.94: 9). *FHM* editor Francis Cottam riposted: 'I have not seen anything that makes me shake in my shoes. We are past masters at irreverence and already fulfil pretty comprehensively the market sector they are talking about' (*Press Gazette*, 31.1.94: 7).

loaded's distinctions were apparent when it arrived on news-stands in April 1994. *GQ*'s most recent issue had included articles on the Child Support Agency scandal, HIV, cricketer Michael Atherton, novelists Jay McInerney and Patricia Highsmith, fashion designer Giorgio Armani, and 'are you man enough to cope with PMT?' (*GQ*, March 1994). *Esquire* was fronted by Hollywood actor Tom Hanks and contained pieces on the Jamie Bulger case, boxer Mike Tyson's time in jail, Prozac, 'Dates from Hell', the 'real story behind *Schindler's List*', and 'why dogs are a man's best friend' (*Esquire*, March 1994). *loaded* stood out, with working-class British actor Gary Oldman staring out from a front cover that highlighted articles inside on cult film *Withnail and I*, Italian football team Sampdoria, hotel sex, skydiving, cartoon characters Beavis and Butt-head, rock star Paul Weller and footballer Eric Cantona (see Figure 2).

In his first editor's letter, James Brown fleshed out an identity that differentiated *loaded* all the more clearly from its competition. '*loaded* is a new magazine dedicated to life, liberty and the pursuit of sex, drink, football and less serious matters. *loaded* is music, film, relationships, humour, travel, sport, hard news and popular culture. *loaded* is clubbing, drinking, eating, playing and living. *loaded* is for the man who believes he can do *anything*, if only he wasn't hungover' (*loaded*, May 1994: 3). Inside, the magazine continued to assert its character with a 'platinum rogues' table, 'charting the peaks, pratfalls and past form of a royal flush of bad boys', 'Great Moments in Life', recalling a football

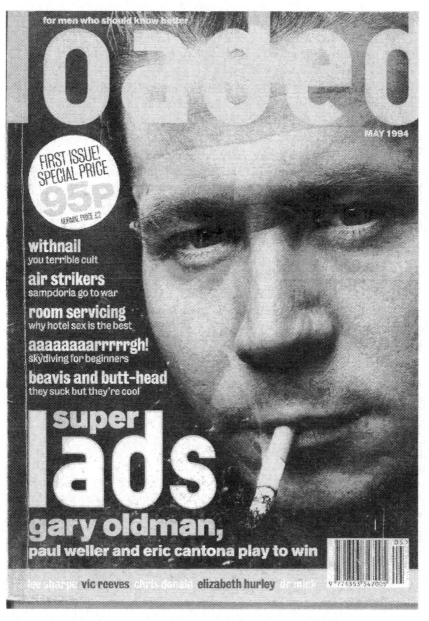

Figure 2 Cover of *loaded*, May 1994, courtesy of *loaded*/IPC.

match pitch invasion by 'junior mods' in 1972, and a 'Greatest Living Englishmen' column commemorating 'Dave' from the 1980s UK television programme *Minder* (pp: 8, 13, 14). In coming editions, *loaded* would honour cult British gangster films *Get Carter* and *The Italian Job*, events such as 'John

McEnroe doing his nut', 'growing a moustache' and 'the Blue Peter Garden getting vandalised', and men including The Likely Lads, 'mad newspaper vendors' and quiz show dummy 'Dusty Bin'. Compared to the list of 'places and things that made my life a life', from *Esquire*'s first issue in 1991 – 'Ben Webster, Ray Charles, W B Yeats, Mexico, Gabriel Garcia Marquez, Casablanca, Proust (unfinished), Hemingway, the World Series and so on' (quoted in *Media Week*, 15.2.91: 38) – the distinctive hue of *loaded*'s cultural references, in terms of nation, generation and class, was all the more evident. First, then, it was distinctively British, and rooted in more recent, populist subculture. Second, these references signalled an identification with elements of working-class culture, in particular an emphasis on street culture and self-gratification. Third, *loaded*'s tone was markedly less earnest and more celebratory in its portrayal of masculine culture than its market predecessors.

Cottam's cynicism was somewhat misplaced. Within only nine months of its launch, *loaded* was selling over 100,000 copies per issue, 60,000 above its original aim and a sales volume that *GQ* had taken five years to attain. Readership figures released in June 1995 also revealed that 73 per cent of readers were from social classes ABC1, a profile putting *loaded* on a par with *Yachting World*, *Empire* and *Esquire* in terms of its value for advertisers looking to target affluent men (National Readership Survey 1995; *Media Week*, 9.6.95, 16.6.95). By August 1995, *loaded* was the biggest selling product in the sector. Meanwhile, encouraged and aided by *loaded*'s progress, other companies had soon joined IPC in producing titles that ignored the template of the first generation of men's titles. In May 1994, Emap had itself begun a revamp of *FHM* that owed much to IPC's gamble, and would eventually create the new market leader. By the end of 1995, the 130 per cent growth rate in the men's lifestyle press was over 100 per cent more than in the next fastest expanding sector (*Media Week*, 20.10.95: 16). A year later, whilst *loaded*'s circulation had reached 365,000, those of *FHM*, *Maxim* and *Men's Health* were over 150,000, 158,000 and 323,000 respectively (ABC, June–December 1996). As I shall now illustrate, the terms and conditions of these new launches had much in common with those of the market's new archetype.

The Launch of *FHM*

The condition of Emap's men's publishing portfolio was much like IPC's at the start of the 1990s. The company's Metro division produced a number of successful entertainment and hobby titles aimed at men, but pulled in no fashion advertising and had been, by its own admission, sluggish in spotting the potential for a general interest men's lifestyle magazine. By 1992, publishing personnel believed that there was growing potential to accrue advertising and circulation revenues from the men's press and that those titles currently reaping them were doing so rather poorly. Editorial personnel were at the same time struck by their own exclusion from the market. Emap Metro MD Barry McIlheney recalled:

> There had been a growing body of feeling, particularly within Emap Metro, that [the existing men's magazines] weren't quite right, and that there wasn't really anything for guys like us to read. We were sort of early, mid-thirties, and the other guys below us were in their twenties, and there was nothing there that turns you on. And therefore we started ... working up ideas for a blokes' magazine. (McIlheney 1998)

Like *loaded*'s creators, Emap's team struggled for some time to give their concept a coherent editorial vision. Certain, though, that a different kind of men's magazine could flourish, and spurred by IPC's endeavours with *loaded*, Emap took advantage of the opportunity to purchase men's fashion title *FHM* in June 1994. Owned by independent publisher Tayvale, *FHM* had existed since 1985, at first freely distributed through menswear retailers and known as *For Him Magazine*. In the early 1990s, the renamed *For Him* was the lowest-selling title in the men's style press, lacking the financial muscle to compete with *GQ*, *Esquire* and *Arena*. When taken over, it was selling only 60,000 monthly copies. Emap's decision to acquire rather than launch from scratch was based on two main rationales. First, it could hook into *FHM*'s established fashion heritage, in particular its relationships with advertisers, which it estimated would take at least a year to otherwise develop. Second, the purchase was a deliberate resolution by Emap to overcome its inertia and concentrate its thinking: a moving vehicle would demand direction.

Emap indeed capitalized on the advertising cushion that the takeover provided. It secured the goodwill of current clients by reassuring them that it would invest heavily in the title, and that their interests remained fundamental. At the same time, Emap planned a significant editorial revamp that it knew could alienate the interests of some advertisers. In the past, divergences from conventional fashion editorial had resulted in adverts being withdrawn. But Emap now reasoned that, since advertising and sales receipts were both relatively meagre, a sales-focussed overhaul was a low-risk manoeuvre. It also knew that advertising support would be forthcoming if the magazine began to sell in large numbers.

Around a year was spent trying to tune the magazine formula. Focus group research substantiated the development team's hunches that the existing sector was, in McIlheney's (1998) words, 'too metropolitan, self-involved' and narrow for most men, whilst *loaded*'s success was taken as further corroboration of the deficiencies of the current market. An editorial team was recruited, led by Mike Soutar, previously editor of Metro's pop music title *Smash Hits*, whom senior editorial personnel like David Hepworth considered a fitting appointment: 'Mike was a guy of a certain generation … mid-twenties. And he just had a feel for it, and had a bit of a vision for it' (Hepworth 1998). Broadly speaking, the strategy was to position *FHM* somewhere between *loaded* and *GQ*, and to appeal to men 'with one eye on their youth, and one eye on their future': 'the bloke in his twenties who would still go and paint the town red with his mates, but then would have to get up the next morning and carry on with his career' (Soutar 1997; and in the *Independent*, 7.7.97: Media, 7).

Focus groups had identified three types of male readers: 'those after specialist info; those who dip in and out of titles; and those who need general info to make lifestyle decisions' (Rich in *Marketing*, 21.9.95: 39–40). *FHM* would target the latter. The editorial team largely ignored the small amount of further research undertaken by the company, instead modelling the magazine on an *ad hoc* basis. Its core brand values were defined as 'funny, sexy, useful', a motto that became the editorial filter through which every page was passed, along with the vision of the 'average 25-year-old man'. Whilst clearly influenced by *loaded*'s recipe of humour, hedonism and heterosexuality, *FHM* largely eschewed its drink and drugs references and its focus on football and music. Drawing instead on the format of comparable women's magazines, and in contrast to the dense text of the style titles, it carried short, light features crammed with practical advice for readers on a range of issues including relationships, sex, holidays, personal health, fitness and fashion.

Emap also exploited its experiences in women's publishing by investing in a clear, consistent and high-cost cover strategy. *FHM*'s convention of featuring sportsmen and male Hollywood stars was soon replaced with a policy of 'attractive positive women', ideally, a woman previously considered unsexy photographed in 'sexy ways' (McIlheney 1998). After the sales dive that met comedian Frank Skinner's cover appearance in September 1995, and the success of the following month's 'World's sexiest women' supplement, which took circulation beyond 100,000 for the first time, the magazine's women-only rule was set in stone. Design, paper quality and photographs throughout the magazine were, similarly, given the kinds of resources that Tayvale could not offer, the latter costing around £24,000 per issue (an amount that was often recouped through syndications to tabloid newspapers). Considerable effort was also put into the title's coverlines and captions to ensure that they conveyed the magazine's core values. The editorial team deemed humour the publication's key mode of expression, always offsetting discussions about relationships, sex, health and careers with banter intended to prevent readers from becoming either bored or uncomfortably self-conscious. Such inflections fitted into the magazine's more generalized tone of 'blokeish' editorial and what McIlheney (1998) saw as 'a kind of intelligent populism … not too pretentious but not too stupid'.

After several months of tweaking, *FHM*'s revamp was formally announced to the trade press in February 1995. Editorial coverage would be extended to emotional issues and sex, and the magazine would now include a health and fitness section, 'Pulse' (to offset the launches of *Men's Health* and *XL*), a general section called 'Reporter' with 'how to' advice and articles covering motoring, cookery and other male-interest topics, and a separate fashion section. With the latter appeasing advertisers' disquiet about the magazine's new direction, *FHM*'s advertising team continued to reassure clients that a new masculine culture would welcome a title aimed at 'regular guys' (McIlheney 1998). Backed by a £400,000 marketing push including poster and national press advertising, these hunches paid off as *FHM*'s circulation steadily, and then exponentially, grew.

The Launch of *Maxim*

Dennis was a medium-sized consumer publisher at the start of the decade, primarily producing technology and computer magazines and occasional, self-contained 'one-shot' publications. Financially dependent on these sources, senior Dennis executives decided early in the 1990s that the company's long-term interests necessitated diversification into other markets. Women's sectors appeared relatively static and dominated by 'massive companies with big pockets' against whom it could be extremely tough to compete (Sawford 1999). The men's magazine market was felt to represent a more viable sector for expansion. Since the readership of Dennis' computer portfolio was mainly young men, the company already had some expertise in addressing male audiences, an opportunity to cross-promote a new men's lifestyle title, and a roster of potential advertisers. More importantly, the men's sector was recognized as holding considerable potential for ventures aimed at audiences to whom *Arena*, *GQ* and *Esquire* offered little appeal.

Dennis' interests remained indistinct until early 1993, when it was approached by two freelance music journalists, Mat Snow and Lloyd Bradley, with a proposal for the magazine which would eventually be produced as *Maxim*. In a forty-page document, they argued that there was no general interest magazine aimed at thirtysomething men like themselves, and that a single publication could fulfil the functions that normally required them to buy up to six separate magazines whenever they took long journeys. Whereas other London publishers had rejected this idea with the accepted lore that men were only interested in specialist publications, Dennis contracted Snow and Bradley to turn their outline into a dummy. After around a year, a prototype aimed at 35–40-year-old men was tested in focus groups. However, the tepid reaction of older research respondents scuppered Dennis' initial plans, and the development team retreated, sensing that it could only 'launch something to a market [of consumers] which [was] still prepared to accept something new, and then grow with it' (Sawford 1999).

Whilst Snow and Bradley were released, Dennis maintained its commitment to producing a mainstream men's title with a slightly older reader than the style press consumer, but lowered the age of its anticipated reader to around thirty. By this stage, Eric Fuller had been recruited as publisher and development manager of what still remained, in his words, little more than 'an idea on the back of a fag packet' (*Campaign*, 21.8.98: 18). With a long track record as a rock journalist on *Sounds*, and publishing positions on music and fashion titles including *Draper's Record*, Fuller had ideal credentials to develop a mainstream men's lifestyle title. *loaded*'s appearance, and some rudimentary market research, provided further basic guidance. As at IPC and Emap, then, Dennis found widespread dissatisfaction with the aspirational consumerism of the style press, which it condemned as 'full of $300 paperweights and $2000 linen fashion suits shot on location in Cuba' (Fuller in *Marketing*, 13.4.95: 27–9).

Looking for a suitable candidate for a more 'approachable' title, Fuller hired Gill Hudson in November 1994 as editor-in-chief to steer *Maxim* to its launch. Until this point, Hudson's career had been in women's magazines. Notably, as editor of *Company* and *New Woman*, she had successfully reinvigorated weary titles using a 'common touch' and a recognition of the selling power of sex in the wary post-Aids era of the turn of the decade. Hudson's personal reservations about men's magazines being 'crap and irrelevant' (Hudson 1998) were apprehended by Dennis' identical concerns, and by the modesty of its aims: a settle-down circulation of 50,000 copies per month by the end of its launch year (*Press Gazette*, 2.7.99: 18). Hudson recalled subsequent developments:

I came in, and basically had to start from scratch. So, it was a complete leap of faith, and I just thought, 'I dunno, I'll just do it for the kind of men I know'. And that was it. We had no research, no dummies … no roughs or anything; the first issue was just it.

So literally there was no research?

Well, not really, not on what I've done. There was lots of negative research … but I just binned that. So very, very, very – some would say – foolhardy, but at the same time I absolutely knew that there had to be [a market]. There were so many men out there, there had to be a market for it. It's like the male equivalent to Cosmopolitan.

How did you know that?

Well, it's logical [laughs]. Men are supposed to know all these things, they're supposed to have all these life-skills. [But] where would any man find out how to get a salary raise? How to check his balls for cancer? How to do anything? How to have sex, actually? … Where are guys going to get information from? Women have read about this stuff for years ... So I just thought, 'well why not?' ... and it was very much a *Cosmo* for men. (Hudson 1998)

As details of *Maxim*'s launch were subsequently released to the trade press, the contours of its identity became more apparent. In common with *loaded* and *FHM*, its consumers would be 'the heterosexual majority', and Hudson, typically, would not shy away from using sex to attract them (*Campaign*, 23.12.94: 13). However, the *Maxim* reader was imagined as someone who had 'outgrown' lad mags, or was the 'big brother' of a *loaded* fan (*Press Gazette*, 19.12.94: 9). Hudson explained how its content would therefore differ from these titles: 'We will be slightly older. When men hit 30, they are less interested in Hollywood stars and getting sloshed with the lads. We will address men's lives and concerns like financial and health matters, family and practical issues. We will be looking at men who are already comfortable with buying men's magazines' (*Press Gazette*, 19.12.94: 9).

Fuller elaborated on the demography and lifestage of the typical reader:

ABC1, certainly in a career rather than a job, and with aspirations to move on in his career. In a relationship, not necessarily married, but ... quite possibly living with a girl; more likely in an office job ... than to have a manual job. Old enough to have responsibilities and to be thinking about the future, maybe to have a mortgage ... but also still young enough to be interested in spending money on clothes and beer and exotic holidays and not to have lost the spark of youth completely; but, equally, old enough to be a grown-up. A grown-up with spirit! (Fuller 1998)

Like *FHM*, *Maxim* would position itself broadly between *GQ* and *loaded*, whilst seeking to lure readers from the style titles with 'broader editorial content', 'straightforward clothes' for men 'more interested in real life than the catwalks of Milan', 'real and approachable features [and] practical assistance' and 'humour and attitude' (*Campaign*, 23.12.94: 13; *Marketing*, 9.3.95: 11; *Press Gazette*, 3.4.95: 7; *Media Week*, 16.12.94: 11). Hitting the news-stands in April 1995, backed by a £750,000 promotion campaign, *Maxim*'s front cover featured a little-known model, a covermounted blues cassette tape, and cover-lines including: 'She wants you ... You're married, now what? Sex and morals'; 'Tyson exclusive'; 'Computerphobia'; 'How to: pull a rich wife, beat the taxman, fax God, save English cricket', 'career crisis: 30 more years of *this*?' and 'Stick 'em up! the greatest pin-ups of all time'. With a column inside by Rory Bremner, and features on beer, electronic organizers, 'sexy cars', and film, book and music releases, *Maxim*'s target market was clearly signalled. Within three years, the 'gentleman's *Cosmo*' was selling six times its original target and almost two-thirds the circulation of *Cosmopolitan* itself.

The Launch of *Men's Health*

Believing that there was a market niche for a general interest title with a health and fitness facade, sports publisher Rodale Press first produced *Men's Health* in the US in 1986 as a one-off pilot. Rodale's faith was soon upheld, as sales grew from 200,000 monthly copies in the late 1980s to over 1.2 million in 1994, doubling the circulations of the US versions of *Esquire* and *GQ* without plundering their readers. Looking to develop the brand globally by the early 1990s, Rodale calculated that conditions were ripe for a British version of its US market leader.

In pre-launch research, the UK team identified a male cohort that it regarded as the domestic equivalent of the typical US reader: the health-conscious baby boomer. A 'certain type of guy', aged around thirty-two (five years older than the average consumer of UK *GQ* and *Esquire*), he was 'young at heart' and keen to stay active, but concerned about his body and personal health, and aware that age, career and personal relationships were putting increasing strain on his ability to do the things that he had previously taken for granted (Boon 1999). Ambitious and relatively advanced in personal and professional life, he recognized the need for a healthy and balanced attitude towards both his physical condition and his work, finances, friends and family. Since *Men's Health* had always used health and fitness as a hook for general lifestyle issues rather than as an end in itself, such a figure represented the magazine's ideal consuming public. However, research indicated that this target group had little desire for a magazine that represented its interests. With regard to health and fitness, focus groups indicated that British men 'either did it … or they didn't want to know about it. A magazine didn't really have a place in their lives' (Long 1998). Yet, as advertising director Ralph Boon (1999) recalled, a 'commonality of attitudes and issues' amongst the launch team provided anecdotal assurance that *Men's Health* would capture men of a specific lifestage with its accompanying dilemmas. Rodale therefore pushed on with the launch, convinced that the magazine would find an audience.

Launch publicity presented *Men's Health* as an accessible magazine offering 'achievable aspirations' and 'practical, friendly editorial' on health, fitness, sex and fashion (*Media Week*, 9.12.94: 8; *Campaign Report*: 9.4.99: 18). Publisher Nick Williams suggested that its advice on sex, psychology and relationships was what 'men may have previously got from looking through women's magazines' (*Marketing*, 13.5.95: 27–9). Any danger that the magazine might strike consumers as 'too self-aware and self-conscious' (Long 1998) – potentially branding them as vain or feminine – would, in theory, be effaced by its ostensible focus on health and fitness, and its self-deprecating humour. Ideally then, men would be given permission to buy an informative, 'service-based' magazine without them 'really admitting that they're concerned about those invaluable pieces of information which you'd probably have never asked your dad about, and certainly wouldn't want to talk to your sister and mum about' (Long 1998).

Initial descriptions and the title's unveiling in January 1995 met almost universal cynicism within the publishing community. *loaded*'s publisher director (already able to command the attention of the industry because of the success of his magazine) announced that British men would not want a publication that took itself so seriously and was 'solely devoted' to health and fitness issues (*Media Week*, 20.1.95: 20–1). Advertising commentators expressed similar reservations about the translation of an American concept into the British male arena, parroting the conventional industry maxim that British men were less comfortable with issues around the body, diet and appearance than their Atlantic counterparts (*Media Week*, 4.11.94: 13, 20.1.95: 20–1). In presentations by the launch team, advertising agencies were supportive of *Men's Health*'s ambitions, but equally doubtful that British men were ready for a title of its kind (Hilton 1999).

Indeed, Rodale itself was only cautiously optimistic. Having assembled a small launch team, including three former Fleet Street journalists and former *FHM* editor Francis Cottam, it initially released *Men's Health* as a bi-monthly, supported by a £250,000 press and poster advertising campaign. The first issue, its cover showing a man nervously trying to look at a fly on his forehead, with the strapline 'Tons of useful stuff' and coverlines 'Get rid of your gut', 'Sex at work', 'Sex at play', 'Miracle mood-lifters', 'guide to scuba diving' and 'low ways to win arguments', was given a sales target of only 75,000 from a 150,000 print run. When Rodale soon announced that over 100,000 copies had been sold, and the magazine posted a first six-month audit of almost 115,000, it was as much to the surprise of the magazine team as to the publishing industry at large (Hilton 1998). *Men's Health* was the most successful launch of the year and the largest ever in the men's lifestyle magazine market. By August 1995, its circulation was almost 250,000 copies per month (Audit Bureau of Circulation, August 1995) (see Figure 3).

The New Phase in the Men's Magazine Market

The influence of the market's new pioneers, and *loaded* in particular, was discernible throughout men's publishing in the remaining part of the decade as a frenzy of further launches sought to imitate their characteristics and capitalize upon their achievements. Within previously 'specialist' sectors such as sport, music and car magazines, the editorial tone of the 'lad mags' (as *loaded*, *FHM* and *Maxim* were quickly branded) was promptly enlisted. Emap's *Total Sport* was thus notable in originating from the company's entertainment rather than specialist publishing division, in using film and music writers as much as

Figure 3 Cover of *Men's Health*, November 1996, courtesy of *Men's Health*/Rodale Press.

conventional sports journalists, and in initially launching as an *FHM* supplement. Similar attempts to bridge the gap between lifestyle and specialist markets, and to entice '*loaded*-style readers' (*Press Gazette*, 24.7.95: 8), included *Goal* and *Total Football*, a host of short-lived comedy titles (*Comedy, Comedy Review,*

Deadpan), and, in later years, car and motorbike glossies such as *Redline* and *Petrolhead*, the latter described as 'a combination of *FHM, Top Gear* and Italian *Men's Vogue*' (*Press Gazette*, 23.1.98: 2).

Attempts to extend the men's lifestyle press also adopted the market's new blueprint. IPC's *Eat Soup* represented itself as a bid to 'liberate' food, drink and travel journalism through the *loaded* idiom, for 'the pleasure seeking bachelor', 'who'd rather spend £100 on a meal cooked by Marco Pierre White than on a new lawn-mower' (*Guardian*, 9.9.96: 14; *Campaign*, 20.9.96: 15). Dennis Publishing sought to apply the new principles of men's publishing to the electronic games, multimedia and Internet-entertainment market, aiming *Escape* at 18–35-year-old men 'more at home reading *Maxim, FHM, Empire* or *Time Out* than *PC World* or *PC Format*' (*Media Week*, 11.10.96: 4). John Brown Publishing's *Bizarre* cast the same tone onto its Web-inspired content of cults, conspiracies, strange experiences and 'weird sex'.

By the end of 1996, market fragmentation began to reveal a number of discrete sub-sectors. *Stuff* and *T3: Tomorrow's Technology Today* had carved open a niche of 'gadget magazines' profiling consumer goods such as cars, computers, hi-fi equipment, clothes, tools and sport and leisure accessories, alongside lifestyle features and pictures of young women. The success of *Men's Health* had meanwhile precipitated the growth of a 'healthstyle' sector, which, despite seeing more failures (*XL, GQ Active, ZM, FHM Bionic*) than successes (*Men's Fitness*) continued to be seen as a rich publishing seam.[4]

With the lad mags continuing to experience substantial growth between 1996 and 1998, publishers also looked to append the market mainstream. Wagadon tried its hand, unsuccessfully, with *Deluxe*, a general interest magazine with a music bias for twentysomething men who were neither 'laddish' nor 'elitist'. Cabal Communications' *Front* proved somewhat more effective in finding space in the burgeoning market. Positioned 'beneath' the existing titles, it sought to scavenge younger readers and draw a new teenage cohort into the sector by applying the attitude and humour of the lad mags to areas including gangster culture, street sports, affordable fashion, television, and what one newspaper summarized as 'sex, tits, drugs and rock'n'roll' (*The Times*, 10.10.98: 20). With *Front* soon attracting well over 100,000 monthly buyers at this end of the market, IPC looked to provide a title for men graduating at its older boundary: the 'affluent but average' 25–40-year-old man, 'swapping kebabs and dead-end jobs for a decent career and some of life's finer pleasures' (*Campaign*, 16.4.99: 18; *Later*, 'first issue': 3). Launched in April 1999 with the tag line 'success, money, women', *Later* looked to slot into the market as an option for those men increasingly embarrassed by *loaded* and *FHM*, but reluctant to turn to the men's style titles.

The endeavour brought into sharp relief the maturity of the market and the speed of its transition. With a first ABC of over 90,000, *Later* only just failed to match expectations that would have been considered preposterous only five years earlier. In fact, by the standards of the end of the decade, IPC's target of 100,000 was relatively modest, reflecting the fierce competitiveness of the market. Whilst *loaded*'s promotional budget in 1994 had been £300,000, *Later*'s launch campaign cost £2.5 million. The intervening period had seen the market grow by 674 per cent, compared to 4 per cent in the women's market (Mintel 1998),[5] and metamorphose from a marginal sector serving a metropolitan elite into a genuinely mass market. In 1990, sales of its members, even broadly defined, aggregated to only 250,000 magazines per month. In August 1998, when *FHM*'s circulation crested, those of *loaded*, *Maxim* and *Men's Health* were over 456,000, 300,000 and 245,000 respectively and monthly sales in the sector, narrowly conceived, topped 2.3 million (Audit Bureau of Circulation, August 1998).

Sales declines at *FHM* and *loaded* in 1999 prompted cries that the lad mag era was over and the men's press bubble had burst. In fact, the sector had reached a plateau after a period of extraordinary expansion and the market leaders were suffering from increasing competition within the market (despite the high number of failures). The perpetual announcement in the UK of new launch plans for magazines aimed at younger men, older men, the mass market and men dissatisfied with lad mags (amongst others, *Ego*, *Quest*, *Gear*, *M2K*, *Limb from Limb*, *Mondo*), rather weakened claims that the market's day had passed. Emap and IPC could, in any case, take comfort from the profits of their spin-off publications and web sites (*Girls of FHM*, *FHM Collections*, *FHM Online*; *loaded Fashion*, *uploaded*), and brand extensions such as an *FHM* credit card, *FHM Holidays* and *loaded*'s range of hair products and eyewear.

Emap's attentions were also turned to the expansion of *FHM* into foreign markets. By the end of the decade, market-leading titles had been established in Singapore, Australia and South Africa, using local twists on the 'funny, sexy, useful' formula. In Australia, the magazine was raunchier and included more sports editorial. In Singapore, personal finance content was increased. However, the company was forced to tone down its representation of women after having its publishing licence revoked by the authorities after five issues for being too explicit (*Press Gazette*, 8.1.99: 12–13). Women in bikinis could only be featured if they were photographed on beaches *(Press Gazette*, 9.4.99: 1). Similar sensibilities had to be taken into account in the US, the market that Emap was most keen to penetrate. American advertisers were highly sensitive about sexual imagery, and were also relatively more powerful than in the UK.[6] Yet, as in the UK in the early 1990s, publishers believed that a vast portion of the male population was not being served by a sector dominated by *GQ* and *Esquire*, and that, with fewer national newspapers covering men's interests such as sport and fashion, the market might be even more profitable than in the UK (*Sunday Business*, 16.1.00: 12).

In developments that mirrored what had already taken place in the UK, US *Maxim* had already begun to redefine the boundaries of male taste. The American version had been launched in 1997 at a reputed cost of $20 million, with the manifesto: 'leave the toilet seat up proudly'. Responding to early criticism from the upmarket style titles, managing director Felix Dennis declared *GQ*, 'for men who like socks more than sex' (*The Sunday Times*, 1.8.99: Focus, 13). After his title became the most successful launch since *Martha Stewart Living* in 1990, selling nearly a million monthly copies within two years, both *GQ* and *Esquire* began to imitate *Maxim*'s racier cover policy. American commentators attributed the success of US *Maxim* to a backlash against political correctness, and the locker-room culture of 'frats' and 'jocks' that had first been portrayed in the 1980s in movies such as *Animal House* and *Porkies* (*The Sunday Times*, 31.1.99: 7). Echoing terms used only a few years earlier in the UK, the editor-in-chief, Mark Golin, proclaimed: 'We have been through a long-drawn-out "sexual harassment witch-hunt culture", where everyone must be on their best behaviour and men are getting bored with it. We are willing to say what is on our mind and damn the consequences' (*The Sunday Times*, 31.1.99: 7).

Such 'regular guys' or 'frat boys' were seen as the counterpart of the 'British lad', and, reversing the pattern of a few years earlier, when American publications and personnel threatened to conquer both sides of the Atlantic, it was British editors who were deemed most qualified to represent them. 'A guy's a guy wherever he lives', claimed Ed Needham, former editor of UK *FHM*, as he launched the US version in summer 1999. Mike Soutar, his UK predecessor and now his main rival as editor-in-chief of US *Maxim*, agreed: 'being a guy is a fairly universal state of mind' (*The Sunday Times*, 1.8.99: Focus, 13). The market appeared to confirm such views. By early 2000, after just over three years, *Maxim* was the best selling magazine in the American men's press with over 1.5 million monthly buyers.

In the UK, it was unambiguously clear that a fundamental shift had occurred within men's consumer publishing over a period of barely half a decade. If this needed capturing in a single incident, Emap's estimated £20 million buy-out of Wagadon in 1999 supplied a powerful symbol of the period's transitions. As the publisher of *FHM* took over the company that had first laid the terms for the re-establishment of the men's lifestyle sector, the deal confirmed both the triumph of the lad mags over the floundering style titles, and the eclipse of the new man by the new lad.

Concluding Comments

By the end of 1995, all four major UK consumer publishers, Condé Nast, NatMags, Emap and IPC, owned a men's lifestyle title, and the sector's new entrants had established it as the industry's 'hottest market' (*Campaign*, 10.2.95: 21–2). Some important points can be drawn from this chapter's consideration of the events that governed this development. First, it is worth noting the debt that these magazines owed to the monthly women's market, as well as to their predecessors in the style press. *Arena*, *GQ* and *Esquire* certainly primed retailers, distributors and advertisers for the market's second phase. However, whilst, editorially, the style titles served largely as negative models for the mass-market publications, that is, examples of what to avoid, women's glossies provided more positive sources of inspiration. *loaded* learnt from their technique of toasting rather than reproaching the gender of its audience; *Cosmopolitan* was evidently the model for *Maxim*; and *FHM* treated its readers like those of Emap's women's titles: in need of information that could help them make lifestyle decisions (*Campaign*, 12.4.96: 7). It was also the women's market, with Gill Hudson a key protagonist, that legitimized the use of sex in magazines that was such a central part of the lad mags' editorial composition.

The wider implications of this influence are arresting, suggesting a convergence between men's and women's interests that was not always apparent from the magazines themselves. Certainly, though, a common explanation amongst senior Emap executives for *FHM*'s popularity was that men were becoming more like women in a number of important respects. Emap Metro chief executive Tom Moloney reflected notably in 1997 that men seemed to have become increasingly interested in many of the issues that had driven the women's market, including their relations with lovers, friends, bosses and their own bodies. 'Traditionally, men didn't have that angst. Their attitude was "I'm a man – I drink, I fart, I exist". This is a new phenomenon' (*Campaign*, 28.2.97: 36–7). Other market practitioners hypothesized similarly that men's increasing concern with fashion and appearance, their growing self-consciousness, their integration into service sector industries, and their developing interest in family life were directly associated with their renewed interest in lifestyle titles. As I suggest in forthcoming chapters, however, such general claims were hugely speculative and the degree to which they were consciously fed into daily production practices was probably minimal.

The influence of the British music press on these second-wave men's magazines was also notable. Many of the key figures in the consolidation of the market came from positions in the music sector, including James Brown and Tim Southwell, whose backgrounds I discuss in greater depth in Chapter 5, as well as *FHM* editor Mike Soutar. More senior decision-makers at both IPC and Emap, such as Alan Lewis, Barry McIlheney and Dave Hepworth, also had backgrounds in entertainment titles, particularly music publications. It was out of their publishing divisions, those anchored in post-war British popular culture, that the market's most successful launches derived. Only *Men's Health*, the most distinct of the four titles I have discussed in this chapter, stemmed from roots outside the UK.

Third, to restate a crucial point, until the mid-1990s, very few industry personnel had any faith in the feasibility of a mainstream magazine for men or any idea about how to address its possible consumer. The mass market was, in this sense, almost inconceivable; or, at least, the way in which it was imagined ensured its constriction. Doubts amongst both advertisers and publishing houses about the mass market were not simply *illustrative* of industry opinion. Imbricated in the industry's institutional knowledge, and thus in its production possibilities, these were discourses that held back the expansion of the men's lifestyle press. As the initial experiences of *Maxim*'s originators suggested, publishing houses were, for some time, almost unquestioningly disparaging of the notion that general interest magazines beyond the style press were commercially operable. Rod Sopp recalled similar difficulties when the idea of the men's style title had been first touted: 'Industry punters ... all agreed there was a place for women's fashion magazines because women were always trying to better themselves. Men, on the other hand, always believed they were perfect. And that was, in a nutshell, why men's fashion titles wouldn't work' (*Campaign Report*, 19.9.97: 8).

The almost wholesale shifts that subsequently occurred in industry conceptions of 'the market' and the 'men's magazine consumer' reflected both the power and make-up of industry dogma, and the uncertainty that characterized attempts to understand the market. Even in those companies that regarded its bare spaces as fertile rather than barren, efforts to visualize the target reader had little focus for some time. Publishing companies were broadly guided by calculations about advertising revenues and general assessments of shifts in lived male cultures. However, vague publishing plans for the magazines I have described appeared to take shape only when editorial figures were introduced to development operations. When progress was made, it was not so much through formal research undertaken by publishing companies, but mainly via the intuition and faith of certain editorial personnel. Indeed, focus group and market research was often overruled or ignored by editorial figures in their decisions to push on with market launches and in their formulation of magazine identities. Personal motivations, preferences and expertise were significant here, as intimated in recurrent antipathies towards the style press and the sorts of credentials casually expressed in Hepworth's endorsement of Soutar as 'a guy' of 'a certain generation'.

Finally then, the difficulty of knowing the tastes and cultures of consumers, and the key role of the 'gut understandings' of editorial producers in articulating their identities and interests, upheld the authority established by individual figures and specific magazines – most notably, James Brown and *loaded* – to define certain aspects of the men's press in the 1990s. Whilst *loaded* rewrote many of the conventions of men's magazine publishing, laying the path for *FHM*'s subsequent ascendancy, it was Brown who could most lay claim to what had been highly elusive knowledge about the means by which to conceptualize and appeal to the mass male public through a lifestyle format. I shall return to and develop themes I have highlighted here throughout the book. Initially, I want to expand upon the observations I have made about the knowledges and strategies that informed some specific launches in the men's market by looking at such endeavours more generally.

Notes

1. At this time, the main competition faced by the style press in terms of advertising revenue came from the weekend review sections of national newspapers. Although the gay press targeted the same sorts of affluent young men as the upmarket style magazines, and *Attitude* cited *Arena* as 'as much a rival as any gay title' (*Media Week*, 7.1.94: 20), mainstream magazines rarely cited the gay press as a threat to their income sources. Many advertisers, keen for their brands to be associated as exclusively heterosexual, were reluctant to support overtly gay titles and advertised only in more mainstream publications. Certainly though, a significant proportion of the men's style press audience was gay. *GQ* was known as 'Gaily Queerly', 'Gay and Queer', 'Great Queen' and 'Gay Quarterly' because of its similarity to gay male erotica and the high number of homosexual readers it was purported to attract (*Media Week*, 29.7.94: 21).

2. Emap's *Q* was the market forerunner in the monthly music sector that *Select* and *Vox* joined. Launched in 1984 with a target circulation of 40,000, *Q* was selling almost four times that volume by the start of the 1990s. Along with *Empire*, it stood out in the Emap roster throughout the early 1990s whilst other titles slumped. Other specialist titles competing for the elusive male reader included youth entertainment magazine *Sky*, and more marginal (and often short-lived) style and cult magazines such as *Dazed and Confused*, *G-Spot*, *Don't Tell It*, *Mixmag*, *Phat*, *Zine* and *The Herb Garden*.

3. *Phat!* closed after three months, doomed after a controversial first issue led to WHSmith refusing to stock further editions.

4. Many launches failed. *Eat Soup* lasted only from September 1996 until August 1997, and *Escape* from October 1996 till January 1998. *Bizarre* was rather more successful, recording a first ABC of over 70,000 after its launch

in February 1997, and climbing to over 120,000 by the end of the decade. In the healthstyle sector, Stonehart's *XL*, following *Men's Health*'s launch by only a few weeks, tried to appeal to consumers through a sports and adventure focus, accessible advice and the style of the music monthlies; and Condé Nast introduced *GQ Active* in 1996 for high-earning, high-adrenaline 'go-getters'. Both failed to match *Men's Health*'s trajectory and were pulled from the market by the end of 1998. NatMags' *ZM* pursued an audience almost identical to those outlined by *Men's Health* and *XL*, men in their thirties with long-term partners and professional careers, demanding advice on how to organize and balance health, fitness, work, finances and relationships, but lasted only from the end of 1998 until January 2000. *FHM Bionic* was axed at the end of 2001 two years after its launch, and less than a year after it had moved from being published twice yearly to monthly.

5. By the end of the decade, the comparatively static women's press was itself looking to the vibrancy, humour and cultural nostalgia of men's magazines for inspiration. Clear examples here included *New Woman*, *Company* and *Minx*.

6. The US market was based on subscription rather than news-stand sales. This created huge postal distribution costs, making circulation sales a loss leader, and advertising the main profit generator.

–3–

The Logic of Market Launches

When we launch a magazine, we follow a formula. I'll tell you what it is. Before launching *Q*, we relied on quantitative research. We produced a dummy. We did qualitative research, assessed the advertising market and planned distribution for the first two years. Then we took a chicken onto Dartmoor at midnight during the full moon, slit its throat and read the entrails. And if I had to choose just one of these methods, it would be the chicken every time. (David Hepworth, Periodicals and Publishing Association (PPA) 'Magazines '91' Conference, 1991)

As editorial director of Emap Metro, former editor of *Smash Hits*, and the launch chief of *Just 17*, *Looks*, *More!*, *Q*, *Empire* and *Big!*, Dave Hepworth was considered one of the industry's most qualified launch experts. Yet, as *Press Gazette* noted, his address at the 1991 PPA conference was not just a swipe at 'publisher pomposity', but a reminder to delegates of the golden rule of magazine publishing: 'nobody knows anything' (13.5.91: 7).[1] Hepworth's dismissal of the value of using formal research tests, appraising potential advertising revenues and evaluating other market conditions highlighted the industry's official view of how to set about launching a new title. According to these 'golden rules', using market research as a route map or simply looking for obvious gaps in a sector were dangerous and unproductive strategies. Instead, authorities like Hepworth suggested, what was essential was to start with a strong hunch, a coherent editorial idea and an instinctive grasp of the target readership (*Campaign*, 25.5.90: 38).

Like Brown and Southwell, Hepworth had an editorial background that guided his interest in promoting 'creative' skills, rather than 'scientific' methods or rational financial calculation, as integral to the formation of new magazines and markets. Equally, like their story of the genesis of *loaded*, his allusions to the business's magical unpredictability were an exaggerated and partial version of a slightly less romantic truth about the workings of the industry that I will continue to examine in this chapter. Relatively un-formulaic, un-researched and unanticipated launches, such as those of *Q*, *loaded*, *The Face*, *Viz* and *Hello!*, entered publishing folklore partly because they conformed to the industry's preferred self-image of dynamic creativity, and reinforced the mystique of 'gut faith' that I analyse in due course. Furthermore, magazines driven by 'instinct' in defiance of industry common-sense and research intimations were self-evidently more likely to be market trailblazers. Thus, although their launch terms were unusual, their accomplishments fortified an industry ideal that was often taken to be representative. As I demonstrate, though, most new titles had histories that were rather less glamorous than those of the industry's crown jewels.

Nonetheless, by exploring in this chapter the different publishing logics and dynamics upon which men's magazines throughout the 1990s were founded, I suggest that the launches that I detailed in the previous chapter had many characteristics that were relatively typical. Although I want to concentrate in this chapter on the forms of knowledge that were at the heart of launch processes and the practitioners who mobilized them, the organizational structures and strategies that I more fully delineate in Chapter 4 are also of significance here. The amount of research a publishing house conducted, the frequency of its launches and the slant of its titles were influenced by a range of broader institutional and economic factors that included the state of the market and the size, character and expertise of the company. It is with these organizational, economic and market factors that I shall begin, before discussing in more detail the launch practices and research exercises with which this chapter is primarily concerned.

The Institutional and Economic Context

In individual companies, launch logics were often based at what Murdock (1982) defines as the 'allocative' level, where decisions are made about the overall policies and strategies of a corporation and its deployment of productive resources. The developments of the UK versions of *GQ*, *Esquire* and *Focus* were bound up not simply with calculations about shifts in advertising markets and cultures of masculinity, but also with board-level strategies relating to the global expansion of magazine franchises. Corresponding with such ambitions to build brands considered 'trustworthy' by the international advertising community, Condé Nast and NatMags launched titles less frequently and with longer-term commitments than other companies. NatMags managing director Terry Mansfield quipped that whilst his company produced its jewels 'like Tiffany's, one at a time', some other publishers were 'more like Ratners, displaying all their wares at once' (*Media Week*, 1.6.90: 15). In contrast, in the publicity that accompanied its establishment in 1998, Cabal Communications announced its intention to produce a launch for every month of the coming year. Although not fulfilled, Cabal's pledge characterized an attitude towards launches that also saw it condemn the 'fear of failure' of more cautious publishers and open and close titles with more regularity and less reticence than was customary elsewhere.

Before its expansion by the early 1990s into a huge, cross-media organization, such had been the policy pursued by Emap. Moreover, in its early days as a small independent publisher, Emap's allocative decisions had been driven mainly by the aims and interests of its key editorial personnel: hence the launch origins of magazines including *Smash Hits*, *Q* and *Empire*. Compared to NatMags and Condé Nast, Emap and the other goliath of consumer publishing, IPC, remained relatively prolific in terms of launch regularity. Ironically though, given the fervour with which they publicized *Q* and *loaded* respectively as titles launched on the basis of 'gut instinct' alone, these were the companies in which the most research was conducted and where its influence was strongest. One senior figure at Emap Metro observed that research results could govern up to 60 per cent of the decision to launch or forsake a title. This relationship between company size and research-based vigilance related not just to the prudence that escorted organizational growth. It also reflected the high cost of research exercises. John Brown, chairman of John Brown Publishing, declared that the only means of accurately testing a magazine's validity was: 'to do a huge amount of quantitative research, and, quite frankly, you might as well just publish the bloody thing!' (Brown 1998). For even smaller publishers such as Wagadon, research was almost prohibitively expensive.

However, Wagadon's negligible use of pre-launch research was not just related to cost. There seemed little point in asking 'punters' how to produce cutting-edge, trendsetting titles when one employed journalists to *know*. Meanwhile, its desire to sanction only certain kinds of fashion-oriented, left-field titles was illustrative of how the launch origins and subsequent character of a magazine were often, in effect, jointly determined. Publishing companies had particular cultures, advertising relationships and forms of personal and institutionalized experience and expertise that directed the sorts of titles they looked to develop. Just as these benefited IPC, Dennis and Emap when entering the men's press in the early 1990s, they also structured the launch logics of more upmarket publishers such as NatMags and Condé Nast. The latter's orientation towards monthly publications of only a certain 'quality' was expressed throughout the company, from the presentation of the managing director, Nicholas Coleridge, as a charming, well-bred, Eton-educated, haute bourgeois to the classic design of its meeting rooms, walled with black and white photographs of the glamorous, famous and rich. One Condé Nast writer recalled being asked to change an article that featured a pub because of this company brand: 'he said to me "Couldn't you make it a wine bar? Pubs aren't very Condé Nast"'.

That *Q* and *loaded* proceeded on the basis of less market research than the more recent Emap and IPC publications that I chart below was also connected to their positions as market forerunners. As I noted in relation to *loaded*, vacant market areas held much smaller financial risks for publishing companies than crowded ones. Attempts to penetrate the latter were seen to demand considerable certainty, whilst concepts could not be claimed to be so ahead of their time that research would be pointless. Conversely also then, as I explain further below, it was considerably easier to ignore or overrule research results in comparatively empty sectors.

As well as fostering more intensive research climates, the risks of launching into highly competitive sectors mititated against smaller publishing companies. Indeed, an overview of the decade was striking in revealing the power of the larger publishers to dominate the men's press. Although each of the big four consumer publishers, and rising power Dennis, experienced failures with individual titles (*Eat Soup*; *XL*; *GQ Active*; *ZM*; *Stuff* and *Escape*), they also maintained a hold on circulation and advertising revenues whilst smaller publishers struggled. Repeatedly, independently backed magazines were grounded by inadequate production, distribution and promotional resources (advertising deals, cross-title marketing, news-stand positioning, reader promotions etc.) that could not compete with the economies of scale and experience of the sector's major players. After Wagadon's failure to break the men's press in 1998 with *Deluxe*, in part because of an underfunded marketing strategy related to the collapse of the company's women's glossy *Frank*, the company's sell-out to Emap in the following year underlined the difficulties of independent survival when marketing and advertising budgets were spiralling, and global and online publishing were the new profit motors of the industry. However, that it was IPC that reinvigorated the men's lifestyle sector does warn against a crude conflation of size with conservatism. IPC's financial security was critical in encouraging the kind of radical venture that *loaded* represented, and in allowing the ambitious monthly print-run increases that exposed the magnitude of the market.

Economic factors were also significant in framing the number of launch attempts across the publishing industry as a whole. The recession of the early 1990s induced a noticeable slowdown in the release of new products, and it was not coincidental that the titles I discussed in the previous chapter were published as consumer spending was on the increase, both on magazines themselves and the goods advertised within them (*Media Week*, 15.11.91: 21, 24).[2] This revitalization was, of course, culturally as well as economically induced, based on shared representations of the state of 'the economy' that circulated around the industry. Nonetheless, it is important to acknowledge that perceptions of economic health were central to the renewal of interest in men's publishing. Industry expansion was also encouraged at this time by a Monopolies and Mergers Commission ruling that forced wholesalers to supply magazines to supermarkets and petrol stations, significantly boosting the number of retail outlets for all press products.

The range of magazine identities offered by the industry was also circumscribed by underlying economic forces, or, at least, perceptions thereof. Since publishing profits depended upon advertising as well as circulation revenues, it would be fatuous to suggest that the absence of certain magazine sectors was not related to the lack of advertising interest in certain segments of the population. Publishers and editors were doubtful, for example, that a monthly magazine aimed at men from social classes C2DE would be viable given this grouping's relatively weak spending power and the existence of more effective media through which to target its members (particularly television and tabloid newspapers). At the same time, it would be equally reductionist to see the market's development merely as a function of economic precedents. Although it could not have been sustained without the availability of advertising revenues from fashion, fragrance and grooming products (themselves some of the prime beneficiaries of the growth they underwrote), neither could it have emerged or could advertising markets have become functional without the critical input of editorial personnel. It is this key role of editors and particular forms of editorial knowledge that will become clear in the remainder of this chapter as I look more closely at launch developments, before further elucidating in Chapter 4 the relationships between advertising and editorial personnel and priorities, and the organizational structures and operational modes of the industry.

Launch Origins

The launch principles that Hepworth outlined in his PPA speech conflated two stages of the formation of new products that were often separable, and are most fruitfully analysed as such. These were the processes by which publishing companies decided to enter new markets and those through which they developed their ambitions to do so. Whilst highly innovative magazine ideas could precipitate a publishing company's resolve to tackle a new sector, more often, as in the launch histories I have outlined so far, vague plans had already been formed about the viability of a market area before a product took on any definite editorial shape. Although there was no shortage of plausible ideas on offer to most companies, and it was an undeniable truism that magazines germinated, in some sense, through 'ideas', it was the initial receptivity of a publishing house to a product concept that generally pre-structured its development. Haymarket's head of research and development estimated that around thirty coherent ideas floated around the company at any one time, of which between a half and two-thirds were discarded without any detailed examination (*Press Gazette*, 28.1.97: 14). It is how publishing companies were oriented to make such decisions that I first want to discuss.

A striking characteristic of the launch histories outlined in the previous chapter, and those throughout the sector, was that certain forms of wide-ranging and longitudinal research into men's lifestyles and attitudes played no part in editorial practitioners' evaluations of markets or in their development of new products. Although one might have expected publishing houses to track general shifts in the social and cultural climate through ongoing research, such assessments were simply not undertaken in this form. Nor were the findings and resources of marketing organizations and advertising databases such as Mintel, the Henley Centre and the Target Group Index (TGI) considered useful in market evaluations. Likewise, magazine ideas were not built on the basis of advertising and marketing categories such as 'the new lad' or 'millennium man' – terms that most magazine professionals considered clumsy and irrelevant.[3] Whilst publishing and editorial practitioners absorbed a large amount of formalized data on contemporary cultures and lifestyles, they did not use such material in a proactive or direct manner to seek out new sectors.

Where such research was significant was in the relationship between advertising/publishing practitioners within magazine companies and interested parties in the advertising community, with indications of shifts in consumption and leisure patterns used to generate support amongst advertisers for forthcoming titles. For example, in pre-launch promotion for *Traveler*, Condé Nast's sales team drew on market research that had identified the increasing number of independent and long-haul holidaymakers. In the men's market, publishing personnel pointed to the growing number of men joining gyms, cooking or buying aftershave to suggest transformations in male cultures, as appropriate to their products. It was only, though, in the post-production period, after a magazine's identity had already been fashioned, that this information was used.

Intuitive rather than research-driven reasoning was, then, the primary means by which companies decided to enter new markets and develop new products. However, launches were not truly founded on 'pure creativity' untainted by the calculated identification of market gaps, the pursuit of advertising revenues or the evaluation of competition. One obvious spur to the cultivation or acquisition of new titles, and, as I discuss below, a guide to their development, was the state of existing markets. In the case of *Front*, for example, Cabal Communications' primary impetus was an urge to enter the men's press before the market became too crowded, and therefore expensive, to penetrate. Likewise, its inspiration derived from a direct comparison of the men's and women's magazine markets. Cabal executives reasoned that the men's press would evolve in the same manner as the women's market, and that publications equivalent to teenage girls' titles (*Minx, More!, Just 17*) would prosper as the men's market expanded. The anticipation of market maturation was also influential in the launch of *Eat Soup*. Ambitious to capitalize on the success of *loaded*, and already having tested three possible concepts (including one title aimed at a gay readership), IPC executives were extremely receptive when journalist David Lancaster approached them with his almost fully formed plan. Lancaster had himself been guided by the identity of *loaded*, recognizing that it brought a new edge to his idea for a men's food title.

Market considerations could also relate to wider publishing and corporate strategies, as in the respective attempts by IPC and Emap to capture post-*loaded* and post-*FHM* consumers with *Later* and the 1996 acquisition of health and fitness title *XL*. Both endeavours represented attempts to protect prize titles by surrounding them with buffer publications, and to steer ageing readers from one company magazine to the next in the portfolio – strategies that had proved particularly successful for both companies in the music sector. Readers were not, though, the only considerations in such policies. Publishers were well aware that relationships established with advertising clients through one magazine could be harnessed relatively easily for subsequent others. Indeed then, despite publishers' denials that advertising markets were the launchpad for new products, magazines such as *GQ Active* and *ZM*, and brand extensions such as *loaded fashion* and *FHM Collections*, were clearly formulated with advertising revenue streams partially in mind.

With *loaded fashion* and *FHM Collections*, one advantage of 'spinning-off' from the main title was that advertisers who could not afford the ad-rate increases that accompanied circulation climbs were offered a cheaper alternative. *GQ Active* and *ZM* had rather more complex launch logics. *GQ Active* was originally inspired by the unexpected popularity of *Men's Health*. Rodale's achievements alerted Condé Nast to an opportunity to extend the *GQ* brand with a health and fitness magazine that could draw on men's booming interest in adventure sports and healthy pursuits, whilst securing advertising support on the back of the *GQ* heritage. The company envisaged that a spin-off would attract advertising from existing fashion, fragrance, sport and car clients, from specialized fitness-product companies and the casual clothes ranges being produced by fashion houses like Polo Sport, Armani and Tommy Hilfiger, whose upmarket apparel already featured in *GQ* (Read 1998; *Marketing*, 21.8.97: 23–4). Past *GQ* supplements featuring outdoor activities had already proved popular with both readers and advertisers (*Marketing*, 21.8.97: 23–4). Meanwhile, research with *GQ* readers that had found that half were keen for more health and fitness editorial, and half keen for less, suggested that a separate title might be beneficial for all concerned (*Guardian*, 24.2.97: 8).

ZM's roots were much the same. Terry Mansfield had felt for some time that he needed to boost NatMags' standing in the men's sector with a more mass-market product than *Esquire*. He had noted the growth of *Men's Health* and the success of NatMags' women's health and fitness title, *Zest*, and sensed this to be the sphere in which a new men's title might best be positioned. This belief was also stimulated by an observation that international fashion, fragrance and sportswear producers had begun to make goods for both sexes. As well as implying a shift in men's interests, this development indicated a highly lucrative advertising opportunity for a men's health-style publication. Indeed, twinning *ZM* with *Zest* provided an invaluable handle for appealing to the companies that already advertised in the women's title and could be bound into cross-publication advertising deals. The eventual magazine was only called *ZM* rather than *Zest for Men* because research revealed men's reluctance to buy a magazine associated with a women's product (Mansfield 1999a).

A magazine's name was a feature that was usually determined and refined well after the initial decisions that I have outlined above. It was in these subsequent stages that different forms of knowledge and expertise became more significant in the development and clarification of magazine launches. These were, first, the various kinds of formal research practices that most publishing companies conducted, and, second, the informal knowledges of editorial personnel.

Launch Developments

I suggested that the launches of *loaded*, *FHM*, *Maxim* and *Men's Health* progressed only when relatively crude conceptions of market possibilities were fleshed out by editorial personnel. However, basic launch ideas were often shelved before editorial figures became involved with them if quantitative market projections, based on anything from simple demographic data and Likert scale questionnaires to sophisticated modelling devices, indicated that the number of consumers who appeared to fit the basic conception of the target consumer were insufficient to make a title profitable. As one editor summarized, if a company came up with an idea for 30–35-year-old divorced family men, but calculated that only 5,000 such people existed in the general population, the magazine would not be worth pursuing.

Development plans could also be hindered at this early stage if focus group research pointed to an absolute lack of interest in a possible area of development, as in *Maxim*'s initial research, or found very little dissatisfaction with the existing magazines in a sector. Conversely, it was this kind of assessment exercise that encouraged the publishers of *loaded*, *Maxim* and *FHM* in the early 1990s that there was a thirst for men's magazines beyond the men's style titles. As their examples demonstrated though, this was essentially 'negative' research: more a guide to consumers' discontents than their desires. Early focus group testing of embryonic ideas functioned, then, as a gateway to further development, rather than as a refined editorial scalpel. For example, in evaluating demand for what would become *Later*, IPC solicited approval from a group of target readers for an 'artist's impression' of its thoughts (using cut-outs from other magazines) before progressing onwards. More often though, such research became operative in launch decision-making only once a more advanced dummy was developed.

Significantly also, it was in this phase, in moulding the magazine from a basic concept into a material form, that editorial expertise came into its own.

Thus, it was after the sanctioning of the skeletal *Later* prototype over which Alan Lewis had presided that he brought in Phil Hilton to take over the daily progression of the dummy. Hilton recalled that much of *Later*'s eventual content originated in his very early thinking once approached by Lewis, in particular during a train journey before he had even left his previous post as editor of *Men's Health* (Lewis 1998, 1999; Hilton 1999). Much as the *loaded* nucleus defined by Brown remained intact whilst peripheral elements were added and adjusted, the issues of career, money and relationships that Hilton resolved to make central to *Later* prevailed throughout its further composition. Likewise also, these were themes that were salient in Hilton's own life, as a 35-year-old career-minded professional living with his girlfriend. Similarly, at *ZM*, it was editor Paul Colbert who sculpted the magazine's identity into a distinct and discernible form, and it was many of his personal concerns that came to define the title. In particular, the magazine's championing of 'me-time', and its overriding sensitivity to the time pressures that he believed to be increasingly regulating the emotional, physical, occupational, domestic and social interests of the 25–38-year-old man, were contributions for which Colbert claimed responsibility.

Of course, a magazine's editorial development was piloted to a certain degree by the market location intended for it. *Front*'s content, and its use of the humour and attitude of *loaded* and *FHM* without their references to work, homes and serious relationships, were relatively logical steps given its desired position in the sector. Similarly, once acquired by Emap for the lad-mag graduate, *XL*'s relaunch was steered both by the tone of the younger title and the expertise of the company and its personnel. The magazine was repositioned as a 'more fun', approachable and 'sexy' title for the thirtysomething man 'who can't get over his hangover anymore' (*Press Gazette*, 7.2.97: 16). Here again, though, the personal logic of the editor was decisive in configuring the product, as former *FHM* editor Mike Soutar indicated in outlining the rationale behind the magazine's address: 'The only reason I will do things that make me fit and healthy is so that I can go out and do all those things that are bad for me … Having a healthy lifestyle doesn't mean you want to stop having fun' (*Marketing*, 21.8.97: 23–4).

Research trials were at their most significant once a full dummy, with live editorial, had been formed. Focus groups were the most commonly conducted form of assessment at this point, normally involving between six and twelve participants in six to ten groups held in various towns or cities across the country. These generally included questions about how participants saw the magazine in relation to others, whether they would be likely to purchase it, and the intended name, price, cover policy and design features such as typeface and masthead colour. Facilitators and other interested observers also looked for more general signs of how the dummy was received and interpreted by participants: whether they understood its layout and features, empathized with its identity, and approved of the range and balance of its editorial coverage. A number of alternatives or additions to focus groups were also used. *Front*'s pre-launch testing consisted of one week of scrutiny by what was effectively a 'friendship group', twenty young men including friends of editor Hernu and his brother (Hernu 1998; Sutcliffe 1998). Dummies of *Later* were not focus group tested, but given to over 300 men who were then interviewed individually about all aspects of the magazine. If conducting a 'microtest', IPC would leave a magazine with around 150 target consumers for a period of a week, canvassing their reactions to it at the start and end of the period (Tame 1998). *GQ Active*, like *Deluxe*, received no pre-launch focus group trial. Condé Nast had already looked into the sports and fitness markets, and chose to proceed slowly by releasing two stand-alone pilot issues to assess advertiser and reader interest before advancing to a full launch (Read 1998).

Clear-cut plans could be shelved or significantly reconfigured on the basis of research findings. IPC was forced to suspend a version of an older men's magazine that it researched a year before *Later* when indications were discouraging. At least three major publishers were rumoured to have abandoned concepts for young teenage boys because of insufficient enthusiasm amongst focus group participants. However, despite being mediated by research exercises, launch developments were by no means dependent upon them. The launches of *loaded*, *Q*, *Viz* and *The Face* were unusual in the degree to which they countered, bypassed and ignored research indications, but representative of an industry-wide attitude towards research that requires further explanation.

Attitudes towards Research

That many market pioneers had defied research signals and gone on to create and dominate new sectors was one of the most powerful symbols within the magazine community of the uncertainty that was a defining characteristic of its endeavours. The stories of titles that had confounded individual scepticism and collective derision were embedded in publishing consciousness. Those, like *The Hit*, *Nova*, and, in the recent men's press, *GQ Active*, *ZM*, *Eat Soup* and *Deluxe*, which had launched with huge self-confidence and industry support only to be quickly deflated by deficient news-stand sales testified in the same way to the unpredictability of consumer markets. Most practitioners could also think of specific examples from their own careers where research indications had proved inaccurate. Paul Simpson recalled pre-launch research for Haymarket's failed television and entertainment title *The Box* indicating that the magazine would sell very well in London and not very well in the North, when in fact it did the opposite. Another editor noted that Emap claimed to have research models that could predict sales of new magazines to within 2,000 copies, and yet had only recently failed in its bid to launch a television magazine in France.

There were more specific reasons why research was treated with considerable suspicion by industry practitioners. In particular, a host of customary concerns were routinely expressed about the quality of focus group methodologies and data. As Lewis suggested in relation to *loaded*, in pre-launch tests in particular, one could never be sure that participants represented an accurate sample of the target market, or, even, that they consumed any of the media they were being asked to discuss. Such worries were aired amongst the broader market research community in July 1999 when attention was drawn in the trade press to 'focus groupies': 'professional' consumers who would do or say anything just to receive a participation fee (*Campaign*, 2.7.99: 22). The artificial nature of the research environment was also often seen to compromise the accuracy of its findings, and was one reason why many publishing houses had begun to experiment with one-to-one interviews and friendship circle samples. Groups were frequently dominated by the views of individual members, or, according to some publishers, polluted by competitive bravado that encouraged men to exaggerate their demands for 'masculine' editorial content (Long 1998; McQuillan 1998). Equally, through trying too hard to be useful and impressive, and because of their growing media literacy, participants frequently tried to analyse or second-guess the company's publishing strategy, rather than simply respond to it as desired. Researchers were also accused of filtering their analysis through assumptions about what publishers wanted to hear.

Such conventional criticisms of focus groups were regularly rehearsed in the market research trade press (*inter alia, Marketing*, 23.1.97: 18, 13.2.97: 18, 13.3.97: 30). However, some doubts about the utility of research as a whole, and focus groups in particular, were more suggestive of the role of editors in patrolling the production and consumption domains that they sought to articulate. Thus, potential consumers were considered poor sources about their own interests: unable to predict their purchasing motivations or to see beyond the products that already existed in a sector. Significantly also, it was claimed that, in a volatile and capricious commercial culture, what most consumers asserted about their current tastes and preferences was almost immediately outmoded. Consumers and magazine markets were, therefore, not only considered unreliable and unpredictable, but were also assumed to be better understood, anticipated and interpreted by editors and publishers than by themselves. This was not simply that 'consumer fantasies', such as repeated calls for more 'ordinary' cover stars, were overruled by publishing dogma.[4] The notion of asking focus groups to generate original creative concepts was anathema to editors' sense of their own cultural expertise and their innate skills in understanding consumers, markets and the rules of publishing. As *Maxim* editor Chris Maillard strikingly proclaimed, 'If you need a bunch of people sitting in a room telling you what you should be doing, then you're doing the wrong job' (*PR Week*, 22.11.98: 10).

It was for this reason that research groups were not used as proactive agents of creativity, but as reactive checks on editorial expertise. Their role was mainly to check, refine and confirm magazine ideas that were already formed, as well as sometimes to negate them, as I have shown. Rarely were focus groups recommended as offering anything more than indications of what *not* to do and where markets did *not* exist. At most, as NatMags researcher Steven Sturgeon claimed, research functioned 'a bit like a lamppost to a drunk. You either use it as something to lean on, or something to illuminate the way' (*Press Gazette*, 19.6.98: 14). Yet, as I have highlighted, development teams did not always want to be enlightened. Research findings could be dismissed if editorial and publishing personnel already had sufficient faith that an idea was worth pursuing. Hepworth recognized that 'research might tell you that the market isn't there, but it kind of depends whether you're listening or not. Because there will always be an emotional argument to counter whatever the rational one is' (Hepworth 1998). With the criteria for when research was worth listening to vague and flexible – many concurred with the *loaded* team that strong negative reactions could be interpreted positively as suggesting that an idea had 'bite' – magazine practitioners acknowledged their tendency to accept those aspects of research findings that upheld what they already felt, and to ignore those elements that did not.

There was one other sense in which research functioned as 'support' for editorial intuition. Publishing staff within large, bureaucratic companies, particularly those answerable to shareholders, often demanded research backing to convince senior executives of the good sense of their plans. In such situations, research was much more consequential in the protection of publishing judgement than in the moderation of the editorial knowledges whose leverage I have highlighted.

Summary and Concluding Comments

It is important to digest the main points developed in this chapter. A key ambition has been to highlight the relationship between formal and informal knowledges in the orchestration of publishing markets and the actualization of magazine ideas as cultural forms. The recent history of the men's lifestyle press attests to findings in other commercial contexts that producers may approach consumption markets primarily in a state of uncertainty and doubt (Piore and Sabel 1984; Buckingham 1987; Lien 2000; Negus 1992). In seeking to enter new sectors and launch new products, publishing companies were often highly unsure about whom they were producing for and how they should do so. I have shown that formal research practices were generally considered to be unsuitable and insufficient tools for the mapping of unpredictable consumer markets and the development of magazine ideas. Proactive and ongoing research of a general nature into consumer attitudes and socio-cultural trends played a negligible role in launch logics in the men's magazine market during the 1990s. Thus, whilst Nixon suggests that the sector's development in the previous decade was given 'considerable impetus' by the identification in advertising industry research of new consumer segments such as 'innovators' and 'avant guardians' (Nixon 1996: 102; Nixon 1992), similar findings played no discernible part in its later phases.

More specific research, such as focus group explorations of existing markets and dummy products, was more influential in delimiting the direction and tone of launches. However, as in other commercialized cultural sectors including the newspaper industry (Tunstall 1996), the music business (Negus 1997), advertising (Nava 1992) and television (Buckingham 1987), such practices were treated with considerable scepticism. This was not so much, as Nava suggests in reference to the advertising industry, because the quality of the research was 'by academic standards surprisingly disreputable' (Nava 1997: 40). Indeed, many of the methodologies employed within publishing were highly sophisticated and innovative. Rather, it was the 'elusiveness' and unpredictability of consumer markets, as well as conventional doubts about research techniques, that subverted most practitioners' faith in the predictive capacity of 'scientific' devices. Research served mainly to frame editorial developments rather than to guide them. Although used to offer negative indications that might lead to concepts being rejected, it was considered incapable of generating ideas for new titles or replacing the 'vision' and cultural expertise of editorial personnel. Formal and tangible evidence was thus far less significant in launch developments than intuitive assessments, informal knowledges and personal faith. In this respect, although the emptiness of the existing sector meant that the magazines I discussed in the previous chapter were less governed by research than most launches, the general contours of their development were not abnormal.

This specialist knowledge wielded by editorial practitioners is crucial to this book's argument. The sparks of unbounded creative genius celebrated in the industry's most self-congratulatory launch tales were clearly exaggerated: commercial and strategic calculations based on market conditions, commercial strategies and advertising prospects were always, in some form, already made before creative concepts actualized them as discernible cultural forms. And certainly, as Jackson et al. (2001) have also suggested, some editors exaggerated the degree to which magazines developed organically, instinctively and spontaneously, whilst downplaying the input of research and commercial imperatives. However, whilst clearly navigating publishing houses in certain directions, such foundations offered only rudimentary outlines of the magazine identities for which they suggested support. Unless they could be appropriately translated through conceptualizations of target readers into coherent and concrete forms, market possibilities remained, in effect, immaterial abstractions. This upholds Nixon's (1992, 1996) assertion that the production of magazine forms must be seen to be dependent on economic relations that are only constituted and operationalized through specific representational practices, languages and vocabularies that are intrinsically cultural. However, it is editorial personnel, rather than advertising buyers and magazine advertising managers, who should be recognized as being at the heart of such relations. Whilst evaluating the basic viability of a magazine idea was largely a job of publishing personnel, taking it forward was an editorial one. It was editorial personnel whose expertise was the provision of flesh and form to basic market opportunities, the addition of cultural and symbolic meanings to commercial briefs, and the intuitive understanding of consumer values and lifestyles. As Hepworth summarized, the dependence on editorial contribution meant that magazine outcomes could be closely traced to specific editors: 'You could have taken the idea of *loaded* and you could have given it to ten editors, and you would have got ten totally different interpretations. And one would have been really successful, one might have been even more successful, one might have been only selling 40,000 out there. It's interpretation, it's feel, it's personality' (Hepworth 1998).

As I have suggested then, the production dynamics of the magazine industry were delineated by the division of occupational functions between editorial and publishing personnel. Such distinctions structured the different attitudes towards and uses of research that I have noted. Editors often ignored or were unaware of the research data that preceded their employment on magazine projects, as in the case of Gill Hudson with *Maxim*. Often regarding market researchers as 'stiffs in suits' who stifled creative vision, they did not always attend focus group sessions, even when their ongoing employment could depend on their outcomes (*Press Gazette*, 19.6.98: 14). It was advertising and publishing personnel within magazine companies who had the greater concern with such readership data, although they were neither inclined nor authorized to use it to inform a magazine's editorial identity. Instead, they used research indications in negotiations with advertising agencies and clients, relationships that were central to the economic success of new titles, but not necessarily their composition. Nixon's (1992, 1996) emphasis on the importance of advertising-derived conceptions of the stylish young man in defining the terms of establishment of the men's style press may thus derive from his focus on the advertising–publishing rather than editorial–readership axis of launch dynamics.[5]

I have argued, then, that editors held a privileged position in the development of magazine identities, thus far examining their influence only in launch situations. At the same time, by highlighting the influence of a range of advertising and commercial strategies and practitioners in these endeavours, I have also illustrated that 'creative' personnel worked in specific roles and within certain boundaries. The different interests, responsibilities and orientations of magazine practitioners demand further attention, as do the terms within which editorial expertise was exercised. Not only do we require a more nuanced and less monolithic account of production conditions than those normally suggested, but an acknowledgement also of the schisms, conflicts and divisions that pervade production processes (Negus 1992, 2002). It is these issues that the next chapter will address, examining in more detail the space, scope and nature of editorial power and the structural, organizational and commercial factors that channelled, constrained and upheld it in the daily operations of the industry.

Notes

1. This phrase is generally credited to Hollywood scriptwriter William Goldman, who used it to mock his own industry on similar grounds.
2. Some magazines, such as *Vox*, actually performed better during the recession than after it. *Vox* was primarily a music magazine, but also covered films, television and record collecting. As a genuinely more *general*-interest title than most, it thrived when consumers were looking to buy only one title per month and suffered when they could afford to purchase more. Other products were said to sell well in recession conditions if they could present themselves as 'cheap treats'.
3. Many reproached journalists, advertisers and market researchers for creating this terminology of 'fictional archetypes', 'media fabrications' and what Simon Geller called 'handy labels for phenomenon that they don't understand or can't be bothered to try and understand' (Geller 1999).
4. According to Terry Mansfield, publishers of women's magazines were constantly being told by consumers to put more normal looking women on the covers, but attempts to do so had always resulted in circulation losses (Mansfield 1999b).
5. Fleshing out to advertising parties a suitable image of the intended reader was particularly important when new markets were being established, as clients often had little conception of who consumers would be. In the publishing–advertising nexus, figures such as the 'new man' and the 'yuppie' may therefore have been much more influential in sketching the emerging style press reader than were analogous portraits in the sector's later years.

–4–

The Terms of Editorial Power

In February 1999, after a brief episode consumed with relish by the national press, James Brown and *GQ* parted company, the terms of their divorce unclear. Brown's exit as editor had been provoked by the contents of the magazine's just-published March issue. Focussing on 'men's twin obsessions', 'Sex and Violence', the magazine featured one photo shoot showing a naked, trussed-up woman in a bathtub full of blood, and an item on 'style icons of the twentieth century' which included Rommel and 'The Nazis' (*GQ*, March 1999) (see Figure 4).

Brown had been poached by Condé Nast two years earlier precisely in order to inject some vitality into their title. *GQ* had been left behind by the extraordinary growth of the lad mags, and its original response, a more serious and reserved editorial tone, had failed to attract readers in sufficient quantities to satisfy senior company figures. Brown certainly fulfilled their expectations, not just in the magazine – which, one month, carried a CD-ROM covermount showing two staff members licking custard from the breasts of a model – but also in the company's prestigious offices in Soho. Brown's exploits in Vogue House during his early months, before he began a drink and drugs detoxication programme at the suggestion of Condé Nast executives, included an incident in which he threw a bottle of champagne through his office window, showering the street below with glass (*Independent*, 19.2.99: 5; *Guardian*, 22.2.99: Media, 4). The promise of Brown's editorial talent, seen to reside in his exuberant personality and to depend on its free expression, secured latitude for such conduct for some time. But with his behaviour and editorial preferences becoming increasingly embarrassing for his employers, Brown had become, in their eyes, more of a burden than a messiah: inflammatory and reckless rather than provocative and innovative. Brown himself conceded that, after 'Rommelgate' and the accompanying media coverage, his partnership with Condé Nast was no longer functional. Reaping the status, profile and wages of the editor's position also meant 'taking the fall' when things went wrong (Brown 1999b).

March's *GQ* proved the best-selling issue in the magazine's history. Indeed, the release of the ABC circulation figures that covered the final period of Brown's tenure showed that he had increased *GQ*'s sales throughout his time there. In a phase when many other men's magazines were faltering, including *Esquire* and

Figure 4 Cover of *GQ*, March 1999, Willy Camden © GQ/Condé Nast Publications Ltd.

Arena, *GQ*'s advances under Brown were impressive. However, his appointment and his own eventual defenestration had highlighted familiar publishing trade-offs between sales, advertising support, brand identity and editorial freedom. Brown had been offered editorial *carte blanche* by Condé Nast only to find it repeatedly retracted when it threatened the values of the magazine and its owners, and the advertising revenues upon which both depended. For Condé

Nast, an upmarket publisher more reliant than others on advertising incomes, hiring Brown and promising him editorial freedom had been particularly risky. With many of its clients owned by Jewish and conservative business-people, Rommelgate and *GQ*'s increasingly graphic sexual content were especially unwelcome.[1]

Played out in the pages of the national broadsheets (including the *Observer*, the *Evening Standard*, the *Independent* and the *Guardian*), the incident brought to light some of the competing imperatives of the publishing industry, and the ultimate sanction on editorial autonomy: retention of the job itself. A closer look in this chapter at operating circumstances in the men's press will reveal the dynamics and balances of these demands and the relationships in which they were embodied. Those between publishing directors (or, more often, simply 'publishers') and editorial figures were particularly crucial in steering magazines and circumscribing editorial roles, and it is the nature of this partnership that is explored in the first section of this chapter. I then describe in more detail some of the different organizational structures and operational modes found amongst companies in the men's market. In doing so, I chart the lines of communication and authority that placed editors in particular relations with other significant decision-makers within publishing companies and influenced the degree of power and autonomy that they held. Having outlined the daily channels within which editors operated, the second section will examine the means by which they gauged their consumers on an ongoing basis. Brown's statement on leaving *loaded* for *GQ* that 'all the best editors put their personality into their magazines, and *loaded* readers aren't going to want to read about me entering my thirties' (*Guardian*, 21.4.97: 6) was suggestive of several editors' claims to edit their titles and understand their audiences by projecting their personal interests onto the pages of their publications, although other strategies were also common. It is important, however, to examine the often unacknowledged effects of advertising and sales imperatives on such editorial operations. Having charted these pressures, and the ways they were managed by editors, I reassess in the third section how editorial sovereignty and knowledge were continually negotiated and asserted within the publishing system.

Publishing Structures and the Editor–Publisher Relationship

It was *GQ*'s publisher, Peter Stuart, who was left to explain Brown's departure to the trade press and to recapitulate Condé Nast's expectations of the title's next editor. Substantiating his role as the long-term guardian of the magazine's commercial integrity, Stuart effectively apologized for Brown's conduct and assured the advertising community that *GQ* would return to its earlier identity as an upmarket publication rather than a 'lads magazine' (*Campaign*, 26.2.99: 8). In doing so, he highlighted the complex nature of the relationship between editors and publishers that the following section begins to explore.

Editing and Publishing Roles

The editor and publisher formed the central working relationship of every magazine in the men's press, and, in an operational sense, each undertook a very different task. The publisher was responsible for the overall profitability and commercial position of the magazine. Fundamentally, this involved maximizing advertising and circulation revenues and redistributing them appropriately in the outgoing expenses of the magazine, such as staff, printing, distribution and publicity costs. Overall then, the job involved directing the distribution, retailing, marketing and promotion of the magazine, managing the relationship between the magazine brand and advertising clients, and developing spin-off products and opportunities. As the 'managing director of the magazine', it was only a publication's editorial direction and content in which the publisher had little direct involvement.

The precise nature of the publishing role depended partly on the current requirements of the title in terms of its life cycle and market position. Whilst an underperforming title might demand a focus on marketing, a market leader called more for a 'street-fighter' to maintain market position, and a successful, glamorous publication that was heavily dependent on advertising incomes needed a 'brand manager' to nurture its name and reputation with advertisers. The definition of the publisher's role also varied between publishing houses, according to the publishing strategies and incomes that were prioritized. Publishers at NatMags were primarily 'brand managers', responsible for marketing and promotion, and focussed mainly on advertising perceptions. Likewise, Condé Nast publishers were 'meeters and greeters', dealing predominantly with advertising agencies and clients. At IPC, such responsibilities were generally handled by advertising directors, leaving publishers to concentrate on circulation and marketing strategies. Emap publishers also spent relatively little time with advertising parties and were largely concerned with market penetration. More radically, on its establishment in 1998, Cabal bucked industry convention by replacing the single publisher position with 'experts' bearing responsibilities for editorial, sales, circulation or advertising, claiming, 'We do not need one person on each title to make sure we can add up. We can all add up ourselves' (*Press Gazette*, 4.6.99: 18).

The editor's main task was to supply the magazine's editorial tone and content, and to define the imagined reader in the daily running of the title. In effecting the concept of the magazine, within the parameters of a publishing budget and strategy, editors were involved with a wide range of tasks. These included planning covers and future issue themes, writing and commissioning stories, directing the layout, designing pages, overseeing photo shoots, motivating and organizing staff, liaising between the magazine's various section editors and departments, and checking the overall feel of the issue and the fit between text, pictures, headlines and captions.

In contrast to the publisher position, the editor's job description was relatively consistent across the publishing industry. Variations between editors were expressed less as functions of the formal roles and responsibilities determined by organizational goals and structures than as the effects of individual editorial approaches and personalities.[2] Although some editors, such as Paul Colbert, launch editor of *Encore, Vox, XL, ZM*, and erstwhile editor of *Focus*, highlighted their *abilities* – in his case, as a magazine 'doctor': an expert in launching and repositioning titles – most defined themselves according to their personal editorial *style*: team-builder, manager or inspirational, benevolent dictator.

The separation of editorial and commercial duties established a relationship of mutual dependence between editors and publishers. In most companies, neither figure officially subordinated the other in terms of power or authority, and each relied on the other to perform their role effectively, as one publisher noted:

> The editor can't do his job if I don't allow him enough money to have enough staff or if the advertising team is hopeless at selling advertising. He can't produce a big enough magazine or a glossy enough magazine or whatever he wants to do. And obviously, if the magazine is hopeless, or addressed to the wrong market, then we can't sell advertising and we can't sell copies.

However, some publishers were formally positioned as superordinate to their editors, and others held effective superiority despite official equality. The 'publishing director' position that existed in some companies tended to incorporate some control over editorial strategy, entailing, for example, active participation in meetings about levels of coverage of certain editorial issues or the creative execution of front covers. More significantly, publishers often sanctioned the choice of new editors and editorial teams or the dismissal of old ones, whereas editors were very unlikely to have an equivalent say in the employment of publishers. Such remits reflected the publisher's responsibility for the long-term brand value of their title, and gave them a certain leverage to regulate the magazine's overall character and objectives.

Publishers also reported that editors came to them for advice on certain decisions, whilst the opposite happened rarely. In managing the overall consequences of editorial and commercial strategies, publishers were required to hold more holistic understandings of their product's overall mechanics than were editors. This was reflected in the professional background that each was likely to have. Publishers entered their jobs through a number of different routes, via positions in editorial, advertising sales, marketing and circulation, but were always expected to have some empathy with the 'creative' elements of print culture. For example, on his way to becoming *FHM*'s executive publishing director, Phil Thomas had written for *Practical Photographer*, before helping to launch and subsequently edit *Empire*. In contrast, editors were never previously employed in publishing positions, held little commercial expertise and always came from backgrounds in some form of journalism.

Nonetheless, the days no longer existed in which editors could deal exclusively with words and pictures, leaving cost and profit considerations to publishers alone. Editors were increasingly obliged not only to be aware of their responsibilities to balance sheets, but to be actively involved in some of the directly 'commercial' aspects of their magazine. The main task here was to pitch the publication to advertisers and clients, explaining its core values, characterizing its readers in terms richer than those provided by industry statistics, and outlining the magazine's future direction. Through their ability to talk authoritatively and fluently about these matters, editors were a valuable part of advertising sales processes. As I have begun to illustrate then, publishing's separation of creative and commercial responsibilities was not absolute. Moreover, the formal terms of editorial and publishing functions revealed only a limited amount about their interrelationship, not least in terms of where power and status truly lay, as I explore further in subsequent sections of this chapter. It is helpful first to delineate the organizational structures in which editor–publisher relationships were located in different publishing companies and the impact of these institutional arrangements on the autonomy of editorial and publishing practitioners.

Editors, Publishers and Organizational Structures

Brown's move from *loaded* to *GQ* had taken him from the UK's largest consumer publisher to an upmarket magazine house with only a handful of titles, at the opposite end of the publishing spectrum from IPC in terms of size, structure and identity. Brown complained that IPC had failed to match his ambitions for *loaded* and his expectations of just reward and status for laying a 'golden egg', the company's 'fastest ever payback' and the most important magazine product of the decade (Radio Four, 16.7.02). He accused IPC of underinvesting in the careers of his staff, in their ideas for brand extensions, international franchises and new magazines, and in the *loaded* office environment as a whole. Industry commentators corroborated Brown's view that, with a stable of over seventy magazines, IPC had been unable to fully capitalize on *loaded*'s promise and accommodate his aspirations, leaving both to their own devices with little direction or support (*Press Gazette*, 20.2.98: 18–19). Brown made it clear that he anticipated considerably different treatment at Condé Nast, whom he expected to devote more attention and resources both to his talent and his title. Ironically, his frustrations at *GQ* stemmed from the very handling for which he petitioned. Whereas IPC's complacency had presented him with considerable editorial freedom but relatively little institutional influence, respect or remuneration, the responsibilities he carried as a Condé Nast editor proved his downfall (Brown 1999a; 1999b). Condé Nast's attentions became stifling and constraining as well as flattering and developmental, denying Brown the creative freedom he demanded and forcing the crisis that led to his departure. The different operating structures communicated in Brown's contrasting experiences oblige further comparison.

IPC's 'Ministry of Magazines' label signified not just its might and ability to generate huge economies of scale, but also its reputation as a sluggish and bureaucratic monolith overburdened by middle-management and committee meetings. Even its full name, The International Publishing Corporation, and the imposing frame of its main office, King's Reach Tower, fitted this image. As the country's largest consumer publisher, it was hardly surprising that IPC was cast in such terms, or that it bore a multilayered hierarchy that placed editors some distance from their boardroom bosses. The first tier had been institutionalized in 1968, when the company's expansion and industry competition led to the creation of a publisher system that soon became standard across the industry. Initially handling the roles that became separate publisher and editorial director functions, publishers were placed alongside and above editors with responsibility for the profitability and long-term editorial policies of individual publications (Ferguson 1983).[3]

By the 1990s, the company's continuing growth necessitated all the more these functional divisions, but IPC sought to avoid being weighed down by the creative stagnation believed to accompany them. It was after the management buyout of IPC in April 1998 that the company's strategic aims and organizational structure were most significantly modified with this objective, and cost-cutting ambitions, in mind. Chief executive Mike Matthew promised an aggressive expansion strategy through new acquisitions and launches, and turned IPC's five publishing divisions into subsidiary companies with separate revenue, circulation and launch targets and individual financial accountability. Around 200 jobs, a tenth of IPC's workforce, were lost in the process. Although mainly from management and service positions rather than editorial or advertising, some industry commentators predicted that such cuts would compromise editorial standards. Matthew, in contrast, presented the transformations as beneficial for editorial power and dynamism, consistent with a long-term policy of 'returning the company to the journalists' (*Media Week*, 4.7.97: 12–13).

The changes were certainly intended to give IPC the air of a more competitive, flexible and creative business. In theory, with previous layers of bureaucracy removed and decision-making devolved to the separate companies, each could be more sensitive to the individual market circumstances of its titles. Given greater personal responsibility for their profits, managers would be more motivated to strengthen their brands. Meanwhile, lines of communication between managing directors and editors would be shortened, with the latter also given stronger representation through selected editors and editor-in-chiefs on the new subsidiary boards, alongside existing senior managers and publishing staff.

IPC's restructuring illustrates how changes at a company's allocative level could feed into the power, support and autonomy granted to editors in their daily working lives, at what Murdock (1982) calls the 'operational' level. I noted in Chapter 2 that board-level circumstances at IPC were crucial in establishing the necessary space for *loaded*'s original foundation. Indeed, with its editorial offices located in a low-rise building outside King's Reach Tower, even *loaded*'s geographical positioning reflected the relatively hands-off treatment it was accorded by IPC senior executives. In fact, as I have suggested, the company's strategic ends both liberated editorial policy and hindered certain aspects of *loaded*'s development. When owned by Reed-Elsevier before the 1998 buyout, IPC's profits were channelled towards growth plans elsewhere in the parent company rather than ploughed back into its consumer magazines. As plans for the expansion of the *loaded* brand through product spin-offs and international launches were thus constantly blocked, Brown's dissatisfactions were institutionally reinforced.

IPC's reorganization aped the structures already in place at its main rival and the industry's other colossus, Emap.[4] There, a decentralized structure had existed for many years and contributed to a company identity of energy, vitality, creativity and editorial empowerment that IPC lacked. The managing director of each of the five separate companies that formed Emap's Consumer Magazines section reported to the overall chief executive, but oversaw a relatively independent organization with its own board of directors and senior management.[5] By the end of the decade, then, men's magazine editors at IPC and Emap were working within comparable institutional spaces.[6] The editor was the title figurehead, working alongside a publisher and underneath an 'editor-in-chief', whose role I discuss below. *loaded*'s publisher himself worked under a publishing director who held authority over a number of similar title-specific publishers and had the power to hire and fire editorial staff. This publishing director was thus responsible for the overall commercial interests of a portfolio of music magazines, web sites and 'special' (new) projects. Above him and the editor-in-chief in *loaded*'s authority chain were the managing director of the Music and Sport division and the IPC chief executive.

Channels were similar at *FHM*, with the Emap Metro stable providing general publishing and advertising services much like the Music and Sport group at IPC. Publishing directors at Metro were likewise charged with a cluster of titles and could make staffing decisions. At *FHM*, though, an 'executive publishing director' combined the normal roles of the publisher and publishing director, working alongside a marketing manager, business development manager, commercial director, planning director, creative director and two production managers at the top of the Metro structure that was run by its own managing director. Above these figures sat the chief executive, editorial director and chairman of the Emap Consumer Magazines section.

At both companies, then, was a stratum of executives situated above the editorial and advertising teams of individual titles, and below a set of more senior managers. One important figure in this layer was the editor-in-chief, the editor's most immediate superordinate in the editorial chain. In IPC's Music and Sport group, this position was filled by Alan Lewis, who oversaw the launches of new magazines and the editorial strategies and repositioning of existing titles by providing general guidance for individual editors and recruiting and managing magazine teams. This included making sure that editorial personnel were performing their jobs properly and contentedly, whilst also incorporating the occasional dismissal of such staff.

With this kind of jurisdiction, editors-in-chief were ambiguously positioned as both 'creative' and 'commercial' employees: Lewis (1999) admitted that he was 'one of the proverbial "suits" now'. Usually, they were successful former editors (Lewis, like his counterpart at *FHM*, Mark Ellen, had previously helmed a number of music magazines), entrusted to mobilize their experience to ensure that the magazine's content would attract readers. Thus, unlike editors, editors-in-chief were not expected to have personal investments in their titles and audiences, or specific editorial axes to grind. Unlike many publishing personnel, though, their primary concerns were not advertising incomes. Rather, they were charged with maximising sales revenues through shrewd editorial strategies. In the development of *loaded*, it was appropriate therefore that it was Lewis who insisted that the magazine needed to include pictures of women, whilst it was publishing executives who lobbied for the inclusion of fashion content in order to maximize advertising revenue streams.

It was mainly the smaller sizes of Condé Nast and NatMags, publishing eight and eleven monthly magazines respectively, that differentiated their formal organizational structures from those of Emap and IPC. Both were subsidiaries of privately-owned American media companies, the Condé Nast International empire and the Hearst Corporation respectively, although each operated relatively autonomously from its parent organization. At both, magazines were steered by conventional editor–publisher relationships, but there was no intermediary layer of editorial or publishing personnel between this partnership and the company MD. Editors and publishers thus reported directly to Nicholas Coleridge and Terry Mansfield, who had more responsibility than individual publishers for the profitability of individual publications and assumed themselves to be the editorial directors of all their titles. Both claimed to see their editors and publishers at least once a day. In also maintaining vetoes over staff matters and direct responsibility for the hiring and firing of editors, each had a relatively powerful influence on the long-term brand identities and editorial directions of their magazines. This was even more the case at small, privately-owned publishing houses such as Wagadon and John Brown Publishing, where Nick Logan and John Brown had considerable input into magazine projects and performed roles that encompassed a range of both commercial and editorial functions.

Other companies were structured along lines between the large, decentralised, layered models of IPC and Emap and the more compact cultures of the smaller publishing houses. However, the formal structures and lines of authority that I have outlined describe only the official configurations of their organizations. As such, they do not fully capture the degree of autonomy granted to editors and the pressures they negotiated in establishing the identities of their titles. How editors judged who they were producing for and what to produce for them in an ongoing sense, and how their editorial ambitions were compromised and constrained in doing so, are the areas to which I now turn.

The Methods, Dynamics and Determinants of Editorial Production

Assessing the Reader

> 'How do you fill a magazine like Later with concepts relevant to grown up men?' I expect you were about to ask. Imagine research teams combing the British Isles; imagine computer-generated graphs or social psychologists with note pads and frankly you'd be fooling yourself. We at Later favour a more intuitive approach. Gut instinct, a bar, bottled beers and 12 or so keen creative minds are all we need. It is out of this kind of informal meeting, believe it or not, that we came up with the idea of asking celebrity blokes about the fighting they got up to at school ... We're still exchanging absurdly inflated tales of playground heroics so feel free to write in with your own similar stories. We'll print them and then screw them up very small and stuff them down the back of each other's shirts. (Editor's letter, *Later*, August 1999: 3)

Phil Hilton's address in the third issue of *Later* may have somewhat glamorized the creative process, but its picture of the intuitive and instinctive methods of editorial production was consistent with how most editors described their daily practices. Moreover, his quip that readers' contributions would serve only a transient purpose was a telling, if unintentional, comment on the role of consumers in defining themselves to those personnel employed to represent them.

After the uncertainties that characterized launch situations, once products were on sale, magazine producers could, at least, draw on the plain realities of circulation and readership figures to assess their achievements and the audiences they had reached. Such data was mainly supplied by two independent organizations, the Audit Bureau of Circulation (ABC) and the National Readership Survey (NRS), the latter segmenting consumers by basic variables such as age, sex, social class and marital status. Further details of the attitudes and consumption preferences of readers was offered by the Target Group Index (TGI), an extensive lifestyle survey utilized throughout the media. Publishing houses also carried out a range of their own formal research exercises into their readerships and markets. Primary amongst these were focus group evaluations and reader profile questionnaires, both of which were used with particular prevalence in the early months of a magazine's life and repeated thereafter according to company policy and commercial circumstances. Thus, NatMags researched *Esquire* on a twice-yearly basis and, after eight months of Peter Howarth's editorship, conducted an in-depth comparison of his version of the title with that of his predecessor. By contrast, in 1999, *loaded*'s editor was unaware of research having been conducted on his magazine since an in-depth 'tracking study' (an evaluation of every article and the front cover) in November 1995. In addition, editors mobilized direct feedback strategies to monitor their progress, welcoming letters and emails from readers. At *Focus*, such contributions were actually organized into a 'panel' of core consumers who assessed each issue's articles.

To varying degrees, these strategies underpinned the undertakings of most editors in the market. Data on the average age and typical occupation of the readership provided the basic terms of the consumer profile, and changes in NRS findings could significantly shift the terms of a magazine's address. As *Maxim*'s median reader age fell towards the mid-twenties in the three years after its launch, it dropped its contributing cartoons editor and science writer and converged somewhat in tone and content with *loaded* and *FHM*. Sector circulation figures also informed general redefinitions of the 'men's magazine reader', in particular, the floating consumer so crucial to monthly sales. Although some publishers and editors claimed that 'watching the opposition' was anathema to their creative ideals, in reality, they had little choice but to pay attention to the market's signals of what appealed to consumers. *GQ*'s employment of Brown, like the expansion of its 'Body and Soul' section and the addition of a sex column in the months after the launches of *Men's Health* and *loaded*, was a direct response to the rethinking of the men's press audience that began in the mid-1990s. As I discuss further below, the ubiquity on the sector's front pages of slim, young women from the light entertainment industries, such as Zoë Ball, Gail Porter and Jenny McCarthy, likewise reflected the apparent demand – primarily evidenced by the success of *FHM* – amongst consumers for coverstars with heterosexual rather than iconic appeal.

The blunt interventions of monthly readership figures, reader feedback via letters, emails and questionnaires and formal research exercises also informed producers' underlying senses of 'what worked', revealing matters such as readers' purchasing motivations and favourite features. In the research he observed in his early days at *GQ*, for example, James Brown – now editing by 'science "husbanded by instinct"' (*Press Gazette*, 11.12.98: 15) – was struck by the importance to readers of the magazine's fashion coverage. *Men's Health* learnt from its analysis that 95 per cent of buyers were influenced by its coverlines rather than cover image. Everyday output and monthly content were also guided and formatted by the various rules and formulae that most magazines developed. *FHM*'s editorial sieve of 'funny, sexy, useful' and *Men's Health*'s pledge for each article to carry 'takeaway value', some kind of tip or technique, represented the most explicitly and uniformly applied of such prescriptions. The templates that determined each issue's coverage – 'always health, a sex story, possibly a relationship story, nutrition and fitness' (Warwick 1998) – performed a similar role, whilst press releases, seasonal events and the launches of big films and music albums also simplified and routinized certain aspects of the editorial process.

Nonetheless, if readership figures, focus groups and consumer contributions certainly informed editorial production in these respects, they did so in only a limited and partial manner. Moreover, as during the pre-launch phase, research procedures were not designed merely to inform editorial assessments of consumers. The quantitative data of the ABC, NRS and TGI served primarily to lubricate relationships between advertising managers on magazines and advertising agencies and clients. The class background, aftershave preference and clothing expenditure of a magazine's average reader were examples of the kinds of common currency through which such transactions were negotiated. Publishers' own research into the media and masculinity or advertising effectiveness in magazines, such as Emap's 1996 'Men's Study' and IPC's 1994 'Ad Track', was also openly and deliberately formulated to facilitate dialogue between the buyers and sellers of advertising space.[7]

In relation to their efficacy as torches for editorial guidance, the scepticism surrounding focus group testing and market research was less strong once products were in circulation than in the pre-launch period. Publishers could, at least, consult actual members of the readership, rather than just potential patrons. However, issues around the representativeness of participants remained problematic, as Peter Howarth conveyed: 'What five blokes in Swindon think should not sway you; if they think your cover story was shite, you don't go and slit your wrists' (Howarth 1998). Letters, emails and questionnaire responses were handled cautiously because editors were well aware that they represented a very partial sample of the magazine audience, those readers already most committed to the title. Indeed, for the reasons catalogued in the previous chapter, practitioners remained cynical about focus group findings and the ability of consumers to represent themselves accurately and authoritatively. With such doubts pervasive in the industry, research results were 'always discountable' (Stitt 1998), although that was clearly not to say irrelevant.

Crucially, then, the information that could be usefully appropriated from formal and empirical feedback processes furnished editors with what were only skeletal and often ambiguous indications of their consumers. In their ongoing conceptualizations of and addresses to readers, research therefore played a supporting role to predominantly intuitive strategies. Amongst these, two contrasting editorial methods stood out, those of the 'professional' and the 'instinctive' editor (cf. Ferguson's (1983) 'thinkers' and 'feelers'). For the former, the classic means of conceptualizing the consumer was through a model of the target reader: ' ... lives in Streatham, has been married for a year with one child, and drives a car worth so much and pulls in that amount of money' (Sawford 1999). *Focus* editor Paul Simpson imagined a specific acquaintance from his time at university as a beacon for his ideas and accommodated his editorial address with this figure in mind. 'He was a guy who ran the university radio station, from a scientific background, so he had a very no-bullshit approach to anything that was outside that. So if you're doing something slightly different, you have to present it in such a way that grabs their attention very quickly' (Simpson 1998). Simpson's predecessor, Paul Colbert, had adopted a similar approach, making his constructed reader as corporeal as possible: 'we said "how old is he?, what sort of job?"; we gave him a name, we did a cardboard cut-out of him, and we would actually have him in the office' (Colbert 1999).

Men's Health editor, Simon Geller, epitomized the 'professional' approach. Although he felt relatively close to his market at *Men's Health*, he acknowledged that he was not 'the classic *Men's Health* guy ... I'm overweight and I like a drink ... my leisure pursuits are eating, drinking and watching telly!' (Geller 1999). Geller was unperturbed by this discrepancy. His previous posts having been mainly on women's magazines, he had never been able to 'rely on gut instinct' to evaluate his consumers. In his view, the job of doing so was an 'objective, team-leading exercise' (Geller 1999), the key being to instil in the editorial team a consistent profile of the reader.

> You hammer out various attributes, and at least everyone will know who it is they're aiming for. And the reason why that's so important is that everyone out there on the editorial team makes decisions on a one a minute basis: is this the right picture? Do we say girlfriend, or do we say partner, or do we say wife? Is he a dad? ... You sit your entire editorial team down in a room with your latest issue and you go through it page-

by-page, saying 'that's not right', 'I don't think our reader would like that picture'. ... And everyone in the room starts to build up a better picture of who this reader is: he's a man who doesn't like purple, wouldn't use the word 'gorgeous' [to describe a car], whatever. (Geller 1999)

It was in constellating these imagined audiences, with all the nuances suggested in Geller's description, that formal research was an auxiliary but always insufficient tool. It could never provide adequately detailed information about the target consumer's lifestyle, values or imagined identity – take, for example, *Eat Soup*'s 'pleasure seeking bachelor' who 'believes the good things in life are often worth bribing for ... pays by credit because he's got no cash, and drives fast because he's late' (*Guardian*, 9.9.96: 14; *Eat Soup*, first issue: 131) – not to require further elaboration. Focus groups performed a similar, ancillary function. For Phil Hilton, a practitioner particularly conscious of the confines of his lifestyle in spaces such as Soho and the Groucho Club, they were an essential means of keeping in touch with his less privileged readers: 'I accept that my life is very unlike someone running a double glazing business in Lancashire. I'm an English graduate, I hang out in a big urban centre. I'd be making a terrible, terrible error if I felt that I was writing a magazine for myself' (Hilton 1998). Hilton was more receptive to research exercises than most editors (see also Jackson et al. 2002: 60–1). He was also typical of several editors who presented themselves as close representatives of their audiences whilst recognizing that they were older, more metropolitan and more affluent than many readers. *Front* editor Piers Hernu accepted that his personal heroes, David Bowie, Oliver Reed and Ozzy Osbourne, were of a different generation to those of his readers, but maintained nonetheless that the magazine's interest in 'crime and danger and sport' reflected some of his continuing interests. 'I live the life, I always have done ... and I used to work for *loaded* for three years, so I know all about drinking and women and things like that and it's what I enjoy' (Hernu 1998). Editors who considered themselves, in this way, only semi-detached from their readers could often draw on junior staff members to monitor their intuitions: 'if [editors] are not twenty-two years old and going out largeing it every single night – cos they're probably not the best people to run a business – then they will make sure that they're surrounding themselves with young, keen, eager journalists who probably are doing that' (Newbold 1998). It was in this way also that female editors tended to function, using male personnel who more closely represented readers than themselves to hone any arising uncertainties. Work experience volunteers were another means through which 'real readers' could be tracked.

Such mediating mechanisms were superfluous for 'instinctive' editors, who presented themselves as the embodiment of their readers, and claimed simply to write their magazines for themselves and the editorial teams that they generally built in their own images. Thus, for Tim Southwell, judging the right tone and content for his magazine was 'the simplest part of all, because *loaded* has always been ... just whatever inspires us, whatever gets us excited' (Southwell 1999). Like Brown, he declared himself the magazine's reader incarnate, and assumed his own interests, heroes and lifestyle to be exactly the same as those of his audience. Ekow Eshun, editor of *Arena*, explained his editorial technique in similar terms: 'if I think that something's cool, and everyone else does here, then there's a huge chance that, once our readers are exposed to it, they'll have the same reaction' (Eshun 1999). Asked how he knew whom he was writing for, he explained that his consumers were, simply *'our* people' (Eshun 1998), those with the same concerns, values and preoccupations as himself and his editorial colleagues.

Editorial Capital

For both instinctive and professional editors then, there was little practical difficulty in fathoming appropriate content. In the banality of editorial production that most editors recounted, ideas came out in informal exchanges and what Eshun described as 'the cracks in the working day': the everyday, disorganized interactions of office life (Eshun 1998). Ideas also originated beyond the workplace, both in after-hours socializing, and, more significantly, through the entire gamut of social and cultural activities in which editorial staff engaged. Inspiration could thus come from the detail of everyday life, as Howarth outlined: 'Often, it will be something that somebody's just noticed, someone will have been over to America and they'll have seen the new Star Wars merchandise, and they'll say "god, did you know you can get this?"' (Howarth 1999). Brown related his own creative process:

> I've recently read a book about Bruce Reynolds, who planned the Great Train Robbery ... and there are some great passages in the book about just what clothes they were wearing ... you think 'is there anything I can get out of that?' So you can get your ideas from anywhere, from a book, from the park, from other people's magazines. (Brown 1999a)

For instinctive editors in particular, employment was thus predicated on the importation of personal, everyday tastes and cultural repertoires into professional life. Knowing intuitively what was 'going to be big', and having to do so three months in advance of it happening, also relied on stocks of subcultural capital and social networks. These partly represented what Bourdieu (1984) calls the 'habitus', perceptual structures and embodied dispositions that reflect cultural and economic structures and generate an individual's social and cultural practices and preferences. This is not to claim that all editorial aptitudes were simply 'instinctive'. As well as people-management, organizational and decision-making skills, editors had to be able to write well, understand libel laws and so forth. The work of professional editors was also characterized as much by the mobilization of conscious reflexivity (what Giddens calls 'discursive consciousness' (1991: 35–6)), the ability to interpret the nature of and reasons for social behaviour, as of more 'practical' knowledge of the audience. Not only did decoding the motivations, priorities and cultural benchmarks of the reader require considerable reflexive competence. Deconstructing social trends and stereotypes ('The New Old: getting old will no longer mean being old'), cultural signals, habits, hierarchies and dynamics ('how to dress for an interview'; why adults discuss the television programmes of their youth; 'The winners and losers of 1997'; 'the spread of the sick joke'), and interpersonal relations (the 'rules of dating', male friendships) also demanded an accomplished, if not always accurate, awareness of social and cultural space.

Simon Geller presented these editorial abilities as entirely abstract and transferable, claiming that the skill lay in tailoring one's style to the appropriate audience: 'we should all be able to get jobs tomorrow at "Fishfinger Gazette" ... the same core approach should work' (Geller 1999). As I have emphasized though, there were always significant affinities between the identities of men's press editors and those of their readers, suggesting an intimate relation between personal identity and professional position. The boundaries between work and non-work were often therefore indistinguishable. In order to build up connections and keep in touch with contemporary cultural life, editors were almost obliged in their professional roles to attend certain parties, premieres and openings. Popular journalism, summarized Lewis, was 'about keeping the antennae twitching and keeping your eyes and ears open' (Lewis 1999). Equally then, since cultural knowledge and everyday lifestyle were carried over into the workplace, 'private' pleasures, such as watching films, listening to music and even going to the pub were also professional investments. Job adverts frequently highlighted this relationship between everyday taste and employment. A search by James Brown's post-*GQ* publishing company, IFG (I Feel Good Ltd), for 'the best young magazine editor in the business' demanded that applicants, 'Must be able to link Paul Smith, Sven-Goran Eriksson and Honkey Sausages' as well as have 'flair, imagination, experience and a sense of adventure' (*Guardian*, 7.5.01: Media, 8). It was also registered when trade press question-and-answer profiles asked practitioners as much about preferences such as favourite adverts and who should play them in a film of their life as about their careers themselves.

This blurring of personal and professional life defined editorial work in a number of significant ways – as I shall discuss further in coming chapters. As Jackson et al. (2001: 57–8) have also noted, the industry's informality and sociability were often highly celebrated and accentuated (see Nixon (2003) for similar findings in the advertising industry). *GQ Active* editor Simon Tiffin (1999) remarked that: 'having fun can become your job', whilst Piers Hernu (1998) noted that 'even though you do work hard, it doesn't feel like it at all'. Citing American journalist P.J. O'Rourke, *loaded* senior writer John Perry proclaimed that journalism was 'getting money to do what one would spend money to do if one hadn't found a way to be paid for it' (*loaded*, July 1999: 94).

In contrast, the all-embracing nature of editorial work was sometimes portrayed as a burden. Tiffin himself pointed out that the '24/7' nature of the job was a 'drawback' as well as a 'great thing ... it's always on your mind' (Tiffin 1999); other editors reported feeling under constant pressure to think about their products. Meanwhile, a social life that was effectively subsidized was, in other senses, laboured. Socializing after work could feel almost compulsory, whilst leisure practices and personal interests could be effectively colonized by the need to scrutinize them for the sake of the magazine. Nonetheless, most editorial personnel welcomed a job that was not just, 'churning out nuts and bolts and then wanting to go home at five o'clock' (Sutcliffe 1998), even if, as will become clearer, the meanings attached to magazine journalism in relation to manual labour were rather more complex for some practitioners.

Second, the interdependence of career and lifestyle meant that the former could be significantly determined by changes in the latter associated with the process of ageing and the changing responsibilities that accompanied it. Although long hours and high pressure also contributed to the characterization of editing as 'a young person's game', editorial credentials were mainly compromised by lifestage transitions (transitions which themselves engendered changes in masculine investments, as I discuss below). Brown's move from *loaded* to *GQ* was typical, then, of the course that many editors were forced to follow as their lives diverged from those of their readers. When Gill Hudson stepped aside as *Maxim* editor in May 1997, she explained that, as a 42-year old-single mother, she no longer felt comfortable representing the magazine. New editor Nigel Ambrose confirmed why he did: 'the editor should relate to his target reader. I'm thirty-two years old, an AB1 male, single, but about to get married and educated. That's my peer group' (*Press Gazette*, 16.5.97: 1). Mike Soutar's move from *FHM* to *XL* (before editing US *Maxim* and then returning to the UK as managing director of IPC's Music and Sport division), Paul Colbert's trajectory from *VOX* to *XL* to *ZM*, and Phil Hilton's passage from *FHM* to *Men's Health* to *Later* were likewise related to concomitant changes in lifestage and masculinity. The rapid turnover of personnel in editorial positions was not just, then, indicative of professional ambition, but also of the precariousness of expert knowledge in an industry that could not afford to 'lose touch' (see Jackson et al. 2001).

Since their expertise resided in their instinctive perceptual repertoires, instinctive editors were particularly constrained in the pathways that they could tread. Indeed, Coleridge (1999) highlighted this limitation, as well as the limited tractability of the *GQ* identity, in accounting for Brown's 'lapses' as due to his inability to change himself sufficiently to fit the magazine brand. Most editors were more able, or inclined, to make such transitions, but still did so in ways that were consistent with their cultural resources and preferences. For example, in keeping with their interests in forms of upmarket consumption and the business-reader, Paul Keers and Alex Finer, the respective launch editors of *GQ* and *Esquire*, moved into customer publishing, with Keers eventually establishing his own contract publishing company and Finer editing *Hot Air*, Virgin's in-flight magazine. Other style press journalists found daily and weekly newspapers more accommodating to the changing modishness of their expertise. Music magazine editors within IPC and Emap benefited from being able to progress from younger to older titles as their tastes became dated. However, for editors without such opportunities, or for those no longer excited by the editing job, staying within consumer publishing meant gaining a senior editorial post or moving into publishing functions.[8] It should be clear why the opposite change, from publisher to editor, was unheard of.

Third, since popular- and sub-cultural capital was more critical for employ-ment than knowledge disseminated through the education system, entry into the editorial sphere did not require formal qualifications. Many senior industry figures, including Mike Matthew, Terry Mansfield and Alan Lewis, had left school at eighteen or earlier. Dave Hepworth described the top strata of Emap as 'the worst argument for the British educational system you've ever seen ... there have been times when you couldn't summon up a university degree between them' (Hepworth 1998). Although few younger editorial staff had entered the profession without some form of university instruction (less than a tenth of my sample), this said more about the expansion of further education in general than about the demands of the industry. Fashion and art directors tended to have taken courses with direct vocational relevance, such as art and fashion design. Amongst other editorial personnel, formal training was uncommon. Of those who had been to university, over a third had taken degrees in English, and almost half in other arts, humanities and social science subjects, many at top-rated universities. Those who had taken postgraduate journalism diplomas were not seen to have boosted their employability to any particularly meaningful degree. Attitude, enthusiasm and relevant knowledge were deemed much more important credentials. Indeed, in 1991, Nicholas Coleridge declared most training courses 'footling and time-wasting', more likely to drain zest and talent than to develop it (*Press Gazette*, 13.5.91: 7).

If the magazine industry was therefore 'unpossessed' social space (Bourdieu 1984: 147), in the sense that it lacked formal entry criteria, it was not, in any simple sense, 'open'. Entry into and movement within the industry was aided considerably by 'social qualifications', that is, connections and contacts, as well as specific cultural competences (Bourdieu 1984: 152). Compared to most professional and commercial sectors, hiring procedures were relatively informal. Many journalists got initial breaks through speculative approaches for work experience placements or with freelance articles. However, once within the industry, mobility often resulted from casual approaches, or 'poaching', by editors and editors-in-chief. Responsible for the construction of editorial teams, such figures often dragged former colleagues and friends with them when changing titles. Launches offered opportunities for outsiders to penetrate the industry, but connections were again vital here (see McRobbie 1998: 160). Both Piers Hernu (1998) and Phil Hilton (1999) recounted the limited scope of their recruitment sweeps. Alongside a few applicants to official adverts, many of the journalists they took on were friends, friends of friends or people recommended by colleagues. Hernu recalled: 'it was just "Oh fucking hell, who are we gonna get to write the magazine?" So I went through my phone book, and just phoned up all sorts of people that I knew' (Hernu 1998).

When experienced journalists sought new projects, they traded on being known already by the people they approached. Often there was no need to advertise positions formally, with shortlists drawn up based upon such informal contacts and networks. With market developments indefatigably logged by the trade press, and with a small number of companies operating in a relatively bounded world, people in the publishing community were well informed both about possible openings and the employees who might fill them. For editorial practitioners, social capital was also crucial in the performance of the job itself. Eric Fuller described as critical the journalist's 'contacts book, and their relationships with publicists and indeed with celebrities, and their ability to work the system' (Fuller 1998). An upmarket publisher concurred that his staff were expected 'to mix with a certain type of cutting-edge person, whether in business or personally'.[9] Indeed, it was through fraternizing socially with photographers, musicians and fashion designers, including Paul Smith, that Nick Logan had first recognized the opportunity for *The Face*.

The difficulty of codifying and classifying editorial knowledge contributed significantly to an occupational fluidity characteristic of other media and creative industries (McRobbie 1998; Negus 1992; Tunstall 1971). Careers were marked by ill-defined positions and demarcations and erratic forms of mobility, rather than established job titles and clearly defined promotion ladders and criteria (see also Jackson et al. 2001). With no systematic standards or official channels, entry into the industry was rarely smooth and almost never without periods of unpaid and insecure employment in work experience or freelance positions. Although many editorial personnel had advanced incrementally from local newspapers and trade publications into national consumer journalism, or from placements into staff positions, many others travelled more circuitous routes, working in areas including teaching, arts administration, television production and public relations, before finding magazine work. There was no typical pathway. A senior editor at *Esquire* travelled for two years, did six months of community work and was in advertising for eighteen months before initially becoming a music journalist. After then taking a journalism diploma he spent eight years at *GQ*, becoming deputy editor. Three years of freelancing followed before he was offered a contract at *Esquire* for his current position as editor-at-large. An *Arena* staff writer spent a year in his university town after graduating, doing an engineering course and various, mainly manual, jobs. During this time, he secured a work placement with a record label, helping their magazine launch and starting to write freelance articles for *The Face*. As this work became more frequent, he moved to London where he was offered a contract at *Arena* by editor Ekow Eshun when he himself moved there from *The Face*.

Fourth then, the dissolution of work and leisure boundaries was one reason why the industry remained unprofessionalized. The absence of systematic theories, fixed qualification criteria and specialized, intellectual training distinguished publishing significantly from medicine, academia and other established professions (Tunstall 1971: 66). Editorial knowledge was such that separating individual practitioners from abstract, applicable rules and procedures was impractical. Subcultural capital and intuitive 'man knowledge' could not easily be taught, nor was it usually desirable to conceal subjectivity, personal preferences and personality. As I shall discuss further in due course, the 'mystique' of the editor was upheld by this intangible quality of their expertise. Seemingly contradictory claims by many editors that the job was 'not rocket science', yet could only be done by an exclusive elite, served latently to elevate their worth. Thus, whilst, unlike McRobbie's (1998, 1999a) fashion designers, fine artists and DJs, many editors did not present themselves as artistic, cerebral creatives, several distinguished themselves as a certain breed of *idiot savant* by implying the routine nature of their brilliance: good ideas were completely obvious, but only to them.

Such self-portraits glossed over the requirements of work in the men's press that I have described, and, as Jackson et al. (2001) rightly point out, there were elements of bravado and self-promotion in editors' emphasis on the instinctive, creative and spontaneous aspects of their work. Nonetheless, highlighting the subordinate role of research in generating daily editorial produce was by no means deceptive, as I have demonstrated. Producers and consumers in the men's lifestyle sector were articulated not primarily by forms of market research – and this point merits particular emphasis – but by the intuitive cultural knowledges of key editorial personnel. As Emap MD Barry McIlheney, himself a former editor, commented, summarizing industry dogma, 'the best form of research is having an editor who understands implicitly the audience' (McIlheney 1998).

Indeed, the relationship between real and imagined audiences was always some-what ethereal. Since editors reserved the right to accept or reject consumers' self-representations, readers were positioned as 'the stars' (Tiffin 1999) of editorial operations whilst being virtually disqualified from speaking for themselves within them. The voice of the consumer was instead elucidated and mobilized by key editorial personnel whose expertise was precisely to 'represent' it.

However, this representation entailed not just the symbolic definition of the readership but also the defence of its interests. This was required because of the impact of advertising and other commercial imperatives on the magazine's daily production. It is these pressures, and how different editors positioned themselves in relation to them, that I shall now discuss.

Advertising Imperatives and Editorial Conflicts, Constraints and Commitments

In April 1996, US car manufacturer Chrysler was reported to have forced the withdrawal from US *Esquire* of a short story featuring a homosexual protagonist. Unhappy at the prospect of being associated with the piece, the company's advertising agency allegedly told editors that, in future, they were expected to inform Chrysler in advance about articles containing social, political or sexual content that might be considered 'provocative' (*Guardian*, 6.12.97: Review, 1–2). Such direct interventions into specific articles and editorial policies were, however, rare. Advertising parties understood that editorial production should appear free from commercial interference, that attempts to dictate content would be resisted, and, implicitly, that clumsy intrusions were not needed for their interests to be heeded.

More commonly, certain advertisers (fashion houses, in particular) lobbied for the favourable positioning of their campaigns and sympathetic editorial coverage. These appeals were sometimes granted to valued clients, whose solic-itations were laced with the threat of removing support altogether, as one editor recalled:

> We worked very hard at finding two or three things that we could incorporate in a fashion shoot. ... But it just wasn't right ... too young, too radical. And inevitably they say 'well, you're not featuring our clothes; obviously we're not right for your audience. We shouldn't really be advertising in your magazine'. And they'd [the publishing company] say 'well can't we get more [of their stuff] in?'

These threats were occasionally executed. In August 1997, a number of fragrance advertisers expressed displeasure at the market's increasingly downmarket and sex-driven environment, and Chanel dropped *FHM* from its advertising schedule.[10] The following year, the Nationwide Building Society pulled its campaign from the launch issue of *Front*, concerned by the magazine's sexually explicit content.

It was partly because these incidents, and those such as Brown's departure from *GQ*, were so loudly publicized that advertisers did not need to assert their demands directly for them still to compromise editorial freedom.[11] Open spats delivered a powerful message to editors about the expectations of the advertising community, reconfirming the borders of acceptable editorial policy. Advertisers thus benefited from forms of editorial self-censorship carried out on their behalf. Anti-corporate messages and radical sociological or political commentaries were unlikely to be considered appropriate. Likewise, in consumer product reviews, editors tended to stress 'the positives rather than leaping for the negatives' (Sutcliffe 1998) or would 'say nothing rather than totally slate the product' (Long 1998). The heavy presence of fashion editorial and the frequent appearance of wristwatch review features represented another form of accommodation to important advertising markets. Advertisers did not need to actively engage their persuasive forces for content to be skewed in their interests, as *Maxim* editor Chris Maillard outlined: 'It is a commercial business and therefore you do some-times, you put a feature in, or you might structure the magazine in such a way that it's possible to put advertising next to things. Or in such a way that, you might run a feature that will be interesting to your readers, but also advertisers will be into it' (Maillard 1998).

As Maillard hinted, some editors regarded advertising and reader imperatives as relatively non-conflictual. They fully endorsed the commercial objectives of their magazines and tasked themselves only with delivering readers to adver-tisers and sales revenues to publishing coffers. Loyalties lay firmly with the publishing house, rather than with any independent notion of 'reader interest' or personal and creative ambition. Phil Hilton explained:

> I don't really consider it a balancing act. That would imply that you're a creative indi-vidual trapped in a corporate straightjacket, whereas it's not really that kind of endeavour ... Really, your interests are identical with those of the advertisers and the corporate people: it's a big commercial operation: ... the Hollywood blockbuster rather than the European art movie ... it's certainly not a yearning from the soul. (Hilton 1998)

Such revenue-oriented editors recognized the dangers of certain advertising interventions and still normally resisted initiatives such as fold-out front covers designed to carry ad campaigns and the proliferation of advertorials.[12] However, objections were not based on commitments to creative integrity, nor to readers *per se*. Rather, they reflected an overtly commercial consideration, one upheld equally by publishing and advertising practitioners: the concern that readers took exception to titles perceived to be just vehicles for advertising. In carrying the voice of the reader into advertising–editorial negotiations, these editors thus represented the readership more in the sense that they 'understood' it than that they had any idealistic investment in its interests.

Editors could distance their primary aims from those of advertising–publishing executives whilst remaining essentially revenue-oriented. Many perceived their remit to stretch no further than the maximization of copy sales, equating editorial quality only with reader popularity, whilst acknowledging the consequent role of their endeavours in the title's appeal to advertisers. Concurring with the universal view expressed by publishers, these editors saw healthy circulation as a necessary precondition of advertising success. Reader interests were defended as the means to a commercial end, as John Brown outlined.

> Without meaning to sound noble about this, editorial integrity is absolutely, totally, first. ... Magazines work if people want to read them, not if people want to advertise in them. You can fool advertisers into advertising in a fundamentally unpopular magazine for a short amount of time, but not for that long. If you start chasing advertisers rather than readers, you are doomed. I mean, you need to chase advertisers very badly, they're enormously important. But, if you start putting them in front of readers, it's the classic tale of the tail wagging the dog. ... You've always got to put editorial first. (John Brown 1998)

Despite such pledges, editorial compromise could not always be avoided when content that attracted readers also alienated advertisers. The conservatism of some clients and retailers (in particular, international fashion houses and supermarkets) about sexually explicit material thus inhibited content that certain titles would otherwise have provided in order to increase sales: 'so what you've got to try and do is put in enough topless women to please the readers, but not too many to displease advertisers' (Fuller 1998; see also Jackson et al. 2001).

However, for other editors, satisfying and representing the interests, cultures and concerns of readers was a matter of principle rather than profit. Brown and Southwell's dedication to 'a magazine which unashamedly celebrated working-class Britain' (Southwell in *Campaign*, 15.10.99: 34) was a clear example of this kind of commitment, as I shall discuss in greater detail in Chapter 5. Non-revenue goals of this kind – ideological, professional, creative and personal – were seldom untrammelled. The first few months of *loaded*'s existence was, in this respect, unusual. Surpassing its sales aims rapidly and with little competition, and with advertisers at first wary to commit their support, the magazine's editorial team was briefly afforded almost unrestrained scope and space to pursue its interests. Changes in *loaded*'s production context soon brought about the state of constant, though civil, attrition between editorial and publishing personnel that editorial missionaries customarily experienced. As the influx both of market rivals and advertising support soon subjected the magazine's editorial producers to conventional publishing constraints, and personal investments were forced to vie with corporate responsibilities, a number of journalists became increasingly disillusioned.[13]

The main cause of dissatisfaction was not IPC's mollification of advertising sensibilities, but its reluctance to allow the editorial team to ignore the circulation successes of *FHM* and *Maxim*. In the ever more competitive battle for readers, female coverstars were clearly a powerful weapon, and *loaded* was pushed towards the same cover policies that its rivals had instituted. The magazine had initially featured more male than female cover stars, championing the heroes of its staff. As the market peaked, *loaded*'s occasional efforts to deviate from the 'tv babes' norm and return to its earlier stance resulted in the loss of a significant proportion of sales, allegedly over 40 per cent. Southwell declared that, although he 'would rather put Kate Adie on the cover than Melanie Sykes', such a decision would be 'circulation suicide' (*Independent*, 18.1.00: 10). Indeed, his announcement at the beginning of 2000 that the title's woman-only cover formula was to be scrapped was overturned after just one new exertion.

The incommensurability of Southwell's preferred version of the title and the one bluntly suggested by readers through their monthly news-stand behaviour exemplified a frustration that only certain editors faced. The intrinsically partial nature of editorial knowledge meant that discrepancies between editors' conceptions of readers and readers' own demonstrations of their editorial preferences were inevitable. However, only editors with non-revenue objectives experienced such sales imperatives as restrictive. 'Instinctive' editors, like Southwell, who believed themselves to be simultaneously representing their own and their readers' interests could suddenly be confronted with an audience that they no longer seemed to embody.

In such circumstances, claims to be representing core rather than peripheral consumers, to be challenging the readership's 'knee-jerk' impulses, or to be protecting the title's 'brand identity' were last recourses. The signals delivered by readers were so unambiguous, and IPC's hunger to match *FHM*'s sales success was so trenchant, that Southwell's attempts at resistance were futile. However, most disputes between publishing and editorial personnel were less clear-cut, with reader interests rather less transparent. How these battles over the discourse of 'the reader' were normally resolved, and what this revealed about the nature of editorial power, is the subject of the final section of this chapter.

The Negotiation of Editorial Autonomy

In the previous section, I noted the acknowledgement of publishers as well as editors that commercial success was dependent in the first instance upon editorial 'integrity' and freedom. Although I highlighted circumstances in which editors' attempts to maximize sales were curtailed, it remained the case that publishing executives felt their fundamental responsibilities as profit-makers to rely on the delivery by creative personnel of appropriate readers. Thus, as Ferguson (1983) found in the women's magazine industry of the 1970s, respect for editorial expertise was upheld not only by editors themselves but by their employers and senior managers. Even when they were senior partners in the editor–publisher relationship and involved in the editor's appointment, publishers accepted that there were limits to their own capabilities and areas where editors had to remain imperial. *Men's Health* publisher Tony Long's comments were typical of the publisher viewpoint.

> If you've got a good editor, there really is very little point in a publisher trying to get involved in that area. … apart from the fact that the editorial expertise of your editor, his experience, is really what you're paying for, it's pointless having somebody who does not have that experience trying to develop the magazine on a completely different agenda. (Long 1998)

Just as most editors accepted that they had certain commercial responsibilities, publishers recognized the importance of safeguarding editors from unwanted commercial pressures and shouldering the fallout from disputes with advertisers. Although editors were used to establish relationships with advertisers, they were also shielded from financial negotiations that might unduly jeopardize their independence, as *Esquire* editor Peter Howarth outlined:

> I will go and have the odd lunch, or maybe go to the odd presentation [to an advertising agency]. It's much more social where I'm concerned. People want to know where I'm taking the magazine, what I'm doing … and why I'm doing it. The business side of things is left to the publisher, because otherwise, you get into exactly that grey area where there is a conflict of interests, and someone says 'well if you do a 6-page feature on the new Audi TT, we will give you a double-page spread of advertising': you don't want to have those conversations. (Howarth 1999)

More significantly, as one publisher confirmed, it was the editor's special knowledge of the readership – his cultural authority in understanding and defining it – that was the decisive factor in clinching publisher support.

If, for instance, the editor decided to write repeated articles saying Mercedes were hopeless cars, that he hated Germans and that if you bought a Mercedes you were a complete ponce, that clearly would not please Mercedes and they would stop advertising! So, I would discourage him from doing that. ... clearly, I would feel obliged to point out to the editor that this could be commercially damaging. In the end, if he said 'look, this is absolutely true', or 'this is really important for our readers', then that's his decision. And we, the advertising and the commercial department, just have to take the rap for that.

The scarcity of editorial knowledge in relation to publisher knowledge was a crucial aspect of the power relationship between editors and publishers. For not only was the editor's ability to capture an audience the necessary, if not sufficient, precondition for commercial success, it was also more difficult to 'know' readers than to understand the interests of advertisers. The latter were a small number of material clients whose viewpoints were relatively transparent and readily available, if not actively offered. In contrast, the former were a mass of undifferentiated consumers whose collective preferences were elusive and unpredictable. The difficulty of codifying or formalizing the editor's ability to understand this readership engendered the sense of creative brilliance that was often cultivated around their aptitude in 'just knowing'.

Thus, despite their often official subordination to the long-term guardians of the magazine brand, the editor was presented as more pivotal in a product's performance than their publisher. Terry Mansfield's decision to swap around seven of his publishers between NatMags titles in May 1999 illustrated this clearly: to have done the same with a set of editors was unimaginable given their need to empathize personally with consumers. When magazines were successful, editors were given the credit and became significantly more irreplaceable than publishers. Whilst editors were regularly described as 'visionaries' and 'geniuses', publishers rarely received the same accolades or attention. As Barry McIlheney indicated, the latter recognized their normal position in the publishing hierarchy: 'you have to be ... prepared to take a bit of a back seat and let the editors take the glory. ... it's the editors who are nominated [for awards], it's the editors who are stars' (McIlheney 1998). That, correspondingly, unsuccessful editors were highly disposable and editors had shorter average tenures than publishers reflected the critical importance of editorial skill.

Selling Creativity and the Company Context

Whilst 'knowing the reader' was the editor's most powerful tool in negotiating autonomy, its currency varied according to the publishing house in which he or she worked. But it was precisely because publishing executives recognized that their 'commercial' ends depended upon 'creative' personnel that distinguishing the true power and status of the latter was so difficult. Since advertisers were drawn to magazines that addressed their consumers with intimacy and authority, it was a commercial strategy in itself to pledge to the advertising community one's commitment to editorial integrity and sparky, stimulating products. Throughout their public representations then, particularly in the trade press, publishing houses described their cultures and products as 'creative' so recurrently and imprecisely that the term was almost meaningless.

Championing creativity was always possible through some means. NatMags MD Terry Mansfield asserted that, since his own career had been spent in advertising and publishing positions, he knew to leave editors to their jobs rather than interfere in an area in which he had no experience. Mansfield presented himself as a talent spotter and manager, discovering and developing editorial promise rather than claiming any creative expertise himself.[14] His closest industry rival, Nicholas Coleridge, offered the opposite line. Having moved through a range of editorial positions on upmarket magazines with little initial experience of the more commercial side of publishing, he sketched himself as someone whose first-hand experience committed him to an utmost appreciation of editorial sovereignty.

In terms of company image, Emap was particularly successful in presenting creativity as central to its brand values. Despite its growth during the previous twenty years from an independent, regional publisher into a publicly-owned, multimedia, multinational colossus, it had retained a reputation for agility and energy, kept functional units small and self-contained, and avoided the labels that afflicted IPC. Reputation appeared to coincide with reality. Although more profit-motivated than in earlier years, the company certainly fostered young talent and, by finding new magazine projects and posts for successful editorial staff, retained a high proportion of key creative personnel. Many former editors, including Dave Hepworth, Barry McIlheney and Phil Thomas, had risen to senior editorial and publishing positions, and editorial figures were well represented on the company board. Emap's launch and acquisition activity, underpinned by a calculated business strategy of fast and aggressive growth with high operating margins, and its tactic of 'cluster publishing' (producing titles for different age groups within the same sector), both drew on and encouraged this culture of constant change and employee opportunity. Such measures imbued the company with a sense of creativity, editorial empowerment and informality that was reinforced in its policy of having flexible workspaces with few fixed desks and offices (and personal files in lockable mobile bins), a mode of operation to which even chief executive Kevin Hand was committed (*inter alia, Media Week*, 29.3.96: 19; *The Times*, 7.7.99: 42).

Other publishing companies looked to emulate Emap's ethos of creative dynamism, as IPC's restructuring indicated. On its foundation, Cabal Communications introduced itself as 'probably the world's most innovative magazine publisher' (*Press Gazette*, 12.2.99: 15). Chief executive Sally O'Sullivan and managing director Andrew Sutcliffe presented their editorial backgrounds as indications of their dedication to editorial-led publishing and sought to create an organization with few executives, layers of hierarchy or bureaucracy. With no fixed working hours or annual leave, a permit to bring pets into the office, 'mental health days' in which staff could take days off when they needed 'time to think', and free chocolate bars every Wednesday, Cabal clearly set out to generate an atmosphere of casual vitality (*Media Week*, 23.10.98: 16; *Press Gazette*, 12.2.99: 15). Likewise, as a stand against 'corporate breast beating', Dennis Publishing refused to issue a mission statement, instead producing an 'anti-corporate brochure' which condemned stifling bureaucratic procedures and praised lateral thinking (*Media Week*, 8.10.99: 14). Owner Felix Dennis projected his own anti-establishment, maverick eccentricity onto the company, affirming it pugnaciously at the annual Christmas party by shouting 'what are we?', a question to which employees answered 'Outlaws!' (*Independent*, 9.9.95: 22–3; *Guardian*, 18.12.96: G2, 2–3).[15]

As James Brown's experiences suggested though, there were differences in the constraints that editors faced at different publishing companies, and editorial autonomy and editorial power were not necessarily the same things. Editors could be given operational sovereignty without much further status or power within their companies; alternatively, they might be treated reverentially and yet seriously restricted in their daily practices. The revenue priorities and brand strategies of a publishing company were significant determinants of the standing of and pressures upon its editorial figures. Whilst Emap invested in successful creative personnel and projects, it was relatively quick to kill off struggling titles. Editors were therefore placed under considerable pressure to deliver readerships in a short space of time, and could themselves be disposed of with little compunction. Private companies such as NatMags and Condé Nast did not face the same demands to placate shareholders with short-term profits. Instead of pursuing market share or an involvement in every sector, they looked more to 'build' brands, supporting editorial teams over the long run to do so. However, the construction of robust brand identities was aimed to a large degree at upmarket advertisers, and this was indicative of the intimate relationship between the more 'glossy' publishers and their advertising clients. For their editors, this carried a pressure to conform to rather more conservative and restrained editorial policies than at the more circulation-revenue oriented publishers. In terms of general editorial status, Condé Nast did have a tradition of editorial representation at board level. However, whilst NatMags gave fairly sturdy backing to its editors, with little interference from company directors, Hearst policy dictated that editors could not be appointed to the NatMags board, a rule that had created resentment amongst several ambitious editors and fuelled accusations of an overly corporate culture (*Press Gazette*, 22.1.96: 16).

At Wagadon, (before the Emap buyout) the constraints on editorial freedom were of a rather different nature. Wagadon's commitment to only certain types of avant-garde magazines that sparked the interests of its inner sanctum of senior personnel represented an unusual dedication to the primacy of editorial over commercial aims. Fiercely protective of 'quality', the company famously turned away advertisers deemed unsuitable for its titles and was perceived to be defined by journalistic creativity rather than executives, research and meetings. Yet Wagadon's operating ethos could still constrain individual editors by problematizing attempts to diverge from past editorial traditions. With the company owner and many senior staff having previously edited its titles, residual investments formed an unwieldy inheritance for their successors. Nonetheless, Wagadon's commitment to editorial goals was more substantial than that of many other publishing companies. Just as there were differences between the motivations of individual practitioners, so there were important distinctions between companies in terms of their support for creative and commercial ends. At the same time, the power of editors throughout the sector to determine the identities of their titles was dependent on a further set of factors. These related to market conditions, and demand further explanation.

Market Stability and Editorial Value

I have suggested that struggles between editorial and publishing staff over the tone, content and direction of a magazine were fought over competing definitions of the interests and preferences of readers and advertisers. The advantage held by editors in such struggles was in the scarcity and commercial centrality of their expertise and knowledge about the nature of the audience. Naturally then, changes in these components altered the level of editorial leverage, and the editor–publisher hierarchy was dynamic rather than fixed.

Whereas the industry in the 1980s was dominated by 'suits' (advertising and publishing executives), the 1990s saw editors reclaim internal power (*Campaign*, 26.7.91: 14). This partly reflected the changing balance of advertising and sales incomes in the industry's profits. During the 1980s, advertising revenues expanded in relation to circulation receipts as consumer markets flourished. This trend was reversed from the early 1990s, when national recession reminded publishers of the risk of relying upon advertising incomes.[16] As editorial therefore became increasingly important in the overall performance of magazines, editorial talent increased in value in relation to publishing and advertising expertise. Both Emap and IPC promoted a number of editorial practitioners to senior management positions and appointed an unusual number of publishers from editorial backgrounds (including a number of figures who became instrumental in the development of the men's magazine market, amongst them Alan

Lewis, Dave Hepworth and Tom Moloney) (*Press Gazette*, 23.3.92: 7). In 1993, Michael Clayton became the first journalist in eight years to be appointed to IPC's main board of directors, whilst Hepworth became the first ever editorial director of Emap Consumer Magazines in May 1994, an 'editorial voice' in the upper echelons of the company (*Marketing*, 19.5.93: 4; *Press Gazette*, 6.12.93: 1; 23.5.94: 9).

In the men's press, the shifting power relation between 'creatives' and 'suits' was also underpinned by changes in market stability and the redefinition of the sector that has been the main story of this book.[17] At times of relative stasis and when magazine moulds were particularly solidified, such as at the start and end of the decade, editorial value was diminished. Magazines seemed almost to write themselves through entrenched editorial formulae that could be implemented by a relatively large number of practitioners. In contrast, during the uncertain and volatile period of the mid-1990s, as the established mould was broken, editors who could claim to understand the new male audience were in particularly strong positions to assert the worth of their expertise.

In this respect, no one had a stronger sense of their own significance than James Brown, who declared that he had 'discovered America' (Brown 1999a) by unearthing the mass market for men's magazines and labelled himself 'a genius'. This self-image was supported by the credit he was given by practitioners throughout the publishing community, a trade press that fuelled notions of creative individualism in its constant glamorization of talent and personality, and a national press that reinforced the cultural authority of editors throughout the men's press by courting and reporting their views and endeavours.[18] Brown's value was inflated all the more by his ability to claim to actually 'be' the reader that publishing companies were so desperately pursuing. Other lad-mag editors were rather less hyperbolic, but nonetheless advanced themselves by emphasizing their instinctive abilities to comprehend and address the young, mass, male public.

Meanwhile, market upheaval could also be liberating for the editors of upmarket titles. By disturbing the underlying assumptions upon which their publications were built, turbulence could give them latitude to reformulate titles beyond the normal brand identity. At the same time, when radical changes in content were deemed necessary, 'instinctive' editors were particularly vulnerable to dismissal – the innateness of their knowledge making them suddenly obsolete. Brown's predecessor, Angus McKinnon was one obvious victim of the new demands of the men's market. A serious character educated at Wellington and Oxford, keen on Pulp and Prokofiev in equal measure, and described by colleagues as 'donnish' and 'monk-like', his rendition of the *GQ* identity could hardly have been further from the version that his successor was employed to deliver (*Campaign*, 1.12.95: 21; 11.12.98: 25).

Summary and Concluding Comments

The different products that McKinnon and Brown commanded were conjoined by the *GQ* brand that channelled their operational scope as editors. Embedded conceptions of the reader, in which advertising and sales imperatives were immanent, restricted editors' freedom to define their titles with total sovereignty, as Brown's aborted attempt at radical reformulation highlighted. Nonetheless, his efforts underlined the dominance of editorial personnel in the determination of magazine identities, particularly in times of publisher uncertainty. Brown was employed to rearticulate and redefine *GQ* in tune with the times through the unique knowledge that he was perceived to possess about the 'new men's magazine audience'. It was the scarcity and value of this ability and understanding that initially gave him considerable purchase to impose his new regime upon the title. To restate a central claim of this book, magazine markets and products were only actualized through the interventions of editorial figures: it was only through their cultural representations, knowledges and resources that economic conditions were operationalized and commercial enterprises materialized. It was for this reason that publishing companies acknowledged editorial talent as their most valuable asset and, within certain boundaries, upheld editorial autonomy. *loaded* publishing director Robert Tame summarized:

> The 'do's' are, make sure you've got a brilliant editor that has a total vision for the title. … you hire your editors because they are the visionaries and they are the personification of the brand; they should own that brand, very much, and shape it. … On the business-publishing side, obviously we have an input, but you leave it up to the editor. That's why you hire him [sic]. (Tame 1998)

Whilst this chapter's fundamental argument has been that, despite various conflicts and subject to certain constraints, editors represented the key figures in the elaboration of magazine identities, several other points from the analysis should be reiterated and concluded. First, I have suggested that absolute distinctions between 'creative, imaginative' editors and 'economically calculating' publishers were untenable. Although the roles and functions of publishers and editors were in no way interchangeable, most practitioners regarded creative and commercial goals as interdependent and had some involvement in both domains. In offering themselves and their ideas as the guarantees of commercial success in advertising agency presentations, editors were a vital part of the 'marketing of creativity' that, equally, forced publishers to safeguard editorial integrity. 'Advertorials' manifested all the more clearly this blurring of creative and commercial frontiers.

It would be a mistake to argue that 'creativity' and editorial sovereignty were merely facades for a commercial logic and that content simply represented a means to deliver readers to advertisers and was thus 'dominated' by the interests of the latter (Harms and Kellner 1991). To do so would crush the true complexity of the relationships between commercial and creative imperatives and motivations – complexity that is obscured in overly systemic and economistic models of cultural analysis (Negus 2002). Indeed, I have emphasized that there were significant differences amongst editors in terms of commitments to personal, creative and ideological ambitions, and corporate and commercial ends. There was variation also in the strategies through which editors assessed the consumer markets that they addressed. Although all editors functioned primarily through understandings of their audiences based on informal rather than formal knowledges, some did so by imagining themselves as their ideal consumers, whilst others mobilized a more abstract conception of the target reader. These 'professional' editors still, invariably, had much in common with their readers in terms of age, lifestyle and value system, even if they did not quite embody them.

That there was little overt conflict between editorial and publishing staff was consistent with these variations in editorial orientation and practice. Primarily, editors simply came to learn the parameters of what was acceptable to publishers, and the advertising and sales imperatives that they represented. Many editors had no desire to impose their personal interests and values onto their titles, professing only to follow the terms of their commercial brief (although, realistically, there were limits to what most editors would be prepared to print). Moreover, since they tended to closely represent readers, editors were effectively pre-selected not to produce the sorts of editorial that would breach the terms laid down by publishers. As I have suggested, though, these terms were broad rather than specific, and the borders negotiable rather than fixed. Providing that they brought in sufficient readers and advertisers, editors were magisterial in interpreting the magazine's commercial mandate and articulating it to consumers.

Moreover, it was because the readership was always an imagined, discursive form, never entirely knowable or fully definable, that the arrival at a title of a new editor always signalled some shift in editorial policy: either a new way of addressing existing consumers, or a re-conceptualization of the target market. This was the case with professional as well as instinctive editors. An audience could only be conceptualized through ongoing, anticipatory, intuitive judgements that drew on the specific cultural resources available to editors. These incorporated the languages, practices and competences acquired through educational, professional and recreational background, and distributed via channels of class, gender, generation, ethnicity and other such variables. Even for those editors who claimed not to be ideologically driven, these means expressed personal judgements, vocabularies and orientations. Examining the backgrounds, identities, lifestyles and preoccupations of some specific practitioners, and how these informed the magazines upon which they worked, is the purpose of Part III of this book.

Notes

1. Nicholas Coleridge, Condé Nast UK's managing director, reported that his boss S.I. Newhouse, a member of the Jewish anti-defamation league, had not demanded James Brown's resignation, but 'he clearly didn't like it' (*Evening Standard*, 6.10.99: 19).
2. This is not to say that publishers did not have their own personal styles, only that they discussed what kind of publisher they were in terms of formal responsibilities rather than individual character.
3. The publisher position had not existed, as such, until the late 1960s, with advertising directors carrying out most of the duties that publishers eventually absorbed.
4. Figures from 1996 calculated IPC's total monthly magazine sales at 9.65 million, with Emap's at just over 5 million (*Media Week*, 9.8.96: 19).
5. Emap's broad media interests were divided into four sections for much of the 1990s: Business Communications, Newspapers/Printing, Radio and Consumer Magazines. The latter's five divisions were Emap Metro (music, film, men's lifestyle), Emap Elan (women's), Emap Nationals/Images (cars, bikes, computer games), Emap Publishing (sports, pets) and Emap Apex/Choice (gardening, photography, trains). Restructuring in 1999 saw the constitution of four new groups and a digital division. These included Emap Performance, which included music magazines alongside radio, TV and internet interests, and a revamped Emap Elan, now taking in entertainment, men's, women's and youth lifestyle titles. The changes were mainly designed to suit the new media environment and advertisers' wishes for cross-media opportunities, and were not expected to have a dramatic effect on most staff.
6. Positions and structures changed frequently. For the sake of ease, I am offering an outline of arrangements at the time of my interviews in late 1998 and early 1999. At this time, Emap Metro existed as a separate publishing division, and *loaded* was published within IPC's Music and Sport section.
7. The intention of 'tailored' research and qualitative studies of how magazines were read (which measured things such as time spent reading, number of pick-ups and brand relationships) was to provide insight beyond the relatively crude surveys such as the ABC and NRS. However, the incommensurability of the terms and measurements used in independently commissioned research, its potentially partisan nature, and the sheer volume of

information on media and consumption habits thus generated was somewhat self-undermining. Paradoxically, then, whilst publishing and advertising executives continued to demand further, more nuanced research, they also claimed that the amount of information available to them could hamper their decision-making and made them all the more reliant on personal judgements.

8. Emap's commercial director, Steve Newbold, estimated the average tenure of an editor on any one title to be around three years.

9. Such connections were also required of publishers, as Neil McQuillan's explanation of Terry Mansfield's decision to switch publishers between titles in April 1999 highlighted:

I think that you do get to a point where you've sort of exhausted your little black book of the people that you speak to, and the clients that you do business with and have close relationships with. It's perfectly healthy that someone should take a different view of the brand [and] think 'actually, we should talk to these people'. (McQuillan 1998)

10. A few months earlier, telephone sex-lines had been removed and reduced respectively by *loaded* and *FHM*. Citing concerns about the ethical content of these services and the aesthetic impact of their ads on the designs of their titles, publishers were also keen to placate upmarket advertisers who had begun to complain about the environments in which their campaigns were being placed.

11. It is worth noting, though, that advertising interests could be perceived as 'enabling' as well as restrictive in determining editorial tone and policy. As Southwell highlighted, promotional initiatives could fund otherwise unrealizable features.

I think there are ways of using those people like Guinness or Silk Cut or Coors beer, or whoever wants to get involved in that level, and do it on your own terms. So we're going to do a Hollywood issue for our fifth birthday, and we're gonna hopefully get Coors or someone like that to sponsor it. So they will get branding on pages, but the thing is, it's our idea to do the thing in the first place; but we can't afford to do it on our own, we can't have a big party in LA and that sort of stuff … we need a lot of money, thousands and thousands of pounds. So, the way to utilize these scenarios is to go to someone and say 'would you be interested in doing this?' rather than getting them coming in and saying 'we'll give you a hundred grand for thirty pages of branded product pages'. (Southwell 1998)

Advertising imagery was also recognized by many editorial staff as part of a magazine's appeal, an extension of rather than threat to its editorial tone.

12. Advertorials were adverts designed and written as articles by the editorial staff of the host magazine, and, therefore, effectively endorsed by them.

13. Of these, the most passionate and public dissident was Adam Porter, *loaded's* former managing editor, who, in October 1998, at a talk at London's Institute of Contemporary Arts, criticized IPC's 'cosy' relationship with advertisers and its excessive control over the work of writers and photographers. Porter went on to produce *Year Zero*, a news and lifestyle magazine for people 'fed up with PR blurbs' and asked, rhetorically, 'Why bother being a journalist if all you want to do is take orders and interview people?' (*Press Gazette*, 19.11.99: 4–5).

14. One of Mansfield's personal maxims was: 'there are three things that sell magazines: content, content, and content'. It was a phrase he used self-consciously not only in the (1999) interview I conducted with him, but in a session at the Total Publishing Conference in July 1999. In a version of another much-repeated self-representation, Mansfield declared 'I don't see myself as the talent. I see myself as Lew Grade: give your editors the right environment, encourage them to feel good about themselves and cross your fingers' (*Press Gazette,* 13.8.99: 12–13). Indeed, he was acknowledged as a 'hands-off' executive, who, despite his involvement in broad, strategic editorial planning, did leave editors to get on with their jobs without much further interference.

15. Dennis had been one of the defendants charged with corrupting the morals of children in the *Oz* magazine trial in 1971, one of the most famous obscenity cases of the decade. Identifying with other self-styled non-conformists, it was Dennis who invested heavily in the publishing company that James Brown established after his departure from *GQ*.

16. The resilience of magazine sales in the early 1990s, especially in relation to newspaper figures and other consumer goods, also highlighted their low price sensitivity and encouraged publishers to raise cover prices above the rate of inflation (*Media Week*, 7.4.95: 22). Sales remained immune to such rises, and, by 1995, the ratio of advertising to circulation revenue accrued by consumer magazines had reversed from 60:40 to 40:60, swinging back in later years to 50:50 as advertising markets recovered.

17. The overall and ongoing competition between editorial and publishing expertise can be seen as: ' a struggle for supremacy ... in which each category of managers seeks to advance its occupational interests by imposing a scale of values which sets at the top of the hierarchy the functions for which it feels itself best equipped' (Bourdieu 1984: 309–10). This is the same as the general struggle throughout the social system over tastes and values that Bourdieu highlights, wherein 'conflicts of value' reflect 'not only different sectional interests but different scholastic and occupational careers and,

through them, different social recruitment areas and therefore ultimate differences in habitus' (1984–310).

18. With Fleet Street newspapers having become 'heavier in weight but lighter in approach' since the Wapping transformations of 1986 (Tunstall 1996: 46; Curran and Seaton 1997), features written about and by personnel from magazine publishing became increasingly common. The striking growth of the men's press made its editors particularly valuable sources of copy and comment, and, although called upon throughout the media as pundits, panellists and commentators, it was the broadsheet press that was most powerful in underwriting the credibility of their views. Individuals such as James Brown became not only mouthpieces for modern masculinity, but celebrities in their own right, the subjects of newspaper profiles and speculation. Between September 1997 and the end of 1998, Brown was profiled in the quality press at least eight times as well as writing a diary for the *Independent on Sunday*. 'I don't know about the others', he declared, 'but I'm a fucking star' (*Guardian*, 20.6.97: G2, 35).

As Brown's comments made clear, many editors revelled in the public profiles that they could establish for themselves and their titles as repositories of masculine knowledge. Those working on the sector's upmarket products promoted themselves as serious cultural analysts and 'opinion-formers', whilst even editors whose magazines were rarely serious, either in content or tone, became regular spokespersons for their reading constituencies and authorities on young men in general. Amongst numerous media activities including an occasional column in the *Daily Mail*, Brown appeared on *Newsnight*, Radio Four's *Today* programme and the *Channel Four News* to deliberate on women's magazines, juvenile crime and the England football squad respectively, whilst *Front* editor Piers Hernu wrote for the *Daily Telegraph* on young men's attitudes to marriage, the *Observer* about 'single life', and was invited to give his views on young men to the Prime Minister. Editors had little doubt about their right to speak on behalf of the male population on such issues, often doing so in broad, essentialist terms, based upon what *Frith* and *Savage* (1993) have called 'the authority of experience' rather than any more studied evidence.

Part III
Editors and Magazines

I have focussed so far on the structures, conditions and forms of knowledge that delineated the launches and ongoing production of men's lifestyle magazines in the 1990s. In Chapter 2, I examined the development of the four products that redefined the market during this decade, highlighting the general uncertainty amongst publishers about how to address the mass male public. I suggested that, in these circumstances of perplexity, indecision and doubt, publishing houses advanced more through faith and intuition than formal research practices. The informal knowledge of certain editorial personnel was particularly decisive in driving the establishment of these magazines, in terms of providing both the confidence and the direction for their progression. Through exploring the anatomies of other launches, I reiterated the pivotal role of editorial practitioners in elaborating the identities of new magazines, albeit in constant relation with corporate goals and commercial strategies.

Charting this relationship between editorial practitioners and organizational and commercial factors was the concern of Chapter 4. There, I outlined the terms and nature of editorial power and expertise, emphasizing the various determinants that compromised, channelled and constrained editors in the daily production process. I argued that the unknowable nature of 'the reader' was crucial in upholding the privileged position of editors in fashioning the identities of their products. Whilst doing so in constant negotiation with advertising imperatives, sales pressures and forms of audience feedback, editorial practitioners were employed precisely because of their ability to understand and articulate the magazine audience. Periods of market uncertainty and instability such as the mid-1990s, when readerships appeared all the more unpredictable, afforded editors particular sovereignty to forge titles as they deemed necessary. That they necessarily did so through the cultural resources at their disposal, and often though projecting themselves as their own 'ideal reader', has directed me to investigating in more detail the identities, interests, backgrounds, ambitions and stocks of cultural and social capital of some specific editorial figures in the recent UK men's press.

As the magazine that redefined the market, the special significance in this book of *loaded* should be self-evident. The subjects of scrutiny of Chapter 5 are thus its founding editors, James Brown and Tim Southwell. Focussing in particular upon their gender identities, I examine how Brown and Southwell's world views, motivations, cultural repertoires and languages of self-representation imprinted the form of their title. The self-identities of *loaded*'s editors are traced to their social, educational and career backgrounds, and I propose that the journalistic identity that they sought to inhabit, and which informed their work in significant ways, expressed and resolved key concerns that coalesced around issues of class and masculinity. It is appropriate then that, in Chapter 6, I look more closely at Peter Howarth and Ekow Eshun, the respective editors of *Esquire* and *Arena*. These were magazines associated with an earlier moment in the market's formation, and against whose representations and editors Brown and Southwell appeared to define themselves. Chapter 6 therefore marks out the distinctions, as well as similarities, between the social, cultural and gender identifications of *loaded*'s editors and those of a different set of market practitioners whose ethics of style, aspiration and masculinity were also divergent.

Whilst, as I showed in Chapter 2, *loaded*'s editors were handed a relatively open brief in developing their project, Howarth and Eshun took over publications at the end of 1996 with established readerships, histories and conventions. In this respect, one ambition of Chapter 6 is to show how the appointment of new editors on already existing products both reflected entrenched formulations of magazine identities and resulted in their rearticulation. Detailing the interests, identifications and cultural credentials of editors is again instructive here, since these represented the 'qualifications' based upon which candidates were selected and the reserves that were used in reformulating the magazine address. At a time when the growth of the lad mags had unsettled assumptions in the men's style sector about who was being targeted and how best this should be done, the relationship between the personal identities and ambitions of editors and their titles was brought into particularly sharp relief.

–5–

'Men who should Know Better'?
The Editors of *loaded*

loaded was born from the belief that humour, hedonism and crisps were more relevant to 90s man than £15,000 suits ... a magazine that spoke to them and not at them, a magazine which unashamedly celebrated working-class Britain: football, drinking, sex and getting into 'interesting situations' ... *loaded* was the best goal they ever scored, the best shag they ever had and the best party they'd ever been to. (Tim Southwell, Campaign, 15.10.99: 34).

I suggested in Chapter 2 that the introduction of James Brown and Tim Southwell to the IPC development team in 1993 marked the point at which the company's plans for a mass market men's title began to take shape as *loaded*. I noted furthermore Brown's claim that the magazine was simply a representation of his own lifestyle and interests, and those of the people around him. Indeed, *loaded*'s pioneering status, and the freedom with which its producers were allowed consequently to work, did establish for Brown and Southwell considerable scope to fashion the magazine in accordance with their own ambitions, concerns and identifications. Southwell's comments above indicate some of the underlying preoccupations that he and Brown shared. As I will show in the following chapter, these were primarily anchored in issues around class and masculinity that were themselves interrelated. Analytic clarity requires me to identify their roots and manifestations at first separately, before emphasizing how they were jointly expressed in the journalistic identity that *loaded*'s editorial team adopted. I go on to demonstrate that *loaded* can only be comprehended as a cultural form born out of these constituents and their materialization in the discursive repertoires, subjectivities and anxieties of its editorial founders.

Class, Education and Mobility

Brown was brought up in the northern city of Leeds, where his father worked in a university and then as a 'political travel writer' and his mother was a secretary. He was educated at local comprehensive schools, but was thrown out of sixth-form college after a year and did not return to the education system. Brown attributed the expulsion to the difficulties of adapting to his parents' separation, and his detachment from the educational ladder was undoubtedly premature in relation to his social origins, aspirations and precocious intelligence (*Independent*, 8.6.98: 13). Endowed with what Bourdieu would classify as 'strong cultural capital imperfectly converted into educational capital' (1984: 358), it was unsurprising that Brown soon found refuge for his abilities and ambitions in an area that demanded little in the way of institutionally furnished knowledge and formal qualifications, but considerable levels of non-certified cultural capital. He continued to produce and sell the fanzine that he had recently started, apparently for only twenty pounds, covering the alternative music scene, local bands and politics. Moving to London via Manchester in 1987, Brown soon went from writing freelance articles for the weekly music magazines *Sounds* and the *New Musical Express* (*NME*) – 'the Eton of music journalism' (*Press Gazette*, 27.5.91: 12) – to staff positions at both titles.

The *NME* was renowned as a title that drew upon fanzine writers and for which enthusiasm, a certain 'cocky' attitude, love for the magazine and an obsessive devotion to music culture were more important credentials than formal qualifications or training (*Press Gazette*, 27.5.91: 12; 11.5.92: 9). By the age of twenty, Brown was the *NME*'s youngest ever features editor, but left in 1991 after failing to secure the editor's job, whereupon he continued to write and edit as a freelancer whilst touring with a rock band that he managed. On departing from IPC, Brown was informed by Alan Lewis, by then the *NME*'s managing editor, of the company's hopes to launch a 'different' kind of men's title. Told that his ideas about an appropriate editorial format would be welcomed, two months later, Brown presented a basic idea of applying the tone of the music press to the areas of music, alternative comedy and sport. In 1993, with Lewis now in charge of the men's project, Brown was asked to develop further the product that would become *loaded* (see Figure 5).

Southwell's mother was a porcelain artist and his father a computer analyst and lecturer. Between the ages of six and twelve he lived in Australia, after which he attended state school and sixth-form college in Sussex. After a year off from the education system, he studied for a degree in social science at Central London Polytechnic (now the University of Westminster). Having always wanted to be a journalist, but unable to enrol onto relevant vocational courses, it was here that Southwell co-founded a music fanzine. He remained in music journalism for several years at various weekly titles including the *NME*, where he briefly worked with Brown and Lewis, and Emap's teen-pop publication *Smash Hits*. Persuaded by Brown to assist with his initiative at IPC, Southwell became *loaded*'s first deputy editor and, several years later, its editor.

Although their backgrounds did not classify them in traditional terms as working-class, both Brown and Southwell presented themselves as spokesmen

Figure 5 Photograph of James Brown by Ken Sharp, April 1995, courtesy of *Media Week*.

for the working-class male public. Whilst Brown's claims were largely implicit and indirect, Southwell's were explicit and recurrent, requiring a somewhat strained interpretation of class. Although Southwell acknowledged a distinction between himself and 'people who are in poverty, who are genuinely working-class', he also propounded the notion that 'whether you're working-class or middle-class, and you work all day, you're all working-class aren't you? Working-class just means that you have to work for a living' (Southwell 1998). This speculation contrasted with the supposition of most editors that the nation was becoming increasingly *middle*-class. Importantly-though, it signalled Southwell's desire to position himself as an 'ordinary bloke', despite being aware that his affinities with the common man were not entirely unwavering.[1]

Brown's class subjectivity was likewise equivocal. He considered himself neither unambiguously working-class nor middle-class and recognized that his mobility complicated any simple assessment of his status. Indeed, Brown dismissed the general utility of class categories, asserting that 'people who talk about class are ostensibly people who have problems with their own class' (Brown 1999a). He argued that class was a 'bogus' label that obscured potential and did nothing to explain personal failure or success: 'everything comes back to the individual' (Brown 1999b). Such sentiments mirrored Brown's self-stylization as someone unclassifiable, unpredictable and uniquely talented. He took pride in defying expectations, not least because it upheld the image of maverick genius that was constructed around him in *loaded*'s media publicity. If this self-representation of individuality sat uncomfortably with Brown's claims elsewhere to represent the 'ordinary man', it also related to an identification with middle-class notions of ambition and credibility that reflected the status he might realistically have expected and to which he continued to aspire.

Indeed, the interruption of Brown's social and educational trajectory served to accentuate his conviction that his success was self-made, a view shared by Southwell in relation to his own achievements. Brown declared that it was 'all self-taught' (*On the Ropes*, Radio Four, 16.7.02), and that: 'Nobody ever gave me anything on a plate ... I haven't got a leg up anywhere, so, you've got to do it for yourself ... I didn't have any qualifications, didn't have influential parents who could get me a job anywhere; you've just got to get on and do it' (Brown 1999b). In this context, Brown's scepticism about 'class' was more intelligible. His celebratory faith in social fluidity and the ability of ordinary people to prosper derived from the narrative of his own life: his unusually forceful ascent through the music and lifestyle press and his ambiguous sense of his own class positioning. Brown's friends were portrayed in the same terms of self-generated mobility and ambition: 'normal people' who had 'turned their passions and private lives into jobs' in various corners of contemporary media and youth culture including the club scene, fashion, film and sport (Brown 1999b). These forms of 'subcultural entrepreneurialism' (McRobbie 1994) were associated by Brown and Southwell with a specific articulation of Thatcherite rhetoric and the democratic optimism of the post-punk ethic. They endorsed a mode of self-aided opportunism that they believed was assisted, but also necessitated, by the dissolution of class boundaries and economic certainties. Brown evoked a picture of having had no option but to try to get into music journalism, or else go onto the dole (1999b; *On the Ropes*, Radio Four, 16.7.02). Politically left-wing, he and Southwell regarded social fragmentation and the disintegration of the 'old order' as potentially liberating. Cited recurrently by *loaded*'s co-founders, the acid house dance movement was seen to exemplify this possibility, both expressing and galvanizing a sense of boundless expectation amongst a mass public body no longer limited or defined by class. The verity of such assumptions was irrelevant; it was the world view expressed in them that was instructive. Brown and Southwell portrayed in positive terms a society in which success could be significantly advanced by attitude and ambition alone, and where working-class identity was desirable, providing that its material conditions could be left behind.

The individualistic rather than social terms in which Brown and Southwell saw themselves – terms which, in fact, represented long-established patterns of lower-middle-class self-definition, as I discuss in the following chapter – were also manifested in a hedonistic 'presentism' that condemned living life according to other people's terms or abstract value systems as 'inauthentic' and 'dishonest'. Reflection was considered to paralyse one's instincts and betray personal autonomy. Authenticity instead lay in immediate experience. Liberation was thus couched in terms of doing what came naturally and required the least deliberation. Southwell dismissed experience as 'lionising the past and fearing the future' and lauded young people for their 'right here, right now' approach to life (*Guardian*, 21.8.99: Review, 2). The problematic nature of deferred gratifications and intellectual judgements was evidenced further in Brown and Southwell's educational and occupational self-profiles. Southwell appeared embarrassed by his scholarly achievements, glossing over his undergraduate era and declaring himself a lazy and 'useless' student stunned by the 2:1 he attained: 'god knows how the fuck that happened. Someone got my results mixed up with someone else's' (Southwell 1999). Asked 'are you your average reader?' in a trade press questionnaire, he responded, disingenuously, 'Christ no. Some of them have got degrees, you know' (*Press Gazette*, 18.6.99: 19). In discussing his work, he was at pains to describe not just his luck, but his incompetence and lack of preparation. Stories of getting facts wrong and failing to think ahead were told almost boastfully. Editorial staff were described variously as 'a bunch of buffoons', 'English twerps out of their depth' and 'somewhere between the Bash Street Kids and *Carry on Publishing*' (Southwell 1998: 76, 84, 111).

Since many of *loaded*'s journalists were, like Southwell, highly educated, such portrayals were striking.[2] Indeed, the efforts to depict his team as this 'ship of fools' brought out some significant strains in Southwell's identity. Idiotic and incapable conduct was romanticized only in certain contexts. When accusations of sexism and yobbishness were levelled at *loaded*, they were warded off partly through a defence of staff as intelligent and skilled professionals. If this highlighted the ambivalent status of education in Southwell's self-understanding, Brown's explanation of his decision not to continue his education spoke equally conspicuously of his own anxieties.

The teachers said 'go to university, you'll love it. You'll do all these things', and I thought 'well I can go and do them anyway'. I can play football for a club down the street, and I can go to watch the concerts anyway. I couldn't concentrate, I wanted to do something more important. A lot of the things that people found, when they're twenty-two, twenty-three, and they've come out of university, I knew that when I was seventeen. I knew that you got further educated and there weren't going to be any jobs.

I understood that. So by the time that my friends were coming out of university, and they were going to functional, bureaucratic jobs at local councils, or DHSS's, or charities or whatever, and earning nine grand a year, I was in Hollywood with [rock band] The Cult. I didn't go to university because I didn't want to go to fucking university. I'm quite interested now in studying a bit more, in studying for some stuff. But I always thought I'll study when I'm at a level where I'm interested in studying. I thought I would just waste the education. And also I knew that I would disrupt it for everybody else. (Brown 1999b)

At the same time, Brown stressed his cerebral qualities, distinguishing himself from other male identities as he did so: 'I'm a journalist. I don't fucking work on a building site. ... I'm extremely well read for somebody who's never had any further education' (Brown 1999b). Like Southwell then, he cherished his subcultural erudition and demanded to be seen as culturally literate and well informed, but was hostile to the connotations carried by formal education. Significantly too, Brown counterposed his hands-on lifestyle with the deferred benefits of education, and contrasted his knowledge gained from 'doing' things with merely 'thinking' about them. In crowing, 'when other eighteen-year-olds were writing essays in university I was travelling the world and interviewing some of the hottest acts of the time', Brown invoked this distinction and his personal affections particularly clearly (*Financial Times*, 4.9.99: 7).

It was no accident that Brown's differentiations carried certain connotations of masculinity. Many of the key facets of his and Southwell's identities were anchored in an ambiguous and indeterminate class identity that was bound up, confirmed and expressed in specific discourses around heterosexuality and gender. It is to these that I shall now turn.

Masculinity and Heterosexuality

In their immediate impressions, Brown and Southwell embodied a brand of confident and enthusiastic masculine heterosexuality somewhat in line with the 'laddish' personalities they were ascribed in the press. Dressed casually yet with care, without flamboyance or formality, both projected an assured and relaxed masculinity, confirmed in modes of expression that were easy-going and unreserved. Certainly, though, they were not macho, overbearing or aggressive; nor did they exhibit the emotionally inhibited toughness of Roper's (1994) organizational men. Brown and Southwell were frank yet constantly courteous, and happy to express passion for their work and interests. Brown's admissions of emotional fragility rather belied his cocky facade whilst highlighting the energetic candour that exemplified his personality: 'I've always been a very passionate, emotional person, but for a long time I was putting on this white, Colombian overcoat [taking cocaine] and it wasn't letting much out' (*Independent*, 8.6.98: 13). Southwell's (1998: 59–60) declaration that, 'The day we got the magazine back from the printers I felt like I'd given birth ... I was close to tears', likewise displayed a lack of emotional reserve some distance from certain conventional masculine formations. Press interviewers were often surprised by such appearances, finding Brown 'surprisingly dainty ... in fact, almost feminine' and lacking the belligerence and coarseness that they anticipated (*Independent*, 8.6.98: 13; *Daily Telegraph*, 20.10.97: 34). Brown himself was neither shocked nor disturbed by profiles that emphasized these 'softer' sides of his personality, announcing 'I'm a great admirer of women, both intellectually and of the feminine form. If people think I've got feminine attributes then that's fine' (1999b).

This response was suggestive not just because of the comfort he declared with being described in such terms, but in its casual expression of heterosexual desire. An unrestrained and guilt-free sexual subjectivity was central in the identities of *loaded*'s co-founders and in their deliberate differentiations from other masculinities. In particular, it was the 'new man' identity, with its more questioning attitude towards sexual relations, which was distinguished as the immediate antithesis of their identifications. For Brown and Southwell, the new man represented a masculinity whose hesitant attitude towards sexual desire was both insipid and unappealing. They presented their more open and direct expression of heterosexual zeal, and their past sexual profligacy,[3] as components of a more 'honest', and therefore unchallengeable, masculine position. Brown said 'I'm not embarrassed about finding women attractive, I don't see where the problem is, why there is all this miserable liberal guilt' (*The Times*, 18.12.98: 40–1). Southwell stated, 'Men like looking at pictures of women. Big deal. Get over it' (1998: 212). Underlying such dispatches was a striking presupposition that, at least in the sphere of sexual relations, a state of equality was already achieved. Thus, suggesting some form of post-feminist settlement, Brown declared himself uninterested in the 'politics of gender', proclaiming that there was no difference between the sexes, and that, 'All that men versus women stuff is rubbish' (*Guardian*, 21.4.97: Media 6–7).[4]

If assuming this 'post-sex, post-politics' society was certainly naïve (*Independent*, 8.9.94: Living, 26), Brown and Southwell's celebration of it did mark out their values from traditional forms of chauvinism and misogyny. Despite their antipathy towards the new man, they were anxious to prove their enlightened credentials and were relatively fluent in the tropes of feminism. Southwell identified himself with a generation of men in touch with their feelings and prepared to admit that 'girls can run rings round them' (1998: 105). By asserting his domestic aptitudes and identifications – 'I've always done the washing up and I'm sure I could handle changing the baby's nappies. I certainly don't see it as an embarrassing thing to do or purely a woman's domain' (1998:

214) – as well as his emotional competences and support for female empower-ment, Southwell sought to define his laddishness as an appreciation of liberated femininity. Brown likewise regarded his unrepressed fascination with unre-pressed women as a sign of progressiveness. Both upheld the putatively uncom-plicated and unmoderated character of their desires as a more interesting, refreshing and honest masculinity than what they saw as the cool insincerities, awkward ineptitudes and tedious sensitivities of certain other men.

Some objections to the new man identity were bound up with the adherence to impulsive hedonism that I have already identified as fundamental to Brown and Southwell's personalities. The new man discourse was considered not only sexu-ally repressive, and therefore 'dishonest', but also prescriptive and judgmental. Disliked in particular was its perceived attempt to make men inhabit an identity that, since it might require effort and change, was 'inauthentic' as well as unde-sirable. Brown's view that men might change 'on the surface' but that 'the animal, the mammal, or whatever we are, stays the same' (Brown 1999b) illus-trated, albeit somewhat confusingly, one reason why the new man was regarded with such scepticism. Masculinity was conceived of as something ultimately innate and unchanging. The modification of 'instincts' was therefore seen as the denial of true self, whilst laddish behaviour was presented as the expression of essential impulses.

Indeed, Brown and Southwell cast themselves as the subjects of their natural urges both in their pursuit of immediate pleasures and in their ineptitudes and flaws. Such reasoning spoke much of the lifestyles that *loaded*'s writers pursued, with the hectic consumption of drink, drugs and women in their leisure time seeming to render them incapable and irresponsible in other areas of their lives. Such disorganization, like their weaknesses in general, was acknowledged without embarrassment. Southwell stated, 'men haven't got a clue what is going on', and maintained that, far from wanting more responsibility in their lives, men needed women's greater trustworthiness and knowledge to help them make sense of the world (*The Times*, 18.6.99: 28). On the one hand then, these contentions signalled a masculinity that did not demand deference or acclaim, nor claim unflinching authority or male superiority. Indeed, they suggested a self-effacing awe for women consistent with Brown and Southwell's almost childlike venera-tion of the opposite sex. In effect, though, they also represented a masculine discourse that absolved men of responsibility for their own actions. *loaded*'s tone, content and tag line, 'For men who should know better', recognized this all too evidently.

Brown and Southwell's aversion to the new man warrants further comment. His embodiment, in their eyes, was the '*Guardian* journalist', an abstraction they attacked repeatedly for his 'narrow-minded' and value-laden liberalism, his attempt to 'find some utopian path to pure infallibility', his constant 'self-reprimand' and his inability to enjoy 'a spontaneous emotion' (*Guardian*, 23.12.96: G2, 10; Southwell 1998: 207). Brown argued that the new man:

> didn't relate to anybody's lives, apart from a few people who'd come out of Oxbridge, or who were writing columns in newspapers. ... I've got a friend, one of *loaded*'s editors, he brings up his kid on his own, but he's not a 'new man' ... But you can do all those things that are perceived to be feminine and [not] wear dungarees, read The *Guardian*, and lose your character and your sexuality. (Brown 1999b)

References to the *Guardian* were not incidental. They connoted the left-wing vanguardism of the middle-class intelligentsia, as opposed to the mass populism of the tabloid press with its more lustful irreverence and its inflections of working-class culture. Indeed, Brown's comments flagged up his sense that there was something incompatible about masculine heterosexuality and the middle-class identity that the new man was seen to represent. His discomfort with the new man was founded on the inferences of femininity that were bound up with his class properties as much as his actual dispositions. The *Guardian* journalist was also significant in designating a conspicuous occupational identity. As I discuss shortly, Brown and Southwell's antipathy to the new man was intensified considerably by the professional competitiveness herein implied.

In fact, then, whilst Brown and Southwell treated the new man with disdain, they reserved real contempt for the 'truly Neanderthal' louts and misogynists from whom they tried to distance themselves even more plainly (Southwell 1998: 214). Brown and Southwell were perturbed by the media's use of '*loaded* culture' as a shorthand for behaviour such as hooliganism and violence against women. Events on a national '*loaded* tour' reinforced these dissociations, when the editorial team encountered a constituency of readers that it found utterly offensive. 'It made your stomach twist when you realized what you were up against', recalled Southwell (1999). That the existence of these men surprised him was because he and Brown assumed that their audience shared their own post-political masculinities, and that *loaded* would be understood in this context. Evidently, though, Brown and Southwell's 'everyman' identifications had significant limits. Indeed, their repeated assertions about the honesty and authenticity of their orientations projected this unease, resolving it conspicuously through the claim that these were natural and therefore incontestable dispositions.

Occupational Identity

I suggested in the previous chapter that a characteristic feature of lifestyle journalism was its dissolution of conventional borders between work and leisure. For Brown, Southwell and Lewis, this promise was a particularly attractive aspect of the job. It provided a professional identity that resolved the strains between their commitments to lifestyles of hedonism and pleasure and their ambitions to be taken seriously as cultural authorities. Brown thus described his drive as coming from 'wanting to achieve things by pursuing things I enjoy' (1999b). On moving to *GQ*, he declared his identification with those readers who 'probably take their lives seriously, but that doesn't mean to say that they're serious people' (1999a). His diary in the *Independent on Sunday* (27.4.97: 27) brought into sharp relief his dual affinity with a lifestyle of glamour and success and the alternative credibility of a more ordinary, 'gritty' existence.

> MONDAY: ... I celebrate my appointment to the editorship of *GQ* by driving to a benefit for Striking Liverpool Dockers at the Mean Fiddler in Harlesden with two Scouse rascals ... THURSDAY: Meet *GQ* staff for first time. Lunch with newspaper mogul. Electricity cut off at flat. FRIDAY: Wash in hot water from pan. Travel the mile from the *loaded* office to the BBC studios at Bush House in Jason's fibreglass bomb of a Lotus Esprit.

The importance of a job that was not one of the 'serious' professions, with their associations of public service, moral earnestness and sobriety, was exhibited even more strongly in Southwell's representations of the *loaded* work culture in his (1998) book about the magazine's early years. As I indicated earlier, this account portrayed the *loaded* staff simultaneously as idiotic, incompetent and invariably drunk, and as dedicated, hard working professionals.[5] The labour involved in producing the magazine was stressed repeatedly alongside an emphasis on the commitment required for the accompanying lifestyle of hedonism and excess: 'we were either in the pub having a laugh or slogging our guts out in search of the impossible deadline' (Southwell 1998: 44). This 'work hard, play hard' ethos differed somewhat from conventional versions of work-based sociability. Drunkenness and hedonistic behaviour were actually parts of the job, not just what one did after office hours. Indeed, Southwell proudly reported one writer's comment that he 'just wasn't used to magazines being like *loaded*. *loaded* was like being down the pub' (Southwell 1998: 40). Other citations disclosed the fulfilment that Southwell derived from portraying editorial production as a synthesis of work and pleasure, graft and gratification: 'Even when we were at work there was no clock-watching, no one wanted to go home' (Southwell 1998: 111). Through such depictions, he and Brown distanced their occupational identities from the traditional Protestant work ethic and the masculinity that it implied. The very suggestion that the office had become a substitute home, and Brown's references to it as 'his bedroom', indicated the homosocial fraternity in which they revelled. Descriptions of the workplace as a 'stinking pig-sty full of drunken loudmouths', 'a bloke's changing room'

(Southwell 1998: 150) and a 'shit-storm of banter' (Southwell 1999) likewise connoted a culture of collective, masculine disarray.

Much of this culture of sociable excess replicated the traditions of music journalism, where interviews, events and other occupational transactions were oiled with drugs and alcohol, and many writers believed themselves to be more capable when in some way inebriated. Fleet Street had its own history of intemperance and overindulgence (Chippendale and Horrie 1990), but, with so many of the men's magazine market's first editorial cohort having come out of mainstream broadsheet journalism, it was no surprise that Brown and Southwell identified their ancestry elsewhere. Instead then, they presented themselves as followers in the tradition of 'New journalism' that included North American writers from the 1960s and 1970s such as Tom Wolfe, Hunter Thompson and Norman Mailer. Brown described Wolfe's books as his 'further education', and pitched his original proposal for *loaded* as '*Arena* edited by Hunter S. Thompson' (*Guardian*, 16.11.98: Media, 2–3). New journalism had been distinctive in a number of ways, partly by using literary devices to create forms of nonfiction that would read like novels. Committed to undermining notions of objectivity, writers often placed themselves at the centre of their stories, using subjective, first-person narration and inner dialogue rather than the traditional journalistic style of understated, neutral description. Practitioners also considered it vital to be at the centre of the action when dramatic events occurred, to view things with self-conscious originality, and to report with what Wolfe described as 'personality, energy, drive, bravura ... style, in a word' (Wolfe and Johnson 1975: 31).

It was apposite that Brown particularly revered Thompson's 'Gonzo Journalism'. Thompson's was the most sprawling, anarchic and drug-influenced approach of the genre, and the one in which the author was the most committed to the role of *agent provocateur*. Taking on the mantle of these conventions, Brown and Southwell dedicated themselves and their staff to an intense and spirited journalistic involvement in which writers were expected to be parts of the stories themselves rather than detached observers. Southwell described their obligation to the magazine as 'to get into the most interesting situation possible ... and if there isn't a situation, create one' (1999). The language and tradition of New journalism performed several functions for Brown and Southwell, expressing their identifications in relation to the men's press at the time of *loaded*'s launch. Thirty years earlier, New journalism had challenged the norms and practitioners of the American journalistic establishment. In identifying themselves as its heirs, Brown and Southwell could take up a subject-position as peripheral 'outsiders' that highlighted the distinctions they wished to draw between their own perspectives and those of the existing market player. They could register their own sense of cultural marginality and mission. As I suggested in Chapter 2, the sense that their cultural milieux, practices and values had been ignored in mainstream commercial channels was a significant motivation for Brown and Southwell. Through *loaded*, they depicted themselves as conferring value on lifestyles that were widely practised but granted little legitimacy. With *loaded,* Brown commented, 'we took it to the level of the street and the nightclub and the pub, where guys were used to being ignored' (*Midweek*, Radio Four, 23.9.98).

Such struggles for cultural democratization had informed Brown's journalistic endeavours since his first fanzine, *Attack on Bzag*, a self-styled assault on cultural conformity that was already embracing the work of Hunter Thompson (Robb 1999). Brown and Southwell's backgrounds in the music press both confirmed their sense of marginality from the existing men's press and conditioned their journalistic voice. At the *NME* under Lewis, their task had been to bring humour and irreverence to a title felt to have become po-faced and pretentious. The experience was formative as well as representative of their personal preferences: Brown's proposal for *loaded* was partly based on this transformation of the *NME* and his desire to bring its tone of spiky enthusiasm to a sector dominated by journalists from the more conservative fields of news and fashion. Approaching the market with such motivations in mind, *loaded* was styled as an offensive against not only the representations of the existing publications, but against the expertise, identities and tastes of their producers. Brown's aims were couched in missionary terms: 'We deliberately set out to create some generational tension. ... We wanted to make the men's magazine editors feel old and scared. We wanted to make the other publishing houses feel out of date' (1999a).

There was also a class issue at stake for *loaded*'s founders, one haunted by the presence of the Oxbridge-educated, liberal journalists who had, in their perception, monopolized the men's lifestyle press. Southwell's hyperbolic comments on the style press editors were, in this sense, indicative: 'It seemed pretty obvious that if you'd met the editor of any of these mags down the pub – or more likely the gentleman's club – he wouldn't have time for you, unless you knew someone with a chateau he could stay in during Paris Fashion Week. The best I could offer was a week in my uncle's caravan in Tenby.' (1998: 128). In the same spirit, Southwell applauded *loaded* for being the first 'successful working-class magazine', and an 'accurate reflection of working-class dreams' (*Campaign*, 4.12.98: 12; Southwell 1998: 210).[6] Brown was more reticent, and at times contradictory, in using class labels to describe *loaded*'s character and appeal. In both insisting and refuting that the magazine and its producers represented working-class people, he communicated the ambivalence about his own class identity that I have already underlined.[7] His assertion that the title was 'about a devil-may-care attitude, not demographics' reiterated a general suspicion of class categories (*Independent*, 8.9.94: Living, 26). Brown declared: 'you can't pigeonhole people

... a 65-year-old driving a BMW might laugh at the same joke as a 15-year-old who's still at school', and projected the magazine as a 'national fanzine' that would appeal beyond men with 'loft spaces and tailor-made clothes', and would represent the 'guys round the back of the bike sheds' rather than the 'head boy' (*Press Gazette*, 28.3.94: 9).

This commitment to overturning hierarchies of knowledge and authority connected Brown and Southwell with the precedents of New journalism in a second, related respect. The destabilization of objective truth claims engendered by subjective reportage resonated with Brown's belief in the validity of personal experience and his indifference to reflexive thought and normative judgement. He felt strongly that no single perspective had absolute legitimacy, and suggested, 'if you've got an opinion that's based on what you see and hear around you ... then it's worth voicing' (Brown 1999b). This conviction was itself bound up with his editorial style: 'All the stuff I've ever done when I've written about men, I'm just writing about myself. ... I can talk objectively about those things because I have an opinion. ... And I wouldn't profess to know anything about other men other than myself and the people I come into contact with' (Brown 1999b).

Brown's belief in the equal validity of different voices mirrored his dislike of taste hierarchies and his own cultural preferences. His assertion that the magazine would cover 'populist subjects in an intelligent way and intelligent subjects in original ways' without 'trying to push value systems' certainly testified to an intention of eclectic relativism (*Press Gazette*, 28.3.94: 9; *Independent*, 8.9.94: Living, 26). Underlying his desire to accelerate the collapse of social and cultural boundaries that he perceived to have characterized the early 1990s was Brown's own unstable class habitus (cf. Bourdieu 1984) and the resulting cultural identifications that I have outlined:

> It was very similar to punk, in that you didn't have to be a member of an elite ... or educated in a certain way to be somebody that mattered. ... You didn't have to be Peter Stringfellow to run a nightclub; you didn't have to be the head of EMI to have a record label; you didn't have to go to Oxford or Eton to run a magazine. (Brown 1999b; see also Robb 1999)

Third, New journalism's ethic of 'making the story happen' appealed to Brown and Southwell's preferences for action and spontaneity over thought and reflection. Most significantly, it allowed them to inflect their work with a sense of risk, action and danger, and to style themselves in the mould of the author-hero. At the same time, they repressed those elements of their jobs that might reasonably characterize them as relatively passive, desk-bound office workers (see Jackson et al. 2001: 58). Southwell proclaimed that writing magazines was 'infinitely more preferable to doing a nine-to-five job' (Southwell 1998: 9). In quipping that 'there are a lot of hoover salesmen out there' to explain the success of *FHM*, he chose an occupation whose mundanity was designed to emphasize the excitement of his own (*Guardian*, 30.11.98: Media, 2–3). Brown's disdain for the 'functional, bureaucratic' jobs of some of his friends provided a similar foil for his self-representation as a creative libero (Brown 1999b), an image somewhat in tension with his actual position as a salaried member of a corporate organization. Meanwhile, expressions of barbarian pride clearly drew upon their wishes to portray their work as a glamorous and masculine form of leisure: 'We thought we were The Clash, or Leeds United back when everyone hated them' (*Media Week*, 26.9.97: 16–17).

Fourth then, the foregrounding of the individual journalist in New journalism furnished *loaded*'s founders with a professional identity that could carry their sense of individuality and talent, rather than restricting them to the disembodied anonymity of the orthodox reporter. The tradition of *NME* journalists such as Charles Shaar Murray, Nick Kent and Lester Bangs, who frequently presented themselves as more interesting than the bands they were writing about, was notable here given the backgrounds of so many of the men's market's most influential figures. More importantly, it signposted a longer history of romantic masculine individualism (MacKenzie 1987) with which Brown and Southwell evidently identified.

In this respect, declarations of the *loaded* team's identification with '*The Dirty Dozen*' '*The Magnificent Seven*' and '*Kelly's Heroes*' (*Media Week*, 26.9.97: 16–17; Southwell 1998: 44), films in which the dominant themes were individual flair, anti-establishment sentiment, heroic masculine toughness and team spirit, spoke volumes. It underlined familiar tensions between Brown and Southwell's accent on their individual authorial talents and their efforts to emphasize the collective culture of the *loaded* team, tensions in which issues of masculinity, work and class loomed heavily. This crucial point requires further elaboration. A recurrent theme in the self-presentations of my protagonists was an anxiety about how to retain status as men in the context of ambitions, achievements and mobility that they perceived to undermine masculine credibility. Desires to be seen as unique and yet ordinary, intelligent without being formally 'educated', and hard-working and aspirational but not professionally solemn, spoke of a recurrent tension between investments in two different masculine identities. The first was a version of heterosexual masculinity anchored in working-class values of collective solidarity, anti-authority bravado, immediate gratification, hedonism, irreverence and a confident sexual agency. The second was a script that endorsed middle-class notions of individual accomplishment, success and competence, but which lacked the desirable sexual identity that Brown and Southwell demanded.

That the new man identity encapsulated by the style press conformed more closely to the latter of these scripts made Brown and Southwell's professional ideals more transparent. *loaded*'s tag line 'For men who should know better' acknowledged their ambivalence about the new man discourse that, despite their renunciations, they recognized as, in many ways, appropriate. Thus Brown declared: 'The best description of *loaded* ever was ... by the head of an advertising agency [who] said "I love *loaded* because *Esquire* and *GQ* and *Arena* tell me how I should be, but *loaded* tells me how I am. Unfortunately, *loaded* tells me how I am"' (Brown 1999a). Repudiations of the new man identity stemmed, above all, from the middle-class qualities that, from Brown and Southwell's perspective, stigmatized it as inherently asexual. By constituting their work instead as a version of *manly* labour – edgy, active, brave and almost physically demanding (Brown even referred to the *loaded* office as the 'shop floor') – without being merely *manual* labour, *loaded*'s creators negotiated some key personal tensions. Crucially then, through such recastings, Brown and Southwell attempted to reclaim their occupational practices and ambitions as unequivocally masculine.

loaded

We were taking a culture and putting it into that magazine ... The key parts of *loaded* were nightclubs, drinking, football matches, being honest – just admitting that we fancied women. We didn't invent any of those things. (Brown, *On the Ropes*, Radio Four, 16.7.02)

I suggested in earlier chapters that Brown and Southwell saw themselves as the ideal *loaded* readers and undoubtedly regarded the magazine as an expression of their lifestyles, interests and values. The outline of *loaded*'s content, character and target market that I have provided in earlier chapters has already evidenced the intimate relationship between the title's cultural benchmarks and the identifications of its editors. Brown reflected that he simply: 'wanted to write about my life rather than about someone who has just released a new album ... why people keep messy cars, what you do if you get drunk and piss yourself, what it is like to dive off a balcony at a concert' (*Media Week*, 28.4.95: 19). If the magazine was no simple reflection of the subjectivities of Brown and Southwell, it was certainly a terrain on which many of the tensions, preoccupations and fantasies of their identities were played out. Confirming this through a systematic textual analysis of *loaded* is beyond my aims and bounds here. Nonetheless, some further illustration of the correspondence between the magazine's format, tone and values, and the cultural repertoires, ambitions and concerns of its producers, is clearly required.

In defining *loaded*'s editorial voice, Brown and Southwell drew upon much of their previous occupational training and experience. The most obvious debt here was to the weekly music press. It was not only *loaded*'s heightened coverage of pop and rock bands and personalities that distinguished it from the men's style press, but also the editorial identity that accompanied it. First then, Brown and Southwell imported the expansive letters page that had proved successful at *Sounds* in creating a sense of clubbish intimacy between readers and writers. The *NME*'s self-mocking cheek and its ethos of inclusive enthusiasm was likewise conscripted. Danny Kelly, one of the *NME*'s editors during Brown's time at the title, and himself a former fanzine writer, had argued that 'the way to make the *NME* work is to make it plain to our readers that we've enjoyed putting the magazine together' (*Press Gazette*, 11.5.92: 9): Brown evidently registered and retained this belief. *loaded*'s efforts to reduce the distance between journalist and audience that its staff considered symptomatic of style press pomposity were also manifested in the magazine in the pictures of and references to the antics, failings and accidents of the journalists that littered it. Such gestures sought to indicate that the magazine's producers were no different from those men consuming it. This avowal was not insincere given its editors' technique of orienting content towards themselves, and the newness of many *loaded* writers to the journalistic field. It was also an editorial principle in which Brown and Southwell's commitments to seeing themselves as 'ordinary blokes' and their attachments to New journalism were distilled.

Brown also took on Kelly's attempt to emulate the sharp punning style of the *Sun*'s caption-writing under Kelvin MacKenzie, who had edited the paper from 1981–94. One staff member at *loaded* was hired specifically to write its captions (*Media Week*, 26.9.97: 16–17). The *Sun* was influential in several other ways. As well as drawing on *The Face*, the design of *loaded*, a 'scrapbook' style much less clean, professional and American-looking than *GQ* or *Esquire*, mimicked the *Sun*'s striking, chaotic appearance (Chippendale and Horrie 1990). Brown's attention to coverlines and headlines, his insistence on keeping print lead times at a minimum (at one stage, a week), and his desire to invigorate the magazine with energy by running it like a newspaper also referenced the *Sun*'s influence (*Press Gazette*, 23.1.98: 14). Lewis praised the paper's ability to connect with 'what ordinary people thought' and its swaggering, irreverent confidence (Lewis 1998). Brown's emulation of MacKenzie's 'aggressively street-wise "common man" personal style', his anti-establishment pugnacity and his reverence of youth over experience were all significant as reflections of the masculinity that he projected onto his magazine (Tunstall 1996: 125).

Other publishing forms that were cited as influences on *loaded* included football fanzines such as *When Saturday Comes* and *Onion Bag*. Both Brown and Southwell had interpreted football's growing popularity after the 1990 World

Cup as another indication of the integration of previously separate male class cultures. Brown also recalled noticing that 'more and more people I knew who were originally massive fans of music had become obsessed with football again. And I felt that if you could put those two elements into one magazine you might have something new' (*On the Ropes*, Radio Four, 16.7.02). Accordingly then, *loaded* covered footballers and football culture in a manner that was without precedent within the market, commemorating eccentricity, excess and the maverick stars of the past as well as upcoming players who represented the magazine's ethos of youthful self-indulgence.

Another powerful influence was the adult comic *Viz*. Selling over 1.1 million monthly copies in 1991, making it the third biggest magazine in the country (despite negligible marketing), *Viz* was the product that most resembled a mass-market men's magazine before the emergence of *loaded*. Its blunt, offbeat, anti-establishment and often sexually explicit humour, and that of the resurgent alter-native-comedy scene of the period, not only inspired *loaded*'s founders, but provided further evidence that fashion and grooming were not the only ways to attract the attentions of the mass male public.[8] Brown and Southwell expressed their affection for *Viz*, football, and a relatively unabashed form of sexual expres-sion from *loaded*'s first issue. *Viz* editor Chris Donald was given a full-page question and answer profile, whilst nonconformist footballer Eric Cantona received a lengthy interview piece and England captain David Platt introduced photographs of his Sampdoria teammates dressed as airforce pilots. The maga-zine's 'most wanted' feature pictured then unknown actress Elizabeth Hurley in a more risqué pose than the style press convention. References to porn channels, 'soggy prophylactics' and 'rampant sex' in a homage to hotel sex struck home the terms of *loaded*'s sexual identity (*loaded*, May 1994: 39–41).

The launch edition's leading articles bore the imprints of its editors even more markedly. The first was an interview with Paul Weller, former lead singer of 1970s band The Jam and 'godfather of mod', mutual adoration for whom had forged the initial bond between Brown and Southwell when they first met (Southwell 1998). References to Weller's 'barely concealed aggressive discon-tent', the influences of mod and punk culture, and his involvement with Red Wedge (the Labour Party's campaign to mobilize young voters through left-wing pop artists), alluded to familiar political and subcultural preferences (*loaded*, May 1994: 21–4). That the interviewer was Sean O'Hagan, author of *Arena*'s original 'new lad' essay, was telling. So was the issue's other principal subject and cover star, actor Gary Oldman: 'local boy ... made very good' (*loaded*, May 1994: 47), and one of the men cited as a new lad role model in Alex Kershaw's 1991 article (see introduction).[9] In an extended postscript to the main feature, Brown himself paid tribute to an evident personal icon: 'Dangerous, sexy, wild, disturbed, disturbing, out of control, in control, too talented and with character too … But the real passion and excitement that makes him so damn attractive as a role model, a hero, is in his pursuit of excellence … he's deadly serious about his art. But not at the expense of humour' (*loaded*, May 1994: 51).

As inaugural champions, Weller and Oldman were apt. Mod's roots were in the post-war encounter between 'working-class puritanism and the new hedonism of consumption': a resolution of the tensions engendered by the mobility of the white-collar worker through the retention of the language and rituals of the parent culture alongside an embrace of the dress and music of the 'affluent consumer' (Cohen, cited in Turner 1990: 172). Oldman's upward social mobility was, for Brown, an explicit part of his appeal: 'His brother-in-law was shot by villains, his father died by the bottle, his teachers told him he was thick, and he's readily admitted that if he hadn't become an actor he'd probably have become a criminal' (*loaded*, May 1994: 51). Oldman's South London background and his education in a school that he described as 'like a borstal' were also significant factors in Brown's reverence. Such roots typified the actor's distinction from the middle-class thespians Richard Briers and Rupert Everett that Brown disparaged (*loaded*, May 1994: 51). As the magazine continued to champion footballers, boxers, rock stars and alternative comedians in subsequent months, its choices were germane in selecting some of the most glamorous and 'masculine' routes out of the working-class. Brown and Southwell's admiration for men who could represent their work as enjoyable but arduous, and could portray their success as the outcome of unique talent in an everyday field, re-emphasized the gendered intonations of their occupational identifications: 'If anyone's got the guts to get up on-stage and risk ridicule, or train every day to be the best sportsman they can be then they deserve my respect' (Southwell 1998: 187).

The cultural dispositions of *loaded*'s founders were registered elsewhere in its first issue: Hunter Thompson's second-place ranking in the 'platinum rogues' column, the review of the Swansea club scene, Southwell's first-person account of a skydive, the 'hedonist's handbook' review section, an opinion column by comedian Vic Reeves (whose book Brown had edited in his years between the *NME* and *loaded*), and an article on cult film *Withnail and I*. This portrayal of alcoholic anarchism was listed as Southwell's favourite film in his profile on the *Uploaded* web site; in the following months, his favourite band, Oasis, and tele-vision programme, The Simpsons, would also be given cover star status. The main travel feature, Trevor Ward's South American 'rampage', recounted 'cheap cocaine, cheap women', the Miss Guyana bikini contest, and the heady cocktail of drink, drugs, football and women that would characterize the magazine's future reports: 'Venezuela is not very good at soccer. So its lads take pride in the next best thing: the quality of the totty' (pp. 61–4). Interviews in subsequent issues of *loaded* emphasized the central terms of its masculine belief system. Whereas *The Face* had explored areas such as the nature of stardom and the political potential of popular culture with its interviewees (Nixon 1996: 147), and those featured in *GQ* had been probed with earnest interest on the daily rituals of their wardrobe (Nixon 1997), *loaded*'s were more likely to be pressed on their consumption of alcohol, drugs and women.

The excess, 'of an alcoholic, narcotic or energetic nature' (Brown, in the *Independent*, 29.9.96: 19), that distinguished *loaded* from the body-rigour, personal care ethic and urbane self-control of *GQ* and *Esquire* (Bancroft 1998), is illuminated considerably when seen in relation to Brown's ambitions and the almost obsessive nature of his hedonistic dynamism. Brown was irritated when the announcement of his move to *GQ* was met with surprise by press commentators who associated him and *loaded* with an unambitious, lazy nihilism. He and Southwell considered their title to be both aspirational and inspirational, albeit in different ways from the upmarket press.[10] Brown fiercely rejected suggestions that *loaded* encouraged indifference and apathy.

> We didn't say it was alright to be lazy … what I actually wrote was 'get fit, or get fucked up; but do something with your life'. To me at that time it seemed better to either be out there being a sports star, even if it's for your Sunday league team, or go out and push it to the edge in another way … And that was just a call to arms: 'do something with your life. Don't be boring. Don't go to the same holiday resort every single year' … And, I think there's nothing wrong with sitting in and watching telly if you're watching a great film. But there's nothing worse than sitting there just channel hopping [from] pulp tv [to] some crappy gardening show. (Brown 1999b)

Notably then, Brown claimed to be non-judgemental about what other men should do with their lives. The important thing was for them to 'do something' rather than nothing, but Brown purported to be non-directive about what had cultural, social or political value. 'Maximizing one's potential', enthusiasm for life and the passionate pursuit of one's ambitions – 'whether it's collecting toy cars or pencils, or having sex with women, or going down the gym and going rock climbing, or whatever' (Brown 1999b) – were portrayed as goals in themselves. It was in this way that Brown could conceive of ambition and hedonism, defined as 'living life to the full', as non-contradictory ideals, and could regard the pursuit of immediate gratification as consistent with the pursuit of less transient achievements. Brown's admiration of accomplishment through the transformation of personal interests into careers was, again, discernible here.

Of course, the plea for others to 'seize the day' was in itself normative, and *loaded* was certainly prescriptive in endorsing its brand of indefatigable, brazen libertinism. Nonetheless, unlike other men's magazines, it offered no explicit lifestyle guidance or recommendations and no product reviews beyond forms of popular culture.[11] Brown and Southwell condemned market competitors for their lifestyle tips, and mocked their readers for requiring them. Brown declared *Maxim* and *FHM* 'actually quite bland. I think men should aspire to greatness ... they should be inspired' (Brown 1999b). *loaded* was presented as a magazine that simply wanted to legitimize the enthusiasms of its editorial producers, and enthusiasm in general, rather than to assert the superiority of any specific practices. Only by seeing this in the context of Brown and Southwell's general hostility to prescription and reflection is it fully intelligible.

Meanwhile then, and in contrast to the more conservative aspirations of *GQ* and *Esquire*, *loaded* also endorsed the legitimacy of *not* striving, and a less dutiful version of the masculine career script than the self-sacrificial responsibility of conventional renditions. In the same week that *The Face* published a list of the most important people in fashion, Brown co-wrote '*loaded*'s least important people: the slobs, the no-marks, the people who are going nowhere', including cartoon characters Homer Simpson and the renowned actor, drinker and womanizer Oliver Reed. Such initiatives were deliberate cultural interventions, 'to galvanise a nation of men into realising that you didn't have to be ashamed of being a bloke any more' (Southwell 1998: 214). Brown was equally keen for the magazine to be unapologetic about men's instincts and imperfections. The point was to celebrate, rather than challenge or channel, the condition of masculine enjoyment. In thus seeking to be inspirational whilst also assuming that 'men are useless. Everyone knows men are useless' (Brown, in the *Daily Telegraph*, 20.10.97: 34) *loaded* exhibited one of the critical tensions of the identities of its editorial architects. Equally, in championing both the carefree and the creative, the magazine clearly reflected the individualism of its producers.

Brown and Southwell's sexual politics were also significant in framing *loaded*'s representation of women. The models featured in the magazine, often tabloid pin-ups, were 'more girl-next-door than distant stars' (Nixon 2001: 382), their relative accessibility reflecting the inclusive ambitions and class affiliations of its editors. Meanwhile, the magazine's unashamedly heterosexual and promiscuous editorial voice, and often topless and provocative photographs, were considerably more explicit than the style press. As I have already outlined, such portrayals were underpinned by a belief in the 'authenticity' of heterosexual desire, and justified through assertions that, in a post-political sexual climate, issues around representation and objectification were thankfully obsolete.

Cultural commentators who detected such tensions in Brown and Southwell's proclamations tended to interpret them, somewhat simplistically, as middle-class men posing as working-class. *loaded*'s new lad identity was also often described as 'ironic', suggesting a 'studied political incorrectness' or an 'awareness of his own clownish nature' (Moore, in Southwell 1998: 205; Bancroft 1998). Using textual and linguistic analysis of specific texts, Benwell (2001) has argued that the use of irony in men's lifestyle magazines serves to 'continually destabilize' the notion of a coherent and monolithic masculinity. The authorial voice oscillates between those identities against which it defines itself without allowing its own nature to be fixed. Whilst she concludes that this evasiveness 'accommodates multiple audiences', 'provides multiple and fluctuating identities for its readers' and becomes 'ideologically inscrutable' (Benwell 2001: 8–9), my analysis suggests that, in *loaded*'s case, it also conveyed the straining identifications of its originators. In this sense then, the motto 'For men who should know better' was more than just an acknowledgement of knowing irreverence or simply a disclaimer for the magazine's adolescent tendencies. By recognizing that one ought to '*know* better', it not only indicated the relationship between 'thinking' and 'doing' that was a central issue for *loaded*'s editors, but also the ultimate ambiguities of their masculine identifications.

After *loaded*

In their retrospective analyses of *loaded*'s success, Brown and Southwell highlighted familiar preoccupations. Southwell compared the magazine to the rock band Oasis, well known for its proud working-class background and exploits with drink and drugs: 'both experienced massive overnight success, both celebrated life and got people excited, doing everything their own way, not caring what the literati said, cocking a snook at the establishment' (Southwell 1998: 207).[12] Other explanations overtly associated the magazine with Thatcherism and drug culture, claiming that each had expanded the expectations of ordinary people and broken down established social and cultural boundaries (*Guardian*, 30.11.98: Media, 2–3).

These themes remained salient in Brown's vision of the *GQ* reader. I discussed Brown's move from *loaded* to Condé Nast's prestigious men's title in Chapter 4, and it is appropriate to return to this affair. *GQ* had undergone several transitions in its nine-year history before Brown's makeover. As launch editor Paul Keers was replaced by Alexandra Shulman in early 1990, the magazine's original focus on clothing, gadgets and a lifestyle of urban, yuppie sophistication was broadened. In adding more features writing, Shulman also brought in the men who went on to be the magazine's next two editors, Michael VerMeulen and Angus McKinnon. VerMeulen took over in February 1991, and began to ease the title towards the more 'streetwise and blokey' magazine to which it reverted under Brown (*Campaign*, 11.12.98: 24), with an increasing and, for the time, unequalled emphasis on sex and women. It was he who sanctioned the Sharon Stone cover that took *GQ*'s circulation to a new height in 1993, and the prescient cover line 'Sex, sex, sex and more sex'. VerMeulen and Brown had much in common in terms of lifestyle and personality (though, having never met VerMeulen nor read his title, Brown could not be said to have been directly influenced by him). Like Brown, VerMeulen was a charismatic, charming and often brash self-publicist, with a prodigious appetite for drink, drugs and women, a fondness for rattling off quotable soundbites, and a facade of confident, sometimes boorish, egotism. Unlike him though, VerMeulen was American by birth and identification, with a background as a theatre impresario, drama critic, law and financial journalist, a fondness for books over sport or music, and for sprits, wine and American cocktails over pints of beer. Indeed, VerMeulen was more like the gentleman womanizer of a past generation than Brown's updated version of the lad, and a liberal but libertarian capitalist rather a left-wing, populist individualist (*Telegraph*, 30.8.95: 25; *Guardian*, 8.11.93: G2, 17; *The Times*, 21.10.95: 30).

After VerMeulen's death from a drink and drugs overdose in August 1995, it was deputy editor Angus McKinnon who was appointed to take his place. With *GQ* sales levelling out but the lads mags thriving, the dilemma faced by Condé Nast about how to take the title forward was symbolized in its printing of two different covers for the September 1995 issue, one featuring model Helena Christensen and the other the actor Hugh Grant (*Media Week*, 11.8.95: 6). McKinnon himself announced that he would not ditch the magazine's sex coverage, but would 'bring out the Condé Nastness of the title' (*Campaign*, 24.11.95: 8). His reign, informed by the ascetic, cerebral character that I noted in Chapter 4, lasted less than two years, as circulation declined and market competition intensified.

The choice of Brown to rejuvenate the magazine was less odd than some commentators imagined. The appointment was described in one paper as 'as if the editor of the *Daily Sport* had been made editor of *The Economist*' (*Independent on Sunday*, 5.10.97: Features, 4–5). (Brown himself likened it to a first division footballer moving to the Premiership.) Yet, as Brown had aged, the differences between him and his predecessors had become less marked. VerMeulen's preferred social arena, the Groucho Club, became one of Brown's hangouts, whilst a predilection for the *Literary Review* emphasized Brown's new self-image as a man of refined taste. He explained that it was now upmarket magazines rather than *loaded* that reflected his lifestyle: '*GQ* seems a more interesting proposition to me. I'm older, I've got money, I have responsibilities I didn't have before. ... I've got a wardrobe full of Paul Smith suits, I've got cars. When I started *loaded* I owned one suit, I didn't have a car, I lived in a tiny flat in Tower Bridge with three mates' (*Media Week*, 26.9.97: 16).

More specifically, whilst acknowledging that he had grown up – 'when you find yourself wanting to chin someone because they've gazumped you on a house, you know something's up' (*Guardian*, 21.4.97: Media, 6) – Brown also claimed that his attitude and interests were no different from ever before: 'I do the same things I ever did, but I've got better clothes and my seats are more comfortable! That's the truth of the matter. And I don't have to queue!' (Brown 1999a).

It was certainly true that Brown's new lifestyle of champagne-drinking and first-class travel meant that he could no longer claim to be a man of the people. Indeed, his celebrity status meant that, whilst at *loaded* he had prided himself on inhabiting the same milieux of his readers, by the time he was editing *GQ*, he was mixing with the actual stars who graced the title's pages.[13] Brown's efforts to understand his magazine by 'living it' – 'I wander around Mayfair and pop into a tailor on Savile Row, I make sure I get my sports car valeted and I get my shoes from Oliver Sweeney' (*Press Gazette*, 11.12.98: 15) – represented a more self-conscious editorial technique than the effortless embodiment he had exercised at *loaded*. Nonetheless, he remained committed to an instinctive method of imagining his readers and producing his title. Bringing in former colleagues to aid his revamp, he restated his pledge of a few years earlier that his magazine would be 'for me and my friends' (*Independent on Sunday*, 5.10.97: Features, 4–5).

Accordingly then, Brown refreshed the existing image of the *GQ* audience by shifting the target market in line with his cultural resources and identifications: 'There is a new breed of yuppie in Britain – the black market yuppie who used to be a ticket tout and organize raves' (*Press Gazette*, 4.7.97: 3). In this sense, *GQ*'s model reader under Brown was the man who had read *loaded* four years earlier, now with rather more money and the lifestyle to match. With Brown eleven years younger than his predecessor, it was appropriate also that he looked to a considerably younger consumer. Meanwhile, he reinterpreted McKinnon's definition of 'cool': 'The most contemporary evaluation of cool is someone with a good sense of humour … Traditionally cool has been associated with po-faced' (*Guardian*, 21.4.97: Media, 7). Invoking the audience in a way that, again, indicated his own self-image, and rendered the readership rather differently from *GQ*'s earlier brand of conservative-metropolitanism (Nixon 1996), Brown claimed that 'to partake in the *GQ* lifestyle you have to have a sense of adventure and a bit of verve' (*The Times*, 18.12.98: 40–1).

The first issue over which he had full control, in November 1997, was stamped with Brown's identity and preferences. Cover star Paul Weller was interviewed inside the magazine by Brown himself, whose opening questions probed the singer about the anger and passion of his music. Football, comedy and film were covered through profiles of hard-drinking, aggressive Manchester United midfielder Roy Keane, alternative comedian Sean Lock, and *Get Carter*, the 1970s film starring Michael Caine as a drug-taking, sex-seeking hitman. One of the many short music features discussed Jamie Reid, the man who had created the art work and imagery for punk band The Sex Pistols. The motoring column focussed on Rolls Royce, replete with references to the model recently given to Oasis guitarist Noel Gallagher by his record label. Meanwhile, an article on Che

Guevara and a head-to-head interview between National Union of Mineworkers President Arthur Scargill and socialist comedian Lee Hurst indicated the political accent that Brown brought to a magazine that had always been the most blatantly and slickly materialistic in the market. Design and details were also marked by Brown's fingerprints, not least in the letters page he introduced, whilst the use of vibrant, clashing colours on the cover (light blue and orange), and changes in column width and font designed to give the magazine a 'busier and less American' look, were imported directly from *loaded* (*Press Gazette*, 17.10.97: 12). Coverlines such as '12 pages of sexy chicks in pants', 'one off the wrist' (for a photoshoot of watches), and the headline 'There's more to Colombia than meets the nose' (p. 107) also highlighted the new tone that Brown delivered to Condé Nast's flagship product.

Brown's following three cover stars, Vic Reeves (December 1997), Eric Cantona (January 1998) and Oasis' Liam Gallagher (February 1998), underlined his ambition to transform the title and hailed *loaded* as the magazine's unlikely antecedent. Cover lines continued to pledge fresh interests, most notably, cocaine, drink, football and comedy, with sexual content increasingly explicit. The 'Gents' section at the front of each issue identified 'everything a modern guy should know' as ranging 'from drug testing kits to how much footballers earn' (Brown, in *Press Gazette*, 20.2.98: 18). Although 'success with style' remained the publication's unwritten motto, the skew placed on both terms was rather different from in the past. Weller remained a pertinent exemplar, with Brown now foregrounding mod's style code of crisp suits and its obsession with detail. A feature in February 1999 on 'Lock, Stock and Smoking Style', referring to a recent British gangster movie with recurrent post-mod overtones (ska and old soul music, long leather coats, smartly-cut suits), highlighted the magazine's 'geezer chic' identity and its new motif of working-class mobility. Brown's interest in the style choices of Great Train Robber Bruce Reynolds (as noted in Chapter 4) was equally symbolic. And whilst he extended the magazine's fashion and grooming coverage, Brown also expanded the notion of what style might cover: a two-page spread on the badges of English football club typified the magazine's new horizons (March 1998, 210–11).

Other changes were represented through the new freelancers that Brown commissioned. Whilst the BBC's head of foreign affairs John Simpson was not an obvious selection, those such as former *NME* journalist, working-class parvenu and cultural critic Tony Parsons, the confrontational Glaswegian author of drug-culture novel 'Trainspotting', Irvine Welsh, and advertising's Labour-supporting *enfant terrible*, Trevor Beattie, appeared apposite choices. Brown also hired permanent staff from familiar spheres: senior editor Martin Deeson, deputy editor Bill Prince and features editor Iestyn George were former colleagues from *loaded* and the *NME*; others came from *Q*, *Total Sport*, the *Telegraph Magazine*,

Goal and *Mojo*. Contributing editors included original *Maxim* proposer Lloyd Bradley, *Arena* luminary Robert Elms, regular *loaded* model Kathy Lloyd (now employed as a sex columnist) and former drug dealer and *loaded* writer Howard Marks.

Martin Deeson's travel-cum-reportage articles on elephant tracking, Hell's Angels, North Sea fishing, the Yakuza and New Age cults reapplied the New journalist template, although with a less frenzied style than at *loaded* and with a much higher standard of photojournalism. A report in February 1999 by former *loaded* journalist Ben Marshall was even more suggestive of Brown's previous position and the journalist identity with which he still partly affiliated himself. Based upon Luke Rhinehart's 1971 novel *The Dice Man*, in which life decisions were made according to the roll of a dice, Marshall had put himself in the hands of chance with the end result of leaving his job. The piece, though not in itself particularly glamorous, evoked the sense of underworld jeopardy that Brown had first made familiar through *loaded*. Indeed, through a contractual confusion, an almost identical article was actually carried in *loaded* in the same month.

However, Brown's personal maturation was also signalled in the magazine, particularly through Tony Parsons' 'Dominant Male' column that was commissioned as a monthly deliberation on modern masculinity, and one-off contemplations such as Lloyd Bradley's extended feature on 'how to get it together before it all falls apart' ('Changing Man', *GQ*, September 1998: 150–63). The parallels with Brown's life were striking. Appearing on Channel Four's *Girlie Show* whilst at *loaded*, he had rhetorically asked, 'who could get bored of drinking and women?', but had since become a married teetotaller. These changes, and the very fact that he was considered a suitable candidate for *GQ*, revealed the dynamic nature of masculinity that Brown was now beginning to recognize. Usually flippant about gender 'issues', after his detachment from Condé Nast, Brown wrote a long broadsheet article in which he openly reflected on the relationship between football, masculinity and his own life (*Guardian*, 24.7.99: Weekend, 16–23).[14] Acknowledging that he had, until recently, been in a state of extended adolescence, Brown now pondered his future direction and that of his contemporaries:

> Football, like the male species, has never been under such pressure to improve itself … To join the colourful, commercial train to success. Just as there are many who eagerly jump aboard, familiarising themselves with the correct labels, so there are hundreds who revert to type. … Just as men have no right to know where the future will take them, neither do football clubs … Both must go forward, be prepared to change, to accommodate the opinions of others. To use their brains, not just their boots and their turnstiles. This is where we find ourselves. (Brown, *Guardian*, 24.7.99: Weekend, 21)

Typically, Brown would not commit an opinion as to which option men ought to take in moving on. But in the context of an ageing process that heightened the uncertainties I have highlighted in this chapter, the ambivalence he articulated in the article was highly personal.

Concluding Comments

Brown and Southwell's nostalgic recollections about *loaded*'s revolutionary accomplishments became increasingly tinged with bitterness. By April 2000, Southwell had left the editor's position at *loaded*, unhappy with the commercial imperatives and focus groups that were impinging on his editorial autonomy, as outlined in Chapter 4. Joining pop-culture web site Switch 2 as editorial director, Southwell continued to preach the punk attitude that he regarded as the original, but now defunct, *loaded* ethic: 'Don't accept the old order. Get rid of it' (*Guardian*, 23.10.00: Media, 55). In November 2000, Brown launched an assault on the men's press that he had effectively founded, describing the sector as 'stale', 'pathetic' and 'embarrassing' and declaring: 'If I'd known when I started *loaded* that the men's sector would descend into a conveyor belt of old soap stars in bikinis, I assure you I would not have done it' (*Press Gazette*, 17.11.00: 1). In April 2001, the resignation of two senior *loaded* journalists in protest at new editor Keith Kendrick's proposals to make the magazine more competitive with *FHM* and *Maxim* seemed to bear out Brown and Southwell's concerns that intense market competition was compromising the title's original ambitions.

This chapter has examined these aims in relation to a period during which commercial demands were far less pressing on the magazine's editorial formulation than by the end of the decade. The relative absence of commercial pressures was an important factor in allowing *loaded*'s character to be determined to a great extent through the identifications and aspirations of its founders, James Brown and Tim Southwell. I have also shown the importance of the men's style press in providing the masculine identity against which Brown and Southwell posed their professional identities and cultural affiliations, albeit with more ambivalence than was at times apparent. That Brown's affections for *Arena*, *Esquire* and American men's title *Details* had often been concealed related primarily to his resentment that these magazines had failed to indulge his lifestyle, interests and the journalistic identity that he had wished to inhabit. However, Brown acknowledged *Arena* founder Nick Logan as a personal hero and Paul Smith, the fashion designer friend who had helped convince Logan that a men's style title could be successful, as a personal inspiration (*Guardian*, 21.4.97: Media, 7; *The Times*, 18.12.98: 40–1). It was instructive also that Brown originally conceived of *loaded* as a 'younger version of *Arena*'. Of the first generation of men's magazines, it was the one most steeped in British youth subculture, in particular the mod scene with which Brown and Southwell had always identified. Influences such as *Viz*, the *Sun* and punk, and columns such as 'Greatest Living Englishmen', confirmed the distinct Englishness of *loaded*'s identity, at a time when *GQ* and *Esquire* were still guided by American cultural benchmarks.

Moreover, it was the Wagadon writers Julie Burchill and Robert Elms whose subaltern identifications and self-authorized confidence most obviously forebore the affiliations and occupational appetites of Brown and Southwell (Mort 1996). Where *loaded*'s creators diverged most markedly both from these predecessors and from other style press writers was in the Gonzo leanings that informed their journalist identities. Southwell's (1998) book, in particular, paid tribute to an editorial subjectivity of wide-eyed disbelief, accidental heroism and charming incompetence that had little in common with the suave self-control of most writers on the upmarket magazines. It is because these publications and their editors conveyed different editorial voices, ambitions and masculine cultures from those of *loaded*, despite some shared lineage through the influence of Logan, that I want to discuss them in the following chapter.

Notes

1. Southwell's self-identification, and the questionable definition of class status that it necessitated, was shared with other senior figures at *loaded*. Publisher Adrian Pettett, whose parents were teachers, described himself as 'C1 ... in terms of, I'm single, I live in London, high income, all that' (Pettett 1999). Publishing director Robert Tame, the son of a sales executive and a social worker, described himself in a questionnaire as upper-working-class, although he recognized in interview that he was 'probably now middle-class in where I live and the car I drive and the salary I earn' (Tame 1998). Both men were university educated and in relatively advanced positions at IPC.

2. Of seven editorial staff who returned questionnaires in 1999, all had Honours degrees, from institutions including University College London, Sussex University and the University of Liverpool: hardly the 'bunch of berks' that Southwell suggested (1998: 111).

3. By the time that my interviews were conducted, Brown was married and Southwell was in a long-term relationship, declaring that 'the most important things in my life are my girlfriend and my baby' (1999). However, both made clear their pride in pasts that were sexually highly active.

4. Several staff on other 'lad mags' displayed similar outlooks. *Front* editor, Piers Hernu, reasoned (1998), 'I don't think many people count bare breasts as pornography nowadays, do they? You've got bare breasts in virtually any

magazine you look in – you get it in *The Sunday Times* magazine; so that's not pornography'. A senior figure at *Maxim* dismissed accusations of sexism as: 'politically correct bullshit really. I just don't see it. Actually we have had many, many letters – and I'm quite sure that this would be the case with other magazines as well – from women saying how much they appreciate men's magazines in educating men about what women want and so on.'

5. Derek Harbinson, *loaded*'s editor May 1997–November 1998, used an almost identical language to discuss the editorial team, describing them as a bunch of 'animals' whilst emphasizing their ability to work 'bloody hard' when necessary (*Press Gazette*, 23.1.1998: 14). 'You don't create an enormously successful magazine by being a bunch of berks. We are a bunch of berks, but we're also very good at what we do' (*Media Week*, 15.5.1998: 9).

6. Criticism of the magazine was interpreted through similar categories: 'The sort of people who were criticizing *loaded* – they're the sort of people that given a World War, they're calling the shots and they want you in the front line or in the factory packing the gunpowder into the guns' (Southwell 1998: 100). 'Specifically the *Guardian* and the *Independent*, [*loaded*'s success] really got up their backs, I tell you, which was brilliant. If they had their way, we would never do anything; working-class people would never do fucking anything' (Southwell 1998).

7. Brown made the following statements in consecutive interviews:

loaded was primarily created by working-class people. It was created by a working-class magazine company. The topics covered in it were ostensibly working-class interests: football, music, drinking, bagging off with girls, whatever; and wanting to improve, better yourself. (1999a)

loaded wasn't set up as a working-class magazine. ... The mixture of people on the staff, some were from up north, some were from out in Essex, some had gone to public school, some had gone to comprehensive schools, some had gone to corrective institutions; some had done degrees, others had got O levels, others hadn't got O levels. Some had had very successful jobs, others hadn't. *loaded* was [just] a product of the people who created it. It wasn't an attempt to be working-class. (1999b)

8. In May 2001, IFG, the company that James Brown established after he left *GQ*, bought *Viz* from John Brown Publishing for £6.4m, in a deal that also included *Bizarre* and *Fortean Times*. Brown declared that *Viz* was still his favourite magazine, and that he had fulfilled a lifetime ambition by owning the title he used to sell alongside his fanzine in Leeds as a teenager (*Guardian* web site, 25.5.01).

9. By the end of the decade, the 'new lad' had become such a polluted and

pejorative term that Brown and Southwell both sought to distance them-selves from it. Southwell said: 'I've never even met a New Lad, and the reason is quite simple: they don't exist and, like the rest of the population, I have neither the time nor the inclination to embark on a miserable quest to find them' (1998: 107). Brown denied that he had ever used the phrase and dismissed O'Hagan as a 'paranoid Irishman' (*Independent on Sunday*, 21.4.97: 6).

10. Brown noted that: 'The first issue [of *GQ*] had Michael Heseltine on the cover, and I really do think that most guys would much rather be in a room with Caprice [the supermodel and Brown's last *GQ* cover star] than Michael Heseltine' (Brown 1999b).

11. Sending up the more concealed product placement of other magazines, *loaded* thanked companies openly for sending in desirable freebies.

12. In fact, Southwell's repeated attempts to condemn the 'literati' and defend *loaded* from its accusations of sexism seemed to betray his assertions that the opinions of the liberal media elite meant nothing to him.

13. 'Last night I went to a premiere of an Irvine Welsh play. ... And I sat next to one of my heroes, Kevin Rowland, of Dexy's Midnight Runners. Harry Enfield was there, looking really sharp. Mel B from the Spice Girls was there, looking very pregnant and very glamorous. Noel Gallagher was there, his wife Meg was there. All Saints were there. It was a very glamorous thing ... quite an intimate thing, there were only about 100 people there. And then we went to a party afterwards, and you get a lot of people like actors and actresses, and record producers and so on. And I'm familiar with those people, and I think those are the sort of people that people often want to read about.' (Brown 1999a)

14. A review of Tony Parsons' first novel, *Man and Boy*, in June 1999 had already suggested Brown's increasingly contemplative mood: 'Man and Boy is a great read because it's a book about change and how men have to be prepared to change' (*Observer*, 27.6.99: Review, 18).

–6–

Editors in the Men's Style Press

I would like to have the option of putting men on the cover, if it were the right man and the right picture and the right month; [but] the risk you run is so great that it's simply not worth taking it. And that pisses me off sometimes because there are clearly months when Ewan McGregor is the right person to be on the cover of *Esquire*. But Ewan McGregor at the cost of 40 per cent of your sales is too high a price to pay. (Peter Howarth, editor of *Esquire*, July 1999)

In the introduction to Part III, I suggested that the editorial leverage given to Brown and Southwell at *loaded* was somewhat greater than that available to Peter Howarth and Ekow Eshun at *Esquire* and *Arena* respectively. This was not only because the magazines that Howarth and Eshun began to edit at the end of 1996 were established titles, but also because, as Howarth's comments make clear, the ascent of the lad mags was by this time putting commercial pressures upon style titles that neither *loaded*'s founders nor previous style press editors had needed to contemplate. Howarth's contention that Ewan McGregor was 'the right person' for his title symbolized the conceptualization of the *Esquire* identity that he constructed and mobilized in negotiation with the conventions of the magazine and the obligations of the market. In the following chapter, I shall explore in more detail the derivations and determinants of this formulation of *Esquire*, and of Eshun's version of *Arena*. The cultural and professional training, resources, interests and motivations of Howarth and Eshun, and the identities they occupied and sought to represent, are central to this account. For it was largely in their respective self-images as the professional, cultured 'man of taste' and the cutting-edge lifestyle-explorer that the identities of their titles were rearticulated.

Contextualizing these shifts requires me to provide further detail of the histories of the publications involved, for it is important to understand the brand identities that Howarth and Eshun were employed to represent and refashion. I shall therefore chronicle the launch and development of *Esquire* before examining Howarth's personal and professional background and identifications, his qualifications for the *Esquire* post, and the impact of his editorship upon the character of the magazine.

Peter Howarth and *Esquire*

Esquire: *'Man at his Best'*

The roots of UK *Esquire* lay in the US, where the magazine had been hugely successful since its launch in 1933. By the late 1950s, it sold 800,000 monthly copies (Osgerby 2000), but it was in the 1960s that *Esquire* marked itself out as the world's most influential general interest men's magazine, discovering writers including Tom Wolfe and Norman Mailer, publishing Truman Capote, John Updike, Gore Vidal, Ernest Hemingway, Vladimir Nabokov and many other respected authors and 'New journalists', and mixing literary pieces with lifestyle features, fashion, political reportage and glamorous photography. By the start of the 1990s, the circulation of the US edition was still over 700,000 and versions of the title had been spawned in Hong Kong, Japan and Italy. In the UK, however, its editorial formula had been dormant since 1957, when the brief and unsuccessful life of a domestic issue had been terminated.

Looking to extend its men's brand into British publishing, and prompted by its competition with Condé Nast, who looked to be securing a commanding market position with *GQ*, NatMags launched UK *Esquire* in early 1991. The launch was overseen by Lee Eisenberg, himself an American import, and editor-in-chief of the US version in the late 1980s. In his self-presentations as part of *Esquire's* launch publicity, Eisenberg offered a distinctive slant on contemporary masculinity. Wearing smart but fashionable suits with shirt and tie, accompanied by a neatly adjusted handkerchief in his breast pocket, he represented a dapper modern conservatism, at the forefront of professional style culture. Eisenberg had the cool self-possession typical of an affluent Manhattan. He celebrated his own charisma and described himself as 'charming and articulate and glamorous and handsome' (*The Times*, 18.1.91: 24). Such flourishes were avowedly heterosexual. Whilst welcoming gender self-consciousness, and discussing the women's movement and its impact upon men in positive terms, Eisenberg clearly valued a masculine, if not quite macho, image. He deliberated openly on manhood, male self-esteem and the difficulties of modern life for the thinking man, whilst suggesting that modern masculinity's future was a manly sensitivity that could integrate feminist concerns with a respect for what was 'uniquely' and 'valuably' male (*The Times*, 18.1.91: 24).

This identity was informed most evidently by the reading of New journalism that Eisenberg adulated (and that *Esquire* had itself helped to advance); specifically, a fusion of literate sensitivity and gutsy toughness that drew on the masculine narratives of Ernest Hemingway and Norman Mailer. Eisenberg's public presentations sought to reproduce their 'seamless masculinity' (Segal 1990: 113), affixed with a reflective edge born from the influence of second-wave feminism. As editor-in-chief of US *Esquire*, Eisenberg had attempted to maintain the magazine's heritage by routinely commissioning modern New journalism, whilst also authorizing an increased celebration of women as objects of desire. Although by no means a complete break with previous editorial approaches, Eisenberg's policy marked a shift in the magazine's imagined readership from baby-boomer new men who were most touched by feminism and material affluence to more robustly 'masculine' readers whom he summarized as 'men who were really men' (*Guardian*, 28.1.91: Features, 23).

The target reader of UK *Esquire* was, in broad terms, the same kind of affluent male professional that *GQ* was seeking to attract. However, whilst *GQ* foregrounded its associations as an upmarket style title, NatMags asserted the literary tradition of the *Esquire* brand to position the UK version as a cerebral magazine for intellectual high-achievers (*Media Week*, 1.6.90: 42). *Esquire* was also pitched as having a broader range of interests than *GQ*, covering 'fine writing, clothes, cars, wine and food' (*Campaign*, 3.8.90: 34), for a slightly older intended reader: 'Men who are intelligent, educated, successful, relatively affluent, who are moving into their early and mid-thirties, if not older and, maybe, have young children. They are beginning to contemplate the second half of their working lives, and taking stock' (Eisenberg, in *The Times*, 18.1.91: 24).

If this broad demographic profile was uncontroversial, the hue it was given by Eisenberg was more striking. In full-page black and white photographs, *Esquire*'s launch campaign promoted Eisenberg himself, aged forty-four, as the personification of the magazine's brand. And whilst insisting repeatedly that he would tailor the magazine to the British male, rather than clone the American version, Eisenberg projected the experiences of the liberal-metropolitan American man onto his conception of the British reader. British men, he conjectured, had gone through the same social and cultural transformations as their US counterparts, and engaged with the same debates around feminism and male identity. Accordingly, Eisenberg had no doubt that they would welcome articles about relationships, fatherhood and 'the experience of being a man', alongside an editorial approach that would treat them like 'real men' with 'balls' (*Media Week*, 16.11.90: 24; *Guardian*, 28.1.91: Features, 23; *The Times* 18.1.91: 24).

The resulting magazine, with its motto of 'Man at his best' and a young Brigitte Bardot on its first cover, was less emotionally self-conscious than its American progenitor, but duplicated much of its tone through earnest, wordy articles on topics such as shaving, cancer and the conditions of masculinity. These were accompanied by lengthy, often investigative, feature articles, fashion and grooming coverage and – to represent the magazine's literary identity – short stories by modern authors. Eisenberg believed that Britain's literary culture harboured the same tastes as 1960s America, when *Esquire* had first published many of New journalism's most famous exponents. Indeed, he positioned *Esquire* somewhere between the two, both geographically and temporally. One industry commentator described the magazine as like early *Playboy* in its 'club-bable male smugness, particularly about sex and women' (*Campaign*, 16.8.91: 11) – almost certainly unaware that, originally, US *Esquire* had been a significant influence on *Playboy* (Conekin 2000; Osgerby 2001). An article by Eisenberg himself that bemoaned the lack of decent shoeshine facilities in England was a telling indication of his effort to transpose an upmarket American style ethos onto his conception of the British professional man.

With the recession in full flow, economic conditions were hardly auspicious for *Esquire*'s launch. Whilst advertising support nonetheless held up well, the magazine's early problems were rooted in a confused editorial pitch that led to a lukewarm reception amongst consumers and the publishing community. The magazine was criticized as po-faced, snobbish, self-important, overly self-conscious, and, most commonly, as too influenced by its American origins: a shrine to macho reporting and earnest consumerism (*inter alia*, *Press Gazette*, 18.2.91: 5; 9.3.92: 8; *Media Week*, 15.2.91: 8; *Campaign*, 15.2.91: 5; 16.8.91: 11; *Guardian*, 24.2.92: Features, 23). Such reviews arraigned Eisenberg as the main cause of *Esquire*'s problems, in effect outlining his characteristics in their appraisals. Those commentaries not implicating Eisenberg instead drew attention to the expertise of Alex Finer, the editor that he had appointed to work under him. The magazine contained less fashion coverage and denser features than *GQ* and *Arena*, and, in many ways, resembled a newspaper Sunday supplement (*Press Gazette*, 9.3.92: 8). Finer's background was as a features journalist in the mainstream press, where, in a writing career beginning in 1968, he had worked, amongst other places, at *The Sunday Times*, as features editor of the *Evening Standard* and as assistant editor of the *Telegraph* magazine (*Press Gazette*, 10.9.90: 6). Cutting a serious figure in suit and tie and with a thick moustache and carrying a judge's battered leather briefcase (he was a qualified but non-practising barrister), Finer identified himself as a sober and serious pressman who devoured newsprint and was primarily committed to investigative rather than consumer journalism (*Press Gazette*, 30.9.91: 13) (see Figure 6).

From early on, *Esquire* failed to meet its circulation and advertising targets. After a launch issue that sold over 100,000 copies, average sales halved to around 50,000 per month. In September 1991, earlier than originally planned, Eisenberg returned to the US, declaring that the magazine's American tint would soon fade (*Press Gazette*, 15.7.91: 8). Finer took full control of *Esquire* and its now all-British editorial staff, with plans to relaunch it with a review section, pocket cartoons, a crossword, and horoscopes about sex and investments (*Press Gazette*, 29.7.91: 9). But after only five months as sole editor, at the start of 1992, with circulation still languishing well below *Esquire*'s goal of 70,000, Finer resigned. His replacement, Rosie Boycott, had been the magazine's deputy and features editor, and had a varied curriculum vitae in press and publishing that

Figure 6 Photograph of Alex Finer, courtesy of *Media Week*.

included stints on the underground press, pioneering feminist magazine *Spare Rib*, a short-lived travel title, girls' magazine *Honey*, the *Sunday Telegraph*, the *Daily Mail*'s *Mail and Femail* magazine and upmarket glossy *Harpers and Queen*. Unable to offer herself as the typical *Esquire* reader, Boycott instead believed that her ability to understand emotional issues and her transferable editorial skills would qualify her adequately for the task. The circulation growth achieved by Alexandra Shulman at *GQ* was evidence itself that men's titles could be successfully edited by women. Meanwhile, Boycott's brand of feminism was not discordant with editing *Esquire*. She had never shared the strident radicalism of her founding partners at *Spare Rib*, instead pursuing a more populist, liberationist project against sexual stereotyping that could be applied equally well to men as to women. As editor of *Esquire*, she featured female cover stars as happily as rival editors, whilst repositioning the magazine to target a less exclusive market through pacier articles, glossier paper and more recognized writers, including John Simpson, Zoë Heller, Jon Ronson and Paul Morley (*Press Gazette*, 6.4.92: 17).[1] Most significantly, Boycott denounced the product she inherited as having traded on 'American laurels' and announced that content from now on would be 'entirely home grown' (*Media Week*, 6.3.92: 12).

By the time that Boycott was poached to edit the *Independent on Sunday* in October 1996, the men's press had been transformed. Boycott had received consecutive Editor of the Year awards from the British Society of Magazine Editors in 1993 and 1994, and, with circulation up to over 90,000, had sought to challenge *GQ*'s hegemony in the pre-*loaded* marketplace by expanding *Esquire*'s science and technology sections. But in the two years that followed, the established magazines had failed to match the extraordinary growth rates of the market's new entrants and were struggling to work out the appropriate response to a readership culture that appeared to demand more flesh and less sedate editorial content. From 1995, both *GQ* and *Esquire* abandoned their normal cover policies of featuring male icons in favour of female celebrities, and increased their coverage of sex, health and fitness to try to stave off the various challengers to their markets. Despite such efforts, in the ABCs of August 1996, *Esquire* was the only sector member to lose sales. In this respect, Howarth's assumption of the editor position in November 1996 came at a time when the company's conception of the suitable *Esquire* identity was particularly uncertain. To understand Howarth's response, it is necessary first to examine his own background, career path and self-identity.

Peter Howarth's Background and Career

Born in Kensington in 1964 and raised by his mother in Battersea, Howarth spent his pre-university years in London, where he attended the fee-paying City of London School for Boys. Howarth described himself as 'totally and utterly middle-class' (Howarth 1998), his only qualification being that he had been brought up in a single-parent household by an unconventional, Austrian mother. With her being a literary agent and his father a photographer and film-maker, and their relationship having taken place during the capital's 'swinging sixties', Howarth's background could hardly have been more rooted in the post-war metropolitan arts. Indeed, the narrative of the romantic creative was one of two competing discourses that patterned his identity as a young man. The other was a striving to prove himself as a conscientious, mature and responsible adult and an academic achiever. Howarth himself identified these ambitions as the effects of a highly ambivalent stance towards his father, whom he did not meet until aged fourteen. He certainly sought to emulate certain aspects of what he perceived to be a glamorous and enigmatic masculine role model, describing his father as:

a kind of tragic hero. An engineering graduate who could fix cars with his bare hands; a philanthropist who gave away a gun to a black South African priest to aid the struggle against apartheid; a star photographer, published in *Life*, who made a name for himself by being able to get *the* picture whatever the difficulty or the danger; a talent so versatile that he later became an award-winning documentary film maker. (Howarth 1997: 118)

At the same time, Howarth was determined not to ape the man whom he regarded as incapable of handling money or relationships responsibly, and who had been unfaithful to his mother.

Howarth's teenage years were inscribed by his desire to become an adjusted and improved version of his father. He read poetry, painted and played in bands. He bought second-hand clothes, dyed his hair, and went to '*demi-monde*' parties (Howarth 1997: 119). In the meantime, he won a place to study English Literature at Cambridge University and took on a disposition that he acknowledged as 'over-serious', 'precociously earnest' and prematurely and mistakenly adult (Howarth 1997: 120). He read the *NME*, *The Face* and *Blitz* – '*i-D* was a bit surreal and weird ... *Blitz* was a bit more Oxbridge as opposed to streetwise' (Howarth 1998) – as well as serious literature. In his year before going to Cambridge he worked in a bookshop whilst playing in a rock band with friends from the Central St Martins School of Art and Design, and considered becoming a photographer and film-maker seriously enough to apply to art school before resolving to take the more conservative academic path. At university in the mid-1980s, whilst many of his contemporaries were lured into financially lucrative jobs in the city, law and advertising, Howarth remained committed to a broad notion of creative activity, envisaging a career in mainstream publishing.

Instead, Howarth took up a job with fashion designer Paul Smith, who would become an important personal inspiration. Howarth had worked for Smith during his university summer holidays, selling and exhibiting clothes in his Covent Garden store and at Paris fashion shows. Looking to expand his operations, Smith offered Howarth the chance to become a permanent project manager when he graduated, dealing primarily with marketing and public relations. Smith's significance lay in the version of creative entrepreneurialism that he represented. As Nixon has suggested, he 'celebrated a nostalgic image of the shopkeeper in his whole retailing ethos', honouring the quirky individualism and eye for detail of the old-fashioned, independent shop-salesman (Nixon 1996: 56). Smith had reinvented himself from ultimate yuppie designer to Nottingham-boy-made-good in tune with the cultural climate of the 1990s, but retained his commitment to 'taste', quality and the self-determination of the autonomous craftsman. For Howarth, that Smith had remained true to such standards whilst adapting to the style culture of the moment distinguished him as a worthy mentor. Howarth attributed Smith's capacity for perpetual innovation, and his longevity as a respected member of style society, to his faith in the value of ideas:

> Paul just has non-stop ideas about everything, about shop-fittings, about ad campaigns, about how to do fashion shows. Not just about what clothes should look like. And he basically showed me that as long as you've got a creative mind, as long as the ideas keep flowing, then you're fine. You'll just adapt, and you can do anything. And that ideas are currency, they really are. (Howarth 2000)

Smith's application of a critical, aesthetic and innovating gaze to a world of style that extended beyond clothing was significant, for Howarth's interests were likewise diverse. Indeed, it was his keenness to maintain an involvement in literary culture that led to Howarth's exit from the fashion industry. Whilst still working for Smith, he had approached *Arena*, and, later, *Blitz*, to undertake to write for them about books, contemporary authors and other areas of popular culture. This choice of magazines was consistent with Howath's investment in certain notions of artistic integrity and sophistication. *Arena* founder Nick Logan shared many of his friend Smith's creative ideals, most plainly in his commitment to creative independence outside the constraints of large corporate players and his self-promotion as an arbiter of good taste (Mort 1996; Nixon 1996). Such values were in turn reproduced through Logan's magazines, *The Face* and *Arena*. As a contributor to the latter, Howarth could exercise simultaneously his interest in literature and his broader conception of fashionable, modern culture.

This extra-curricular journalism was put on hold for a couple of years when Howarth, still only twenty-two, was poached by fashion house Nicole Fahri to launch their menswear collection. Disliking the job's commercial orientation, and missing the creativity of his journalistic enterprises, Howarth soon reactivated his freelance endeavours, writing for *Arena*, *GQ* and the *Guardian* on style culture and fashion. He reduced his commitment at Nicole Fahri to part-time, and was, in time, made a contributing editor and then style editor at *GQ* when menswear was commanding little attention elsewhere in the sector. Under the editorship of Michael VerMeulen, Howarth became a full-time staff member before being promoted to *GQ* style director. His desire to expand his writing beyond a single sphere soon resurfaced, and, with VerMeulen's encouragement, he began to commission features in other areas. After almost five years at *GQ*, in April 1995, Howarth was sounded out by the departing editor of *Arena*, Katherine Flett, about his interest in taking over her position, one that would give him the full editorial jurisdiction he sought. Once appointed, his primary task was to increase the magazine's frequency from six to ten times per year. After fourteen months, in which he was judged to have facilitated this transition successfully (see section on Ekow Eshun and *Arena*), Howarth was headhunted by NatMags to edit *Esquire* (see Figure 7).

Figure 7 Peter Howarth publicity photo, courtesy of The National Magazine Company.

Masculinity, Heterosexuality and Gender Politics

Howarth's masculine identity was bound up with his investment in the script of the fashionable, modern creative: the man of contemporary taste. To a considerable degree, it was his aptitude as an inquisitor of urban culture that authorized his masculinity. Raised with middle-class, liberal-metropolitan notions of masculine competence, he believed male status to reside in the confident and effortless display of intelligence, authority and sophistication, particularly in the cultural spheres with which he was familiar. Notions of working-class heroism drawn upon by Brown and Southwell played a negligible role in anchoring Howarth's self-image as a man, whilst their celebration of heterosexual accomplishment was, likewise, of marginal significance. Crucially also, Howarth enjoyed the sense of being a thoroughly *modern* man, at the forefront, if not quite the cutting edge, of contemporary gender politics. As the editor of a collection of writing on fatherhood, he highlighted more than just his self-proclaimed stance as 'an unashamed dad evangelist' (Howarth 1997: 11). Introducing the volume as an original contribution to the barely explored area of 'the world of the modern father' (Howarth 1997: 13), he deliberately emphasized its contemporaneity. He took for granted the unusual comfort displayed by his contributors, all experienced writers of some sort, in expressing their feelings about fatherhood and personal relationships. Howarth's chapter was no exception. He openly discussed his love for his son, the complexities of his relationship with his father and his propensity to be made tearful by sentimental representations of male friendships and paternal relations. Here then, Howarth indicated a progressive masculine subjectivity at ease with emotional admission and the self-conscious analysis of personal intimacy and identity.

Nonetheless, Howarth's earnest emotionalism had its limits. In presenting himself as the epitome of contemporary masculinity – urbane, sensitive and self-aware – he was careful not to suggest self-doubt or uncertainty. His reflectiveness avoided any implication of insecurity or instability and functioned ultimately to project a self-possessed, measured confidence. Thus, whilst neither sober and restrained, nor sensitive and self-conscious to the point of appearing 'soft', Howarth exhibited an emotional self-control that signalled elements of conventional masculine subjectivity. His personal sexual politics were situated similarly. Howarth considered himself a forward-thinking progressive, but not 'some mad feminist or anything' (Howarth 2000). Indeed, his relationship with modern feminism was rather ambivalent. Though supportive of its ambitions, Howarth denounced those ideologies that made him and his friends 'feel guilty when we try and look at a good-looking girl, and go out and get pissed' (Howarth 1998). Like Brown and Southwell, he proclaimed his non-sexism as the credential that should permit him some scope to exhibit stereotypically male behaviour. Equally, he challenged the value of a feminist politics that, in his view, had sought to preclude 'the acknowledgement that there are differences between men and women' and the expression of heterosexual desire (Howarth 1998).

In this respect, Howarth welcomed the emergence of what he saw as a less repressive, more honest and more inclusive culture of sexual relations. Nevertheless, he questioned the value of the hedonistic lifestyle that he identified with *loaded*. Whilst preferring its energy and irreverence to the 'po-faced, style-dictated eighties' (Howarth 1998), he censured its immaturity and self-indulgence. In addition, he condemned a 'lad culture' that he considered incomparable with his own enlightened masculinism and which he believed had become 'an excuse for a lot of men to behave very, very badly' (Howarth 1998). There was undoubtedly a subtext about class and education in this stance, and an expectation that men should be able to intuitively discern between appropriate and inappropriate forms of behaviour. Unacceptable laddism was identified with a clearly different male social stratum from his own: 'the bloke ... sitting there in Swansea ... out of work ... and having a shit time' (Howarth 1998). Howarth distinguished himself as an altogether different breed: more cultured, mature and better educated. His terminology itself, the use of 'man' rather than 'guy', 'lad' or 'bloke', underlined this self-perception. As such, he suggested that there was a difference, a natural restraint, in the way that he and his friends exercised the license of lad culture compared with certain other men: 'that doesn't mean we're thugs, or even people standing around on building sites showing our arses and whistling at people. It's actually, we've rediscovered our masculinity, and this is how we're expressing it' (Howarth 1998).

Evident too in this statement, and a recurrent theme in Howarth's self-narrative, was a sense of his identity shifting in tune with the times. It was not that Howarth portrayed social identity as something that could simply be self-assembled. Rather, he was drawn to the prevailing male scripts of the media circles that he inhabited. Immersed in professional and social milieux where modish versions of masculinity were constantly scrutinized, and where personal identity was under a similar surveillance, it was unsurprising that a trend-conscious man like Howarth was in this way somewhat pliable. Although Howarth's personality matched neither the new man or new lad conventions, he had clearly been affected by the currency that each had achieved at particular stages of his working life.

Occupational Identity

What remained consistent in Howarth's self-image were the scripts that had modelled his youth: the mature and educated man, and the fashionable creative. In combination, they formed a professional identity very different from Brown and Southwell's self-projections as heroic outsiders, whilst also deviating from the conventional profile of the style press nobility. Both Nick Logan and Dylan Jones, the most prominent editor of the Wagadon stable, had gone into the magazine industry without university educations, arming themselves instead with uncertified forms of cultural capital that they reproduced in the early codings of the men's market. Logan was a self-declared 'East London mod' (Nixon 1996: 132) who had left school aged sixteen to work on the *West Essex Gazette* before editing the *NME* for a decade. There, he championed the punk movement and hired both Julie Burchill and Tony Parsons, before founding teenage pop magazine *Smash Hits* in 1978, *The Face* in 1980 and *Arena* six years later. Jones studied graphic design and photography at Chelsea School of Art and St Martins School of Art from the age of sixteen, after which he spent two years 'taking photos in night-clubs' and absorbing the cultural offerings of the 'London scene' (*Campaign*, 19.4.99: 19). In 1983, he was appointed editor of style title *i-D*, moving to Wagadon four years later as contributing editor of *The Face*, and editing *Arena* between 1988 and 1992.

Howarth's career route via Oxbridge and the fashion industry was itself almost unique. More significant still was the nature of his social and cultural capital, as already partly outlined, in both its family and educational components. Howarth's father was also a Cambridge graduate, whilst it was his mother's contacts who had gained him access to authors such as Graham Swift and Jay McInerney for his freelance magazine profiles. His education had taken him from one of the country's most exclusive and established public schools to one of its most exclusive and established universities, where his course was one of the most classical English Literature degrees in the British educational system. Howarth therefore entered magazine publishing with very different cultural stocks from the patrons of the men's lifestyle sector. Whilst their *modus operandi* was an 'avant-garde metropolitanism' (Nixon 1996), Howarth's was a less sub-cultural disposition that reflected his relatively more comfortable relationship with 'legitimate' culture. His attitude to modern culture and the world of goods was fashionable but mainstream, rather than cutting-edge. And whilst his personal interests – fashion, books, music, films, art, photography, comedy, socializing, food, sport, travel and politics – were sufficiently eclectic to qualify him for the *Arena* post, they were cast in rather more conservative terms than the magazine's conventional stylings.

Such distinctions were also reproduced in the politics of masculinity that Howarth and his predecessors adhered to and represented through their magazines. The architects of the men's press carried a decisive ideology in which 'style' was totemic, the overarching discourse through which all else was given value (Mort 1996; Nixon 1996). Within their magazines, it was presented as a social and political weapon; and politics itself was considered inseparable from questions of aesthetic judgement: *The Face* could cover 'post-marxist thinkers' because they could be seen as 'chic' (Nixon 1996: 151). The intelligent deployment of consumer goods was thus understood as the ultimate marker of masculinity, and liberation identified with the offerings of consumer culture.

Howarth was an interested observer of style culture, but not its most dedicated champion. He shared with its sponsors a sense that the significance of 'fashion' had vastly expanded, to the extent that it influenced: 'every area of our culture – newspaper design, advertising, TV programmes. It's come to mean not just clothing but books, food, holidays, who your friends are, how you want to live' (Howarth, in the *Guardian*, 25.11.96: G2, 16). However, Howarth's association of style with masculine status was heavily diluted. He denounced the prevailing signifiers of the early men's press – 'a certain amount of money and a certain amount of status ... the right restaurants, the right suit, the right bit of modern art, the right record, the right book ... the right holiday in the right places'

(Howarth 2000) – as false icons, and was scathing about the notion that masculinity should be 'a shopping list' (Howarth 1998). Significantly, Howarth's criticisms raised the standing of knowledge in the hierarchy of masculine traits: goods were no substitute for being intrinsically interesting and intelligent; 'Being sharp is not the same as being smart. ... It has nothing to do with who-you-know and everything to do with what-you-know' (*Campaign*, 28.1.00: 22). As in his condemnation of lad culture, then, Howarth differentiated himself from a commodity-based masculinity by endorsing a more enlightened, sophisticated and mature masculine script in which intelligence was the primary badge of distinction.

Howarth's political attitudes reflected the same hesitant relationship with style culture. Logan and his most celebrated protégés at *The Face*, Robert Elms and Julie Burchill, were all self-proclaimed left-wingers from working-class backgrounds who challenged the complacency of the established Left, Burchill with a form of reactionary populism and Elms with an anti-puritanical *stylepolitik* whose main target was the middle-class socialist tradition (Mort 1996: 34–43). Howarth fitted neither camp. Like the educated middle-class, artsy friends he had made at university (one of whom had become head of the educational programme at the Leeds Playhouse theatre, another an opera director) he was a *Guardian*-reading, liberal left-winger who accepted, without fully embracing, the dominance of the free market: 'I think that consumerism is just a given. I don't think it's a problem for you to want to live in a nice house with nice clothes and drive a nice car. I don't think that means you can't be a socialist. In that sense I'm very New Labour about it all' (Howarth 2000).

Just as Howarth's connection to the first stage of the men's lifestyle press was highly formative in the development of his professional dispositions, his experience of the second-wave revolution was also significant. By the time he took over at *Arena*, he was faced not only with an offensive against his kind of magazine, but also with an assault upon his identity as a lifestyle journalist. I discuss below how Howarth negotiated market demands in this period. More salient here is how he handled the emergence of *loaded*'s editorial voice. As the publisher of many of its original practitioners, *Esquire* had always monopolized claims to guard the New journalist heritage. In usurping many of its conventions, *loaded* challenged *Esquire*'s stranglehold, and questioned the industry's assumption that only writers on upmarket magazines had the right to position themselves as the carriers of the New journalism tradition.

Howarth made no pretence to be the heir to Tom Wolfe, but was an outspoken fan of New journalism and cited 1960s US *Esquire* as his favourite magazine: 'If someone produced a magazine tomorrow which was as good as American *Esquire* in the 60s, I'd be like, "what do we do now?"' (Howarth 2000). He professed nonetheless to be unflustered by the appearance of the tradition's new claimants. First, he identified their Gonzo technique as representing only one of a number of writing styles that existed within the genre. Second, Howarth questioned whether the quality of *loaded*'s output was comparable with that of its influences. He contrasted Thompson's meticulous, political craftings with *loaded*'s trademark tones, doubting how much of his output they had actually read. Third, he considered their attempts ineffective, arguing that most of *loaded*'s readers identified the title with naked women and rock stars and barely noticed the subtleties of the editorial tone.[2] Thus dismissing *loaded*'s efforts and differentiating them from his own aims, Howarth portrayed his occupational investments as unaffected by the emergence of this new editorial identity. The strength and confidence of his criticisms confirmed the centrality of professional competence to his self-identity. Above all, he continued to present himself as a more intelligent, educated and tasteful journalist than other market practitioners. How this identity was significant in relation to *Esquire* in the late 1990s is the subject of the next portion of this chapter.

Howarth's Esquire

In his interview for the *Esquire* post with NatMags MD Terry Mansfield, Howarth insisted that the solution to the company's quandary was not to take the title downmarket, but to build on its brand identity, modernize its content and differentiate it clearly from the sector's 'tabloids'. His interpretation of the *Esquire* heritage was rather different from that of Boycott, who had elaborated its history of investigative features, reportage and 'quality journalism'. Howarth recalled the more visual elements of the 1960s US blueprint, including its pictures of glamorous women and 'fantastic bits of modern art and cartoons and sports photography and lots of photojournalism' (Howarth 2000), as well as its written quality. Boycott's product, he felt, was too much like a periodical or newspaper, with an excess of long, serious, literary features, American writers and Hollywood icons. Howarth presented himself as ideally equipped to produce a magazine of visual as well as textual distinction, pointing out his parents' occupations as amongst the many guarantees of his suitability.

By his own estimations, Howarth's qualifications were plain to be seen. Once ensconced in the editor's chair, he affirmed: 'My principal credential for this job is my sex and my age' (*Guardian*, 25.11.96: G2, 16). Contemplating the *Esquire* audience as he prepared for his interview, he had concluded more expansively that:

> This reader is basically me. I was thirty-two, small child, living with my girlfriend ... didn't necessarily mean that I wanted to be an old fart ... me and my peers still want to buy records, go to films, go out, get drunk, see the world, travel, backpack, whatever, even though we may have mortgages and we may be onto our second or third job. (Howarth 1998)

This assessment was not an objective description of the *Esquire* audience, but the rearticulation of a target market that was always discursively rendered. Measuring himself partly against Boycott's imagined consumer, Howarth also transposed his own lifestyle onto an image of the *Esquire* brand that he therefore effectively reformulated. This was, by his own acknowledgement, the only way that Howarth felt able to edit: 'all I know is how to reflect my interests in the magazine, and the kind of interests of people who are like me ... and I surround myself with people who are basically like-minded, and we produce a magazine that we want to read' (Howarth 1999).

Correspondingly then, Howarth's assumed audience, and the tone of his title, differed from those of his predecessors. His imagined readers were younger, in their late twenties and early thirties rather than mid-thirties to early forties, more interested in popular culture and fashion, and of a less earnest, though still educated, disposition. In Howarth's view, they needed a magazine that was 'more exciting, more fun', with a humorous edge based upon 'the legacy of Monty Python' (a telling choice, given its Oxbridge nuances) rather than the 'bar-room' innuendo of the lad mags (Howarth 1998). Howarth envisaged the readers of *FHM* and *loaded* as 'students, living at home or just moving out of home, in the early stages of proper relationships with girls ... applying for their first job ... buying their first suit ... basically teenagers, rising twenties' (Howarth 1998). The reader he imagined for *Esquire* was a life-stage and mentality ahead:

You are in your second or third job. You've got responsibilities, because you're in a long-term relationship, or you've been in one, or you want to be in one, or you know what one is at least. You've bought your suit, you've decided what football team you support, you've got a mortgage, you're onto your second car. You're still interested in fashion, music, film, lifestyle, things that make you laugh, seeing your friends, and all those kinds of things. You're not an adult, in the sense of a patrician, Victorian idea of grown-up and kids. But you're also not a kid. ... reasonably well-dressed, but not a fashion victim ... my readers are sort of Friday night Channel Four, *Friends*, *Frazier*, *Never Mind the Buzzcocks*, *Match of the Day*, *South Park* ... *Panorama*; if they're reading books it's *The Beach* by Alex Garland, or *The Long Firm* by Jake Arnott, or Rupert Thompson or *Glamorama* or McInerney. If they're going to films it's *The Talented Mr Ripley*, *Gladiator*, *Being John Malkovich*, but they'll be getting a DVD player this Christmas and they'll go out and buy *The Matrix* and *The Italian Job* (one classic and one because they wanna get all the special effects). And in terms of music: Moby, Fatboy Slim, Blur's Greatest Hits, REM whatever ... probably interested in sport, he might even play Sunday league football, or squash, or whatever. But he's not a fitness freak, not down the gym every day. Kind of like the people I know, the people I went to college with. (Howarth 1998)

In terms of taste, Howarth's reader was less rarefied than that of either Boycott or Eisenberg, with an eclectic but mainstream range of cultural preferences. In respect to sexual politics, he was identified as the original new lad that Sean O'Hagan had outlined in his 1991 *Arena* article: a 'half-(new) man, half-lad' (*Arena*, Spring–Summer 1991) quite distinct from Eisenberg's self-conscious but manly urban-sophisticate. Although the urbane, composed, literate, tasteful, heterosexual sophistication that had always characterized 'the *Esquire* audience' remained the kernel of the new characterization, Howarth's reformation of the reader-image was evidently reflective of many of his own values, ambitions and identifications. Meanwhile, the forms of New journalism that Howarth commissioned, including articles on smuggling a girl from a Sarajevo orphanage (December/January 1997–98), tracing hostages in Kashmir (September 1998), running the bulls in Pamplona (October 1999), and boxing against the world light-heavyweight champion (December 1999), pointed to his personal affiliation with a more conservative reading of the canon than Brown and Southwell's. Extracts from Hunter Thompson's lost novel, *The Rum Diary* (November 1998), and a report of Thompson's eulogy to beat poet Allen Ginsberg (September 1999), also emphasized the *Esquire* publishing record upon which he was able to draw.

This is not to imply that Howarth's vision for the title was untrammelled by commercial imperatives or the tastes of a marketplace that had changed significantly since the early days of the men's press. In the changes he made at *Arena* that I discuss further below, Howarth did not simply force his identity onto the magazine, but also recognized the need to drag the title's identity away from a commercially focussed masculine persona that was simply no longer in vogue. Furthermore, he appreciated that the style journalism that had initially been a relatively unique feature of the men's press was now the staple format of weekend newspapers. At *Esquire*, his concern was not just the changing cultural landscape, but also, despite his pledges to disregard the market tabloids, the demands of intense sector competition. It was particularly in respect to cover policy, and the portrayal of women within the magazine, that Howarth's personal objectives were compromised. Competing with the assertively heterosexual representations of the lad mags, *Esquire*'s covers became almost exclusively dominated by glamorous 'babes', who also featured increasingly in the magazine's profiles, photo shoots and the growing number of articles in which sex was the main topic of interest (see Figure 8).

Publicly, Howarth defended his strategy through terms that reiterated his characterization of the *Esquire* brand. He contended that readers would be 'sophisticated enough to see that [the photographs were] handled in an intelligent and amusing' way, and stressed that the photographers employed by the magazine and the clothes worn by the models were more upmarket than in other magazines (*Guardian*, 13.7.98: Media, 6; *Independent*, 18.8.98: Review, 1). A shoot of

Figure 8 Cover of *Esquire*, September 1999.

topless models from the *Sun*'s Page Three were justified through the argument that it had been done by an art photographer who had been exhibited in the National Portrait Gallery. Moreover, Howarth maintained that what he was doing was in keeping with the *Esquire* tradition, pointing out that the magazine had carried similar photo shoots during its halcyon era.

Privately, though, Howarth resented having no option to feature male cover stars and was embarrassed to present women of 'little intrinsic interest' in 'patronizing' styles. Only when NatMags pledged long-term financial backing for a rebranding of the title in early 2000 could Howarth jettison the bikini-girl policy, and redifferentiate his magazine in closer accordance with his vision for the title.

> I think, in the middle there, I lost confidence. I started to second-guess a kind of twenty-two-year-old lad reader. It's really brilliant [now] to be able to say 'who shall we put on the cover in March? Why don't we do Mark Wahlberg? Alright.' Whereas it used to be 'we couldn't possible do Mark Wahlberg. We'd love to do Mark Wahlberg; he is the *Esquire* guy, but actually we've got to do Caprice because it will sell.' (Howarth 2000)

Howarth's announcement of the decision to return to a more 'upmarket' identity, with a monthly photojournalism section, regularly commissioned short stories and more investigative features, was striking. His contention was that 'culture works in pendulum swings' and that the magazine medium was about to experience a consumer backlash against laddism, an 'ignorant, narrow and ultimately restricting' fad (*Campaign*, 28.1.00: 22; *Independent*, 1.2.00: Media, 8). Howarth asserted that being 'seen to scrape your knuckles along the floor' was no longer going to be tolerated by 'your more enlightened friends' or by 'most girls [who] don't want a boy, they want a man' (*Campaign*, 28.1.00: 22; *Independent*, 1.2.00: Media, 8). What was significant in this rationalization was that Howarth's personal values were so clearly embedded in its terms, as was his belief in his own expertise in reading the cultural runes. Indeed, the authoritative definition of the *Esquire* reader and the magazine marketplace that carried Howarth's argument was indicative of how editorial leverage was asserted. That the magazine's 1960s incarnation was now invoked, through the notion of 'quality journalism', as a means to support a retreat from the identity it had been employed to support only two years earlier (now labelled a 'trashy fad') evidenced the authority that editors were able to brandish in negotiating the magazine identity, both to advertisers via the trade press and within the offices of the publishing company.

Howarth's interests were also subordinated to market demands in respect to self-conscious deliberations on contemporary masculinity. In contrast to *Arena* under his editorship, *Esquire* featured negligible, or only indirect, discussion of male identity and sexual politics. Although the question of whether to incorporate into *Esquire* the male confessional writing style that was proving so successful in other media was considered at length, Howarth maintained that the magazine should be full of men's interests without going so far as to be *about* being a man. He reasoned that a magazine like *Esquire* was the wrong place for such dialogue, claiming that men's magazines had to sell 'a *celebration* of what it is to be a man' rather than self-improvement or introspection (Howarth 2000). Personal reflections on modern masculinity were therefore restricted to newspaper articles and his (1997) collection on fatherhood. Howarth summarized: "'The medium is the message." We are a glossy magazine, and if I have to find fault with what Rosie [Boycott] was doing, it was that she wasn't using the medium for what it's intended to be … glossy magazines are there to entertain; they have to be something that you pick up instead of a newspaper' (Howarth 2000). Howarth's citation of McLuhan and Fiore (1967) was appropriately knowing, and, again, emphasized his self-image as a cultural authority with the education to support his articulate confidence. This ease with institutionalized knowledge was one of many features that distinguished Howarth from Brown and Southwell, as I have shown in this chapter. His successor at *Arena*, Ekow Eshun, held an alternative view of the place of masculine self-consciousness in the men's lifestyle magazine, and sanctioned a direction for the title that was related to a different set of personal and professional identifications from those discussed so far.

Ekow Eshun and *Arena*

Ekow Eshun's Background and Self-identity
Born in London at the end of the 1960s, Eshun grew up in what he characterized as 'the drab suburbs of north-west London' (*Independent*, 6.8.00). He remembered the area, Kingsbury, as 'middle-class but dead end, not posh in any sense' (*Independent on Sunday*, 2.3.97: Real Life, 2–3). His family background was also middle-class. Eshun's Ghanaian parents were not wealthy – his mother was a nurse, and his father a worker for Brent Council – but had a firm and long-held commitment to education that he said had achieved them status in Ghana. After attending a comprehensive state school, Eshun remained in London to study Politics and History at the London School of Economics. It was here that he first became involved in journalism, conducting interviews for a magazine programme on then pirate radio station Kiss FM. He began to write freelance features pieces for *The Face* and the women's glossy magazine *Elle*, continuing this work after he graduated until offered a staff job on *The Face*'s arts section in 1994. Rising to assistant editor within the next two years, in 1997, aged twenty-eight, Eshun was appointed editor of *Arena*, becoming the first black editor of a mainstream British style magazine.

Race was a defining characteristic of Eshun's youth and fundamental in the formation of his adult identity, as he repeatedly confirmed in his writings. The casual, everyday racism that he experienced through school, popular culture and

1970s political discourse produced a feeling of marginality that drove two important aspects of his subsequent ambitions. In one respect, Eshun's was a familiar tale of alienation breeding a longing to be heard and for difference to be turned to its own advantage. But Eshun was also acutely aware of having always been, through his visible ethnicity, subjected to the value judgements of others. The result was a desire to be defined and recognized on his own terms, and to use self-knowledge to achieve a stable and coherent identity. Evident in Eshun's constant vocabulary of self-actualization and an avowed project to 'find himself', this aim held a privileged position in both his personal and professional objectives.

In appearance, taste and lifestyle, Eshun was at the leading-edge of contemporary urban culture, and it was this motif of intense modernism that organized many other components of his self. He dressed in a studied smart-casual style, simple and unextravagant, but displaying an evident hipness to anyone sensitive to trends in contemporary menswear. Evidently, Eshun knew the latest markers of urban awareness and could comfortably carry the latest styles. Clothing was more than merely functional or pleasurable adornment. In Eshun's opinion, it was 'a fundamental expression of the self', a tool to be used in the reflexive construction of personality (*Independent on Sunday*, 2.3.97: Real Life, 2–3). Fittingly then, given his urgency to demonstrate autonomous control of his individuality, Eshun declared: 'If my clothes say anything about me, it's that I understand how to wear them' (*Independent on Sunday*, 2.3.97: Real Life, 2–3).

Eshun's leisure practices were of a similar nature: cool, urban and pursued with earnest dedication. As well as enjoying travelling and snowboarding, he described himself as an obsessive peruser of popular culture and an analyst of its 'ramifications and significance … in terms of the individual and society' (Eshun 1999). Here, then, he indicated the intellectual aspirations that organized his interests. Modern film, music, art and literature were all consumed with self-conscious erudition. Moreover, their eclecticism was in itself an important signpost of Eshun's modernism, declaring a cultural adaptability in which he took pride. Eshun's sensibilities as a style-leader also drew him to a particular set of London locales that were united in their expression of contemporary urbanity. The nodal points of his capital city were Bankside, with the creative developments of the Tate Modern, the Millennium Bridge and the Southwark environ, the Saatchi Gallery in St John's Wood, the Institute of Contemporary Arts, mixing 'cinema, art, debate and digital media to create an exploratory space for new ideas' Southall, Brixton and Brick Lane, with their vibrant multiculturalism, and the socially diverse Old Compton Street in Soho (*New Statesman*, 10.4.00: 18–19). By contrast, he dismissed Covent Garden for epitomizing 'the faux-traditionalism and conceited classicism' of the 1980s, and for its inadequate representation of the social possibilities of the present (*New Statesman*, 10.4.00: 18–19).

In his self-presentation, Eshun exhibited a confident but receptive individuality, without machismo or bravado. In conversation, he was earnest and expressive, keen to display a critical and reflexive understanding of his profession, background and self-identity. He was at ease with introspection and self-analysis, portraying himself as emotionally as well as intellectually aware. Like Howarth, this self-consciousness was articulate and controlled, an indication in itself of a particular kind of modern masculine subjectivity that advertised its distinction from the stereotype of emotionally retentiveness, whilst indicating emotional strength rather than weakness. However, Eshun's contemplations were of a less abstract, more personal nature than those of Howarth, suggesting underlying existential angst rather than reflective certainty.

This was not the latent, muffled anxieties of Brown and Southwell, but a deliberate and open form of self-questioning. Indeed, it was a faith in the empowering potential of self-understanding that informed many aspects of Eshun's sexual politics and his interpretation of recent shifts in the norms of masculinity. He had welcomed the debates about the boundaries and possibilities of masculinity provoked by the first wave of men's magazines. His concern with lad culture was that, whilst 'loosening ties and loosening belts in terms of men's attitudes to themselves', it had also foreclosed fresh dialogue, suggesting 'that men are just about lager and women' (Eshun 1998). Thus, whilst disappointed by the shape and inflexibility of the new lad mould, Eshun understood it as an attempt to clarify the ambiguities of male identity that he himself experienced: 'All the stuff about laddishness and blokeishness is really about trying to *affirm* what being a man is by people who don't necessarily know. Because it's confusing times, post-feminist times ... and in some respects it's not entirely clear *how* you can define yourself as a man' (Eshun 1998; his emphasis).

Eshun envisaged the solution to lie in sustained self-analysis:

> I think you can be a bit more grown-up and a little bit more substantial and actually try to understand yourself *in relation to* yourself and in relation to the world around you and in relation to [rather than against] women ... Things are more complicated in a good way. In the sense that you can try and take hold of this new stuff, you can try and ask questions about who you are, and actually you end up with some really interesting answers. You end up with more of yourself really. (Eshun 1998; his emphasis)

By his own admission, then, he himself struggled to find an appropriate way of being a man. Indeed, where the modernism of Eshun's aesthetic sensibilities met with his view of identity as something that could be consciously navigated was in his belief in the paramount importance of ongoing self-reinvention. Such mutations were, in fact, relatively superficial. It was Eshun's belief in their necessity and his faith in their possibility – to 'pilot my life in a way that's meaningful, in a way that's not just about capitulating to what people have done before, or what people do around me' (Eshun 1999) – that identified him as a certain kind of thoroughly modern male. Even Eshun's efforts to disassociate himself from fairly suitable labels for his brand of self-conscious masculinity highlighted their relative aptness.

> A lot of those battles to do with masculinity and femininity, to do with gender and so on, are open to negotiation; that's not just about having to assert that I'm, whatever, 'post-feminist' or 'new man'-ish or anything like that. It's actually about having an open space really, and understanding that just because … previous generations, and even your friends, have lived in certain respects before, it doesn't actually mean that you have to do that. You can actually do things your own way. (Eshun 1999)

As Eshun recognized, his ability to effect such choices was afforded by a particular lifestage, and social and economic position. As an affluent, single and childless thirty-one-year-old man, his lifestyle, career and relationship decisions were unusually uncompromised. This context of opportunity both sanctioned the reflexive masculinity that Eshun exemplified and produced the confusions upon which he dwelt. Ultimately, though, Eshun's privileged lifestyle granted possibilities rather than problems, supporting his overall optimism about the outcomes of gender self-consciousness and reflexivity as a whole.

Occupational Identity

> Can I have a flexible way of working? Can I have a flexible way of looking at the world around me? The issue that faces me, and I'd say faces a lot of men, is to do with personal orientation. It's to do with 'how can you pilot your life, how can you create a life?' Because we have a lot that's within our hands, so how can you make the most of that, and how can you make that meaningful? … How can you optimize your life? (Eshun 1999)

Both the theme of individual self-actualization and the strain to find innovative pathways through which to achieve it were notable in Eshun's professional identity. Although his career route through Wagadon was relatively conventional, Eshun's occupational self-image was much broader than that of most other editors, whose ambitions were generally restricted to the written word, whether in newspapers or magazines. As editor of *Arena*, Eshun relished the license to act as a spokesperson for young British men, whilst he also advanced his public profile in a number of media spheres beyond the requirements of his position. Amongst these activities, he produced feature and comment articles for the *Guardian* and the *Observer*, wrote and presented a documentary series for Radio Four on second-generation UK immigrants, established himself as a regular panel member on BBC2's cultural discussion programme, *The Late Review*, and was a member of the London Arts Board. Issues ranging from the educational performance of ethnic minorities to William Hague's image and the meaning of drum-and-bass music were all subjected to Eshun's didactic, if sometimes rather pretentious, musings.

Such projects were an outlet for Eshun's self-understanding as an all-round contemporary critic and modern day *philosophe de café*, and for those of his interests that could not be expressed through the pages of *Arena*: 'the way I became an editor was by being a journalist. You don't stop being a journalist by being an editor' (Eshun 1999). His projection of his future expressed similar ambitions, and the scope of his cultural interests. Predicting that he would not be a magazine editor for much longer, Eshun anticipated a portfolio career spanning a range of media spheres including new media, television, radio and print. On leaving *Arena* after the Wagadon buyout, Eshun declared his intention to increase his involvement in television and to explore other media opportunities, whilst continuing to freelance for *Arena* and *The Face* (*Press Gazette*, 6.8.99: 5). Within a few months, he announced that he was setting up a brand consultancy with former *The Face* editor Richard Benson, and journalist Miranda Sawyer, and, in June 2001, was appointed editor of Nike's *Much Respect* contract magazine.

Both ventures represented a continuation of Eshun's interest in the relationship between art and commerce, the tense partnership he had needed to negotiate as editor of *Arena*. He disclosed that his ideal alternatives to a career in journalism would have been in advertising or as an artist, and celebrated companies such as the designer-clothing house, Prada, Apple computers and Audi automobiles, which he considered to have retained prestige and integrity whilst achieving commercial success. Eshun had sought to produce *Arena* along similar lines. Such identifications, and his masculine persona, were manifested in a commitment to establishing a creative, collaborative ethos at the magazine:

> I try to have a listening environment. I try and make sure that people are stretched and people are challenged, and people actually want to work. So you give people space to express themselves, you listen to people, you talk to people … you incorporate their ideas into the magazine. And then they feel the magazine belongs to them, that it's the embodiment of their creative principles … The magazine, in the end, is about the unity of expression, it's about the unity of feeling that we actually evolve amongst us. That's what we're looking to create. (Eshun 1998)

At the same time, Eshun reaffirmed the importance he attached to self-awareness as a critical source of personal and professional strength:

> The things that help you usually are just having a clear sense of who you are and where you want to get to, and what you've actually got to say. There's not actually many good

journalists who can turn their copy in on time and, more to the point, have actually got something to say. So background obviously defines self, but the way you articulate who you are becomes the most important single criteria. (Eshun 1998)

Under Eshun's direction, these themes would become familiar topics in the pages of *Arena*.

Arena: *'The Original Magazine for Men'*

Arena's tone, content and representations of masculinity and consumer culture – as initially outlined in Chapter 1 – made it an archetypal product of the booming 1980s. However, by the time that Kathryn Flett took over as editor from Dylan Jones in November 1992, the economic climate was rather less vibrant. Economic recession forced the magazine's tone to be rather more affordable, helpful and informational, and rather less aspirational. Nonetheless, Flett was as deeply immersed in style culture as her predecessors and *Arena* did not change significantly under her control. She had advanced from a receptionist to a staff writer position at *i-D*, before being poached by Logan to write for *The Face*. Whilst fashion and then features editor, Flett contributed to *Arena* as a freelancer and edited the *Arena Pour Elle* supplement, aimed at the female partners of the male readership. During her editorship of *Arena*, the magazine's main development was the launch of the *Homme Plus* spin-off title in March 1994, published bi-annually to coincide with the fashion industry's spring and autumn shows, and focussing almost exclusively on upmarket fashion, new clothing lines and trade and catwalk gossip and reports. Advertising manager Rod Sopp's declaration that 'we want to be known as the men's magazine that is serious about fashion' reiterated *Arena*'s priorities as a title oriented primarily by style (*Media Week*, 3.12.93: 8).

It was under Howarth's editorship that *Arena* broadened and updated its appeal to match a decade's worth of change in commercial and popular culture. Howarth's background outside the Wagadon umbrella was important here in refreshing a publication perceived to be rehearsing old scripts. The kinds of changes he would execute at *Esquire* were first implemented at *Arena*, where Howarth widened the magazine's gaze beyond the world of style and fashion and onto previously disregarded areas and emblems of British popular culture. He recalled, 'They were still putting Mickey Rourke and Sting and Bryan Ferry on the cover in 1995! And I went in there and said "Where's Oasis? Where's Pulp?"' (Howarth 1998). In accordance with his own interests, Howarth expanded *Arena*'s editorial remit, commissioning short stories from authors such as Jay McInerney and investigative articles on figures including Michael Portillo and Tony Blair. Their inclusion indicated a meaningful shift in *Arena*'s focus. Blair was asked, amongst other things, about his university rock band and music tastes, upholding the magazine's 'lifestyle' emphasis. But the Portillo article was novel in being a highly informed, well-researched and relatively heavyweight piece. Articulating a personal position as well as a commercial contention, Howarth argued not only that the magazine's version of 'style culture' was no longer original, but that it was alienating and outdated: 'A magazine has to engage with its readers as more than a mail order catalogue' (*Guardian*, 25.11.96: G2, 16).

A publicity package sent to advertising agencies in August 1996 described the *Arena* reader that Howarth imagined: a late twenties to early thirties, well-travelled, high earner who read Irvine Welsh, the *Guardian* or the *Independent*, and the *Telegraph* on Sundays, listened to Portishead, ate at Wagamama, the River Café and the local chippie, drank 'anything with a bit of character' from Sol to Absolut, liked Italian cars, and dressed in Paul Smith, Dolce and Gabbana, Calvin Klein and Levis (*Media Week*, 2.8.96: 28). This conceptualization, a fashionable rather than truly avant-garde consumer, would soon be refashioned. Howarth felt constrained by Logan's desire to maintain *Arena*'s historical identity as a cutting-edge style title, and was relieved to move to a more comfortably mainstream magazine in *Esquire*. It was in such circumstances that Ekow Eshun was appointed the new *Arena* editor.

Eshun's Arena

As the hip young Londoner, Eshun was an *Arena* editor very much in the tradition from which Howarth had been a minor departure. Like Howarth, though, as I registered in Chapter 4, he was an instinctive editor who appointed and edited in his own image. Readers were assumed to be much like himself and his colleagues.

> Well, rightly or wrongly, we model the magazine quite a lot on ourselves, really. We all have similar lives, and we all have similar tastes, in terms of the clothes we buy, the music we listen to, the places we go. And we assume that our readers have similar views to us ... [They're] *our* people. They're sort of mid-twenties to early thirties, they're urban people, they live in metropolitan areas, they have a certain amount of disposable income, and they have a broad range of interests – in culture and the world around them. We like to think our readers are also interested in exploring themselves a bit. (Eshun 1998; his emphasis)

If Howarth's audience was the early-adopting fashionable-mainstream man, *Arena*'s under Eshun reverted to being the cutting-edge trend-leader, at the apogee of the taste hierarchy. The magazine's 'Spectator' section, outlining the latest contemporary commodities and cultural offerings, made this positioning clear. Alongside reviews of new music, films, books and computer games that were glossed with the terms of the cognoscenti, Spectator profiled the avant-garde across a range of urban arts, including film, design, music and photography. The November 1997 issue, for example, spotlighted Austrian shock-artist Hermann Nitsch, Japanese hip hop record label Major Force and 'Virtual aquariums'. April 1998's edition provided brief introductions to artificially-intelligent sports robots, the Asian underground music scene, a short film documenting life from a camera mounted on a cat, an exhibition about Oriental culture, and dance record label Athletico. September 1999 guided readers to sub-aquatic photographer David Doubilet, cult Swedish film actor Stellan Skarsgård, artists Jane and Louise Wilson, and DJ Dave Tipper.

Under Howarth, *Esquire*'s equivalent section, 'Squire', was characterized by a less worshipful attitude towards a more mainstream subject matter, with jokier features and a less minimalist and lustrous visual style. Its content confirmed the magazine's identity as *Arena*'s less left-field cousin. For example, in April 1998, it included a brief interview with Lisa Faulkner from BBC1's popular drama *Casualty*, short features on young British film director Shane Meadows and comedians Armstong and Miller, profiles of Truman Capote and Idi Amin, a short feature on scuba-diving, and Hollywood director Quentin Tarantino discussing the casting of his latest movie.

With female models and entertainment personalities now perceived to be the only commercially feasible cover stars, the heroes of *Arena*'s editorial team were confined to the magazine's last page. Eshun described these as 'iconoclastic figures rather than iconic ones', his aim being to try 'to develop an alternative canon that breaks the hierarchy of male tradition' (Eshun 1999). In the year for which the column ran before Eshun left the magazine, he championed a range of figures toasted nowhere else in the market, including actors Chevy Chase, Jan-Michael Vincent (for his role in the 1970s surfer movie *Big Wednesday*) and John Cazale (Fredo Corleone in *The Godfather*), black music artists Prince and Notorious BIG, 1980s decathlete Daley Thompson, Roy the Replicant from Ridley Scott's *Bladerunner*, and the comic hero 'The Silver Surfer'.

Small columns accompanying the images of these idols explained the terms of their inclusion. Eshun's ethnic marginality and his preoccupation with self-realization and the condition of modern masculinity were the most obvious factors here. It was not just Cazale's acting talent that was applauded, but also his choice of roles: 'naïve, misplaced' and fallible men who offset intense, assertive male leads (*Arena*, April 1999: 210). Thompson was acclaimed as 'a man who heard his destiny calling and did not shirk … our last true sporting giant' (*Arena*, March 1999: 202). The Silver Surfer merited our awe as 'comic history's first existential superhero', trying 'to make sense of humanity's contradictory impulses towards humanity and cruelty' (*Arena*, September 1999: 194). Roy the Replicant was awarded true subcultural credibility: 'to the uninitiated, it may sound like sixth-form poetry, but to the rest of us, Roy's speech still resonates with sharp painful truths about the texture of memory and the compromised lives the rest of us live' (*Arena*, June 1999: 158). Eshun's ultimate hero, and a rare male cover star, Muhammad Ali, was honoured in the editor's letter for having 'escaped definition as a savage', given lie to 'the belief that black people are born inarticulate and remain so', and, in 'uncertain, shifting times', remained a contrast to 'new lads and adultescents [sic], perpetual boys fighting to grow up' (May 1999: 15–16).

The other area where the magazine most evidently expressed Eshun's personal concerns was in its explicit treatment of identity issues. Just as Eshun stood out from other editors in terms of his interest in current debates about gender relations, so *Arena* was noticeable in its intensive, repeated and overt scrutiny of contemporary masculinity. Whereas editors' letters in other titles tended to outline forthcoming content with a mixture of hype and information, Eshun's was often a short article reflecting on the issue's main theme or feature: the troubled state of masculinity (April 1998), men, sex and relationships (September 1998), how to deal with getting older (April 1999), and the new world of work in the 'information age' (September 1999). Such contemplations were deliberate interventions on the part of Eshun. They reflected both private and professional concerns about representations of masculinity elsewhere in the market and the role of the men's press.

> Effectively, what we're trying to do is think about how you can be in your late twenties, early thirties, and actually enhance the quality of your life, and talk about the nature of relationships, some of the questions that you actually have when you're experiencing that particular stage of your life. ... On a professional level, I react somewhat against the cynicism of [the lad mags], in the sense that they offer people a very limited range of expression, and a very limited way of looking at their own lives. And I think magazines are creative sources, and inspirational sources, and [the lad mags] just feel a little bit deadening. (Eshun 1999)

To emphasize *Arena*'s distinction from the downmarket titles, Eshun changed its tag line from 'The original magazine for men' to 'The grown-up magazine for men'. The gesture also signalled a shift in emphasis from its style-culture roots to an identity that more closely mirrored his personal ambitions. The editorial team was recruited to reflect this vision. An article by Richard Benson in the January–February 1998 edition (pp. 72–6) (see Figure 9) represented the collective sexual politics pursued in the magazine. Titled 'Who is Soft Lad?' the piece was in the magazine's tradition of identifying and claiming cultural authority over patterns of social and cultural change.[3] It began:

> Being a man used to be easy: you went to work, raised a family and watched football

Figure 9 Cover of *Arena*, January/February 1998.

at the weekends. Then the world changed, and so did the role of men. In the eighties, ad execs fantasised about a creature called the New Man. The nineties saw the creation and demise of lad culture. So where are we now? Who the hell is Soft Lad? (*Arena*, January–February 1998: 72–3)

Benson revealed that 'Soft' was an acronym for 'Searching For Fundamental Truths' and represented the position of a significant number of 'post-irony, still-not-too-sure-about-everything' British men in the late 1990s (p. 74). For them, he argued, the traditional anchors of male identity – work, class, a well-defined gender role – had disappeared, without finding satisfactory replacement in recent male scripts, from 'the juvenile self-debasing idiocies of so-called lad culture' (p. 74), to the shallow individualism of 80s man, and the excessive sensitivities of the new man. In a national culture that he characterized as questioning, doubtful and insecure, Benson wondered where men could find the ideals to deliver them from cynicism and provide some kind of guidance. Echoing the assertions of postmodern social theory, he proposed that these would not come from the failed, grand ideologies of the past, or any prescribed narrative. 'We no longer rely on someone else's ideas to interpret the world for us, or to imagine epic stories in which we can cast ourselves as the leading man ... we are learning not to buy other men's designs for our lives quite as easily as our fathers once did. There are new designs of our own to be made' (*Arena*, January–February 1998: 75). Benson provided an outline of this new male identity that would wash away the 'myth of the stiff upper lip' without descending either into 'dumb laddishness' or 'Blairite touchy-feeliness'. It would be emotionally open and expressive, joyful, smart, satirical and independent, the spirit of 'Albert Finney in *Saturday Night, Sunday Morning*, not Bernard Breslaw in *Carry on Camping*; of *Alfie*, not Benny Hill; of Ian Wright, not Paul Gascoigne' (p. 75).

The question of how to manage one's life in an increasingly confusing environment and theme of self-realization stood out not only here, but throughout *Arena* under Eshun's direction. An interview in the 'Soft Lad' issue with media presenter Chris Evans (pp. 54–60) focussed upon his emotional condition (a 'new-found maturity' (p. 57)), his approach to working life, and the state of his personal and professional ambitions. In October 1998, the magazine devoted over twenty pages to dissecting the 'new world of work', framed by an editorial in which Eshun pronounced uncertainty as the defining characteristic of the era. A long feature in April 1999 by Nick Compton (pp. 80–5) examined ways in which men could grow up without succumbing to the current option of being *either* a 'lad' or a 'dad'. Endorsing a novel synthesis ('A Man In Full', as the title signposted), Compton assured readers that fatherhood did not have to mean sacrifice, struggle, and giving up the pleasures of a younger masculinity, so long as one gave up some of the 'army of shadow possibilities'. 'The truth is that fatherhood changes everything and changes nothing. It's up to you' (p. 82), reported one of the article's archetypes.

Another Benson contribution the previous month (March 1999: 86–9) re-expressed the lifestyles and leitmotifs of Eshun's editorial cabal. The social breed they had newly identified was the 'Flexecutive', a 1990s version of the yuppie,

no longer solely interested in income and possessions but in more 'human' gratifications: self-development, and an existence of fun, soulfulness and creativity.
Typically, flexecutives were aged twenty-seven to thirty-eight and could be found
in loft parties in revitalized areas of London, such as Old St (where Eshun
himself lived), taking 'upmarket narcotics' and sporting goatee beards and
designer streetwear: 'clothes from youth culture that could be afforded only by
people whose ages and incomes were not really "youth"'(p. 88). It was an understanding of youth culture and the new demographics of lifestyle that underwrote
flexecutive employment. Cross-media literate and up to speed with style and
leisure trends, 'flexecs' formed a fifth column of professionals who sold their
knowledge, ideas and communication skills to businesses and politicians.
Spurning the terms of the traditional career, they preferred freelance contracts
and short-term project portfolios, 'mixing and matching jobs as event organizers,
website designers, ad creatives, marketing advisors, conference runners, magazine publishers, sponsorship co-ordinators, club promoters, market researchers,
PR officers and various kinds of consultancy' (p. 88). Where yuppies had studied
business and valued money and ambition, flexecs were graduates in media
studies and sought 'creativity and personal authenticity' (p. 89), as appropriate in
'a decade in which hipness replaced wealth as a cultural lodestone' (p. 88). And
just as they multitasked in work, so they multi-lifestyled in leisure, gathering
'authentic' experiences through a broad range of pursuits, including travel
beyond the West, where they might find their souls.

Concluding Comments

It was no coincidence that this portrait was familiar. Eshun used his editorship of
Arena to wrestle with the problems and issues that personally exercised him, and
to promote the cultures and lifestyle that he himself enjoyed. Emap's purchase of
the Wagadon titles, and Eshun's departure from *Arena*, marked a further shift in
the character of the magazine. Eshun certainly anticipated that his personal
preoccupations would be given rather less asylum in Emap's more commercially
stringent publishing regime than they had been by Wagadon, where Eshun had
struggled as much against the company's style-format conventions as against the
new rules of men's lifestyle publishing. Having lost almost 30 per cent of circulation over his last year as editor, Eshun's departure once Emap took over was
expected. In his first issue in charge, new editor Greg Williams assured readers
that *Arena* would retain its stamp of 'quality and discernment', whilst alerting
them to some immediate changes: 'More sport, business, money, interiors and,
of course, sex' (*Arena*, November 1999: 17). Chief amongst these, though, was
the discontinuation of the candid contemplations on masculinity through which
Eshun had distinguished the title. By March 2000, an editorial manifesto

declared *Arena's* new brand values 'money, power and success' (p. 27) and indicated clearly that sex and affluence would supersede self-knowledge as the magazine's defining ambitions. Just as Eshun's installation had modified, though by no means overhauled, *Arena's* principles, so the arrival of Williams, and, perhaps more significantly, Emap, brought about another editorial shift.

As I have emphasized, Howarth's influence on *Esquire* was likewise moderated. Throughout its history, the magazine had presented itself as the 'peerless arbiter of good taste' (Osgerby 2001: 43), targeting a readership always broadly imagined as literate, urbane, intelligent and at ease in a world of consumption. I have shown though that such brand attributes were adaptable, and, as such, were reinterpreted and rearticulated by successive editors. Howarth's projection of the *Esquire* reader recast the moulds of his predecessors in accordance with many of the personal and professional identifications, affiliations and ambitions that I have traced in this chapter. The conditions under which these changes were made are worth re-emphasizing. It was when NatMags was particularly uncertain about how to compete in the men's market that Howarth's expertise was most demanded. The departure of Rosie Boycott marked an obvious moment to reconsider the title's brand, an opportunity made more pressing by the advances being made by the lad mags. But while their rising circulations destabilized the *Esquire* identity, Howarth was constricted by the market demands indicated by their success and confirmed in his product's monthly performances. When competing with the editorial policies of the downmarket titles failed to halt *Esquire's* sales decline, and NatMags had to rethink, Howarth's authority was at its potentially most powerful *and* its most vulnerable. He could easily have been replaced by someone deemed more able to understand 'the reader'. Instead, having assured his employers that he was still best qualified to do the job, Howarth was granted more sovereignty than ever before to define the *Esquire* identity.

In concluding the last substantive chapter of this thesis, it is worth briefly expanding on several issues that will now have emerged more clearly. It is important to emphasize that I have focussed in Part III upon editorial figures who were all instinctive in technique, and whose identities, resources and ambitions were perhaps unusually important in imprinting their titles. I have highlighted the roles of publisher uncertainty, market instability and commercial competition in structuring the circumstances in which shifts in editorial character were sanctioned. When titles were felt to require significant editorial changes, instinctive editors were more likely to be hired to implement them than professional editors. The latter were more frequently brought onto publications believed to be performing successfully, or to have relatively stable and well-grasped audiences. In such cases, the reproduction of the magazine could draw more easily upon established formulae, and was less dependent on the personal 'instincts' of the editor. In these circumstances, where there was little need to rearticulate the reader image, the magazine template and the implicit terms of its production were more easily decipherable.

Such was the case, then, at *FHM, Men's Health* and *Maxim*, the publications whose commercial objectives were most smoothly realized during the period I have covered. When new editors arrived at each title between 1994 and 2000 (twice at *FHM*, three times at *Men's Health* and four times at *Maxim*), their personal impacts were far less perceptible than when *GQ, Esquire* and *Arena* were passed into new editorial hands. With editors such as Phil Hilton and Piers Hernu, who operated neither entirely 'instinctively' nor 'professionally', the imprintation of personal identity was less marked than in the cases I have explored in the last two chapters, though nonetheless clearly detectable. It may only be when *Later* and *Front* are edited by new figures that the importance to their characters of Hilton and Hernu will become more discernible.

The last two chapters have also made more clear the relationship between age, masculinity and editorial competence that I raised in Chapter 4. Brown's departure from *loaded* was an almost inescapable outcome of his instinctive editorial technique and his advancing years, as he publicly recognized at the time. The statement issued by IPC to announce Southwell's exit likewise declared that, as a 35-year-old family man, he was 'not the *loaded* lad he was' (*Campaign*, 17.3.00: 5). Even by the time of my interviews, Brown's weekend plans to 'take the dog to the beach' (1999b), as well as watch his beloved Leeds United, and Southwell's declared interest in playing golf, spending time with his baby, and going for dinner with his girlfriend, as well as surfing, indicated the dispositions bound up with the ageing process.

Yet Brown's belief that his move to Condé Nast was a 'promotion' signalled not some simple 'change of priorities', but long-held professional ambitions that were a consistent, if also personally troubling, aspect of his character. That he was able to move from *loaded* to *GQ* whilst barely tempering his instinctive editorial style was itself striking. It suggested that, although the masculine scripts of the men's lifestyle press were differentiated, they were also in certain ways related. In this respect, it is important to dwell on the similarities and differences between the editors I have analysed in the preceding chapters. The identities of Howarth and Eshun, and those they ultimately represented through *Esquire* and *Arena*, were distinctive in a number of ways from those of Brown, Southwell and *loaded*. The 'upmarket' editors did not, for example, characterize themselves through the forms of heterosexual bravado, hedonism and cultural and social irreverence that were significant in the lifestyles and self-understandings of Brown and Southwell. For Howarth and Eshun, cultural aspiration and authority were more important signifiers of masculine status than sexual aspiration. Howarth exhibited a light-hearted cultural reverence that reflected a background in the metropolitan middle classes and a comfortable relationship with the liberal-educational cultural canon. The ease and confidence with which he presented himself as a man of intelligent contemporary taste, and his commitment to relatively traditional notions of professional competence, also spoke of this class background. He displayed none of the anxious strivings and strained affiliations that I identified in the ambitions of *loaded*'s co-founders, whose unstable class properties Bourdieu (1984) assumes to be a generalizable feature of the new petite bourgeoisie.

If Eshun's self-understanding, cultural identifications and career ambitions were rather more questioning and radical than Howarth's, they differed also from those of Brown and Southwell. Eshun's marginal consciousness derived primarily from an experience of race rather than class or education, and his lifestyle dispositions were avant-garde and self-consciously progressive rather than anchored in long-established scripts of working-class masculine heroism. Indeed, both Howarth and Eshun sought to present themselves as decisively modern, if not quite 'new', men, without displaying Brown and Southwell's concerns about whether the class connotations of such identities were themselves insufficiently manly. Although the assumption of post-feminist positions amongst all four editorial figures suggested a common culture of sexual politics within the men's press, the differences between Eshun's reflexive quest for a progressive masculine role, and Brown and Southwell's refuge in an updated version of a rather regressive identity were also significant. Though Brown's perspective had changed somewhat by the time he was at Condé Nast, the tropes with which he had identified at *loaded* were still significant in his rendering of the *GQ* identity. The birds–booze–drugs lexicon, the geezer-chic iconography and the unifying idea of the punter-turned-star were very different themes from the version of educated, modern cultural urbanity in Howarth's *Esquire* and the progressive, self-monitoring, cultural avant-gardism of Eshun's *Arena*.

There were important differences too in the social spaces with which these practitioners identified and within which they moved. The geographic symbolism of *loaded*'s search for a national fan base beyond the capital's 'loft spaces' was significant here. Characterizing themselves, at least initially, as non-metropolitan, Brown and (particularly) Southwell were less enamoured with London's more salubrious entertainment spaces than many other publishing figures. In contrast to Eshun's movements across the capital's sites of contemporary urbanity and multiculturalism, the magazine's editorial team socialized primarily in the Waterloo 'locals' around the IPC office (Southwell 1998). Meanwhile, they derided the city's cultural self-importance and a media scene that they regarded as exclusive and navel-gazing. In what was presented as part of its general democratizing mission, then, the editorial team foregrounded mainstream provincial nightlife: 'ordinary joes in clubs' (Southwell 1998: 174). The coverage of the Swansea club scene in the magazine's first issue was emblematic of such commitments. Perhaps one – unintended – consequence of this regional focus, and *loaded*'s nostalgia for a canon of English buffoonery and talent, was that, unlike Eshun's *Arena*, the title's ethnic focus was overwhelmingly white.

Such distinctions within this group of cultural intermediaries are elided in more cursory portraits. Yet there were also a number of similarities between these practitioners that demand further comment. Bourdieu's (1984) analysis of the new petite bourgeoisie remains an incisive commentary on some of the shared values of cultural workers. Eshun's lifestyle reflexivity, his concern with self-expression and communication, and his rapacious consumption (and promotion) of the avant-garde were most striking in their resonance with Bourdieu's portrait – and that of Featherstone's (1991) postmodern consumer *par excellence*. But, in their aversion to classifications and hierarchies, and in positioning themselves outside conventional defintions of class, Brown and Southwell were also suggestive of these accounts. Meanwhile, despite the differences between their lifestyle practices, Brown, Southwell, Howarth and Eshun all exhibited a commitment to forms of consumption-based urban enjoyment some distance from the more austere habits of public sector professionals and the rather 'undistinctive' culture of managers and government bureaucrats (Bourdieu 1984: 127).

There is a general point to be made here. For most editorial personnel, part of the appeal of magazine publishing lay in the glamorous, metropolitan social life attached to the industry and the broader appeals of the capital. At one extreme, *loaded* undoubtedly attracted 'a certain type of person who recognized the opportunity to live a very hedonistic lifestyle, and get paid for it' (Brown, *On the Ropes*, Radio Four, 16.7.02). For Phil Hilton, the capital's charms were more cultural. He described himself as a 'reinvented bourgeois Islingtonian' who enjoyed going to galleries and films, and eating out with friends, and had little affection for his Essex roots (Hilton 1998). This mobility motif was a common theme in editors' career descriptions. For many, London both represented and effected upward movement in the social hierarchy. This subaltern aspiration and social longing for the pleasures and prestige of the capital has a long history (Feldman and Stedman Jones 1989), and it was no coincidence that Brown, Southwell, Eshun and a number of other editorial figures came from backgrounds in the lower-middle-classes (see also Nixon 2003). Bourdieu (1984: 370–1) argues that such upward social trajectories engender a disposition to self-educate, and an orientation to popularize the intellectual and intellectualize the popular. Brown's proud autodidacticism and his scorn for hierarchies of taste and authority, and Eshun's elaborate contemplations on modern culture represented different strands of these same impulses.

Such tendencies also help to explain the documented association between lower-middle-class backgrounds and the music journalism from which Brown,

Southwell and many other editorial personnel had emerged. Giles describes the typical male rock journalist as coming 'from a certain hinterland in British culture which is very unstable and rootless' (cited in Negus 1992: 119; also Jackson et al.: 39). This instability in relation to class and culture also fed into the discourses of individualism, self-help and mobility that were recurrent in the testimonies of my main protagonists. McRobbie has highlighted the presence of such rhetoric throughout the creative industries, noting the ultimate byline that 'you can make it if you really want' (McRobbie 2002: 107). Furthermore, she suggests that this neo-liberal faith in talent, perseverance and meritocracy is embedded in the vision of the New Labour government, and its promotion of the idea that it is through work that fulfilment and self-realization are to be found. Again, there is common ground here between Brown and Eshun, in terms of their shared commitment to ideals of creativity and 'self-expressive work' (McRobbie 2002: 101). Certainly, there were important differences between Eshun's lexicon of nurture and creative cultivation, and Brown's metaphors of graft, gratification and collective anarchism. Not least, there were strongly gendered overtones to such associations, as there were too in Cabal's brand of caring flexibility and Dennis' belligerent anti-corporatism. Both editors, though, were committed to the idea of navigating their careers on terms that they could claim to be original, and to notions of originality and authenticity more broadly.

That Brown and Southwell understood their self-styled entrepreneurialism in terms of Thatcherite political discourse points to the longer genealogy of recent discourses of creative work. Indeed, Hugh Hefner's self-promotion in the 1960s as the epitome of *Playboy*'s autonomous, self-made, funseeker underlines that there was nothing altogether new about the self-presentations of *loaded*'s editors (Osgerby 2001). Moreover, this continuity between their social pathways, characteristics and self-understandings and established tropes of class marginality, mobility and romantic masculine individualism is striking partly because of Brown and Southwell's sometime insistence on the uniqueness of their identities. Likewise, drawing on Jackson et al. (2001), Benwell (2003) proposes that the broader circulation of discourses of 'honesty' and 'naturalness' around the new lad phenomenon flags up a rather established discourse of 'masculine authenticity'. Brown and Southwell signposted this themselves in their claims to be representing a constituency of men that was eminently 'real' and long-standing. Arguably, though, the self-consciousness of their self-representations undermined their own assertions of honest and unmediated identity.

A final common affiliation between editors throughout the men's press was an intense and often broad interest in the mosaic of post-war popular culture. In the market's earlier years, editorial practitioners such as Paul Keers and Alex Finer had come from broadsheet newspapers and their magazine supplements, or, like Alexandra Shulman and Rosie Boycott, from the broadsheet press and monthly women's magazines. As was suitable for the magazines of the time, an understanding of style culture was the stock qualification of the sector. By the mid-1990s though, most men's titles demanded expertise in music, film and the subcultural aspects of male experience. Backgrounds on music, entertainment and men's hobby magazines (publications focussed on cars or mountain bikes, for example) became much more essential. These were not only traditionally male preserves (and it was notable that the proportion of female editors of men's magazines dropped throughout the decade, by 2002, leaving only Fiona Jerome at *Bizarre*), but also spheres in which an almost obsessive fascination with the minutiae and trivialities of the appropriate culture was required. Paul Colbert, who took professional pride in his grasp of magazine detail and had sought to distinguish *Focus* and *ZM* through the quality of their factual material, openly confessed to being a 'detail nerd' who loved 'pub fact material' (*Press Gazette*, 5.12.97: 14; *Campaign*, 15.5.98: 19). Colbert's deputy editor at *Focus* described him fittingly as 'the only man I have ever met who knows how many twists there are in the wire of a champagne bottle top' (*Campaign*, 15.5.98: 19).

The significance of post-war youth tribes, and the artefacts, codes and cultures that sprang up around them, cannot be underestimated here. Editors' talk was suffused with subcultural references. It was also germane, then, that in a reflection on 'Rommelgate', Brown apologized for causing offence to people whose lives were directly affected by the Nazi regime, but noted that his understanding of events was entirely mediated by screen representations: 'we grew up in an era where the realities of war were totally softened because they were turned into Hollywood fayre ... it was just men fighting in different uniforms' (*On the Ropes*, Radio Four, 16.7.02). It was also salient here that the title of Brown's first fanzine, *Attack on Bzag*, had been a parody of a Second World War pulp novel, whilst the first issue of *Jack*, the magazine with which he returned to men's publishing in 2002, featured an eight-page piece on 'underdog wars'.[4]

Journalists throughout the sector cited magazines and movements at the heart of mainstream subcultural life as their biggest influences, both personal and professional. More specifically, *Arena*, *The Face*, the *NME*, and punk and club culture were frequently eulogized. Many personnel also had a sense of the cultural and political marriage that consumer culture could support. One style press writer noted (on questionnaire – see Appendix): 'I was very influenced by *The Face* in its early days and the idea that style/youth culture could go hand in hand with serious investigative journalism.' Another registered as his influences: '*NME* 1977–90, especially the politics of the early eighties; the link between pop culture and social responsibility ... *The Face* for its democratization of the underground.' Commitments to commercial individualism and leftist political positions were commonly conjoined (cf. McRobbie 1999a), with around three-quarters of editorial personnel recording Labour as the political party they would vote for (most declaring themselves fairly or very strong supporters), and the *Guardian* proving the sector's preferred newspaper by some majority. In this respect, the connections between Nick Logan, the ex-mod, Labour-supporting, creative entrepreneur who had founded the men's press, and James Brown, the post-punk founder of *loaded* who had advanced it, were again striking. The influence of Sean O'Hagan's seminal *Arena* article on both *loaded*'s early identity and Howarth's *Esquire*, and Brown and Howarth's shared respect for Paul Smith, were equally indicative of some of the common foundational references of the men's magazine market.

Notes

1. Here, Boycott took full advantage of her recognized networking skills, and her contacts amongst the literati (Kingsley Amis and Ben Okri were said to be amongst her dinner party circle) and at the Groucho club.
2. Indeed, the same complaint was made by many *loaded* journalists themselves, who became increasingly frustrated by the failure of consumers to notice the journalistic efforts in which they took pride. Southwell vented his frustrations on the magazine's October 1999 spine message: 'Great writing obscured by a smokescreen of female flesh'.
3. See, for example, 'What's so new about the new man? Three decades of advertising to men' (March 1988), 'All mouth and trousers: The professional cockney' (September 1988), 'The Euroman cometh: The new breed of internationalist' (March 1990), 'Here comes the new lad! The unreconstructed man' (May 1991), and 'The new lass: Girls will be boys' (March 1996).
4. Features in *Jack*'s first issue on motel sex, footballer-turned-journalist Jorge Valdano and football club crisps likewise revisited themes familiar from Brown's past ventures. He suggested that the magazine – 'an orgy of war, animals, fashion, genius and cool' (*Jack*, spring–summer 2002: 1) – was picking up on a booming interest in history, the natural world and exploration, subjects that were engrossing him increasingly (*On the Ropes*, Radio Four, 16.7.02). One journalist described the magazine as 'a cross between *loaded* and *National Geographic*' (*Guardian*, 22.4.02: Media, 8–9). Brown saw it as 'an adventure magazine ... Jon Ronson's [adventure] is a feature where he tracks down the anthrax letter bomber, my adventure was trying to get hold of Robert De Niro and Michael Holden's adventure was to sit and watch every episode of *The Office*. It's a magazine about someone who's in love with life' (*Guardian*, 22.4.02: Media, 8–9), 'a personal celebration that I've found another way to live my life' (*Observer*, 21.4.02: 15). In promoting the magazine, he declared that 'the war between the sexes is over' and argued that 'everything around men has changed', allowing shifts in attitude and

greater opportunity and choice for men than ever before (*The Sunday Times*, 21.4.02: New Review, 5). Brown also claimed that inspiration had come partly from rediscoving the music of his youth: The Specials, The Jam, The Sex Pistols and The Clash, influences that gave the magazine its 'punk ethos'.

Summary and Conclusions

James Brown's declaration that, through the launch of *loaded*, he had, like a media Columbus, 'discovered America', encapsulates many of the concerns of this book. In Chapter 2, I drew attention to the publishing community's scepticism about the likely success of a mass-selling men's magazine, and its belief that the market had already been effectively conquered. Trade debates in the early 1990s repeatedly doubted that the sector could be significantly expanded, even though they recognized the existence of a vast consumer market unserved by the men's style titles. *loaded* certainly opened up previously unexplored publishing territory and gave public representation to the cultures and lifestyles of the large audience of men that the industry had until then assumed to be unreachable. Within advertising, the early years of the decade saw similar uncertainty about how to appropriately address the young male public. The imagery and script to which *loaded* gave rise consequently became a dominant conceptual shorthand through which this audience was understood and portrayed throughout commercial media. Meanwhile, the expansion of the men's magazine market granted significant authority to individual practitioners in the sector to speak as the new public experts on modern masculinity.

It was the unanticipated nature of *loaded*'s entry into the men's press that I highlighted as one of its most suggestive properties. That *loaded* shattered publishing complacency in such an unexpected way raised important questions about the ways in which magazine producers assessed their audiences. Publishing was a highly competitive commercial industry that had always prided itself on its sensitivity to shifts in lived cultures. However, the stagnation of the men's press that was exposed by *loaded*'s success indicated that publishing companies had rather lost sight of their consumers. I have partly accounted for their oversight by illustrating the primacy of informal knowledge in the charting of consumer markets. Previous research has pointed to the role of institutional discourses, informed guesswork and specific cultural languages in setting the terms of cultural production (Mort 1996; Nixon 1996). If anything, though, the significance of informal knowledge has still been underestimated in such studies, with the influence of formal consumer research perhaps overestimated. In the launches I have examined, 'fact-finding' into consumer identities and interests was notable mainly by its relative unimportance. Where formal research was undertaken, mainly though focus group evaluations of existing publications or dummy products, its findings were often discounted. Instead, it was often 'hunch', 'intuition' and other informal conceptualizations of target audiences (though rarely the pure, creative inspiration that the industry romanticized) that governed the determination of new products and niches. In this respect, trade debates did more than merely reflect industry sentiments. As professional discourses, they also structured the ways in which commercial production was liable to proceed. It was for this reason that the shift in men's publishing during the mid-1990s was so paradigmatic. Throughout the early part of the decade, the industry's ideologies and its practices were as good as indistinguishable in rendering unrealizable the formation of the mass market.

Brown's metaphor was also suggestive in asserting his personal centrality in the sector's redefinition of its audience and the market's eventual configuration. The notion of absolute, individual credit that, with characteristic bravado, he often claimed, was not entirely legitimate, for the commercial ambitions of publishing houses were always directed towards certain areas in advance of the input of editorial ideas and personnel. However, the launch anatomies that I provided evidenced the crucial role of editorial practitioners in forging magazine identities and thus actualizing commercial goals. On a practical level, it was editors who transformed broad commercial briefs into specific cultural forms, and whose primary expertise was in giving definition to elusive readerships. In charting the ongoing techniques by which they did so, I distinguished between 'instinctive' editors, who declared themselves to embody their target consumers, and 'professional' editors, who tended to mobilize models of their readers in their daily production practices. In both cases, editors were the pivotal figures in articulating the spheres of production and consumption and in making material what were otherwise only notional market possibilities.

It was the difficulty of such effectuations and the constant uncertainty that characterized market endeavours that meant that the identities of magazines and arising sectors could crystallize around individual editorial figures like Brown. Indeed, the scarcity of knowledge about the audience was significant in determining the autonomy of editors to define the character of their magazines as they deemed appropriate. In times of perplexity, such as when the mass market first emerged, editors believed to understand the redefined readership culture were particularly valuable. Correspondingly, editorial dominance was less assured once the market was more established and the demands of the new male reader were more transparent. The increasing competitiveness of the men's press also imposed commercial imperatives upon editors that were more pressing than when the potential volume of sales had been less obvious. The ability of an editor to hegemonize decisions about a title's tone, content and overall direction was also dependent on a number of factors relating to the operating practices and strategies of publishing companies. These included revenue priorities and attitudes towards research that were themselves connected to size and ownership structures and the creative and commercial aims of senior executives.

In the continual negotiations about a magazine's character, readers existed, as McRobbie has summarized, 'as much as concepts and strategies as ... active consumers' (1999b: 60). Even established readerships were constantly in flux, and therefore never fully knowable. It was for this reason that editors made assumptions on behalf of their audiences with little input from actual consumers themselves. In this respect, 'the reader' and the 'magazine identity' were discursive conceptions whose definitions were always unstable. Although magazine brands circumscribed the remit of editors, they were always also rearticulated by these key personnel as notions of the readership demanded ongoing reformulation. Whilst the degree to which such redefinitions took place depended upon factors such as publisher uncertainty, market volatility and the strength of a magazine's commercial position, the ways that they were made relied on the particular cultural resources of editorial practitioners. Thus, whilst editors were not necessarily imperial in determining the scope of editorial changes, they were certainly monarchical in orchestrating them.

The cultural repertoires, competences and languages that editors drew upon in their operations were rooted in social, educational and career backgrounds, and in current lifestyle dispositions and milieux. Indeed, editorial work was distinct from most occupations in the extent to which work and non-work life were inseparable, with personal interests and preoccupations and professional expertise often overlapping. Editors did not, as Ferguson suggests, simply learn the editor's role through 'anticipatory socialisation' (1983: 24), although, as with Brown at *GQ*, they might need to incite themselves self-consciously to 'live the magazine'. More often, they were hired precisely because of their intuitive ability to inhabit, express or embody a magazine's projected identity in line with their own. Even 'professional' editors in the men's press broadly resembled their audiences in terms of class, age or lifestyle. This had important implications for the careers of editorial practitioners. Remaining culturally aware and in touch with audiences demanded forms of cultural and subcultural capital that were relatively transient. Employability was therefore circumscribed considerably by age and lifestyle. Crucially also, it meant that the identifications, ideals and concerns of editors were given habitual public expression through their titles.

In Part III of thesis, I explored in more detail this relationship between the backgrounds, identities and ambitions of editors and the characters of their titles. It was clear that, although magazine identities were not simply reducible to those of their producers, the interests and expertise of editors imprinted their publications in significant ways. Brown and Southwell's backgrounds on fanzines and the music press, their identification with assertively heterosexual post-feminist sexual scripts, and their celebration of selected aspects of working-class masculinity were amongst the most conspicuous of their personal resources and affiliations that came to mark *loaded*. I suggested that there were notable tensions in these identifications, with Brown and Southwell highly ambivalent about the masculine connotations of their upward mobility and ambitions. This had clear consequences for the gender and work identities that they inhabited, not only in exaggerating their outward hostility to a new man script with which they hesitantly identified, but in guiding their masculinization of the magazine-journalist identity through the protocols and practices of the Gonzo tradition. Both the ambivalences in Brown and Southwell's self-identities and their attempts to resolve them were inherent in *loaded*'s editorial voice.

At established titles *Esquire* and *Arena*, the cultural resources, knowledges and identifications of Peter Howarth and Ekow Eshun were crucial in qualifying them as editors, as well as being central in how they recast their products. Howarth's identity as the assured, contemporary, tasteful professional both fitted and redefined *Esquire*'s brand of discerning, literate urbanity. The cutting-edge, reflexive modernism that characterized Eshun's lifestyle and self-understanding likewise both suited and inscribed *Arena*'s brand of avant-garde metropolitanism. Bound up with specific social, educational and professional experiences, the languages and modes of masculinity that Howarth and Eshun represented were of a rather different nature from those of Brown and Southwell. Indeed, one rationale behind scrutinizing *loaded*, *Esquire* and *Arena* was to contrast the most influential of the market's second-phase titles with two of its founding publications.

This not only allowed me to explore how the men's style titles responded to the arrival of the lad mags. It also enabled me to highlight the range of magazines and masculinities that existed in the market, and the differences between those editors responsible for them. Too often in journalistic accounts of the period, the men's magazine market was discussed as a monolithic entity. Although James Brown's transfer from *loaded* to *GQ* underlined some of the similarities between magazines at apparently opposite ends of the marketplace – or, at least pointed to the roles of age and mobility in bridging their differences – it does no justice to the different values and cultures expressed across the sector, and the motivations of some of their originators, to portray it as an undifferentiated mass. This is particularly the case when, following Mort and Nixon, commercial culture needs to be recognized as a location where an expanding and differentiated range of gender identities are reflected and re-presented to consumer markets with increasing intensity.

It is important to stress that the editors to whom I paid particular attention were not typical cases, but were the most pertinent for illustrating some of the interconnections between commercial imperatives, personal and professional aims, identities and qualifications, and the formation and reformation of magazine brands. I have acknowledged that, since Brown, Southwell, Howarth and Eshun were all instinctive editors, their personal identities were more closely connected to those of their publications than in many other cases. Nonetheless, it is worth re-emphasizing that professional editors worked on products whose initial editorial templates were themselves often intimately related to individual figures; and that they were more likely to be employed at times when the underlying terms of the magazine's identity had little need to be redefined.

It is important to take further stock of how previous research has been advanced by some of the findings I have summarized. One significant revelation was the way in which cultural producers and consumers within the magazine industry were articulated via certain forms of informal and ongoing editorial understandings of 'the reader'. I have been keen to emphasize that, unlike in the art markets that Bourdieu (1993) dissects, where producers can feign disinterest in the buyer, in highly competitive commercial fields like magazine publishing, assessments of consumers are always enveloped in production decisions. Both practically and conceptually, therefore, it makes no sense to bracket off the spheres of production and consumption from each other. As I have repeatedly highlighted, though, actual consumers played a rather spectral role in defining their own interests and outlining their own identities. True though it was that they could always determine what was and was not commercially successful, and that publishers had to be responsive to public demands and tastes, I have shown that 'consumers' were invoked by producers as assumed constituencies with their actual voices often ignored. If this suggests that editors' assessments of consumer interests and identities were prescriptive and productive as well as descriptive and responsive, then this would not be to overstate the point. In offering to readers particular social explanations and scripts through which to understand and negotiate their lives, and in a medium in which guidance is such a pervasive mode of address, the discourses that emerge from the magazine industry may be highly normative; in arbitrating celebrity and cultural kudos, editorial authority may be particularly powerful. This would be the case regardless of whether editorial practitioners acknowledge that they may be pursuing specific objectives through their products.

It has not been the power relationship implied here that I have dwelt upon, although the complexity of the producer–consumer relationship has certainly been worth underlining. Rather, it is the discursive specificity of the representations produced by this mode of articulation, and the critical role of editors in solidifying them, that I have been able to highlight. One advantage of the empirical, case-specific approach that I have employed is its ability to be sensitive to such details in ways that political-economic and some other production approaches generally are not. In part, this has reflected my belief that the output

of the men's magazine market was of intrinsic interest, and not simply significant as an indication of a more abstract theoretical claim. Some of the key interests of political economy and the production-of-culture paradigm have proved to
be influential elements in the dynamics of the magazine industry, particularly
factors such as advertising markets and producer competition. However, I have
understood these determinants not as concrete laws but as limitations and
constraints which, as entities whose terms are discursively defined, are effectively negotiable – which is not to say inescapable or somehow unreal.

It is useful to reiterate how my account challenges the adequacy of approaches
that regard cultural objects as the outcomes only of social group practices and
organizational needs. I have shown that the emergence, development and character of specific products within the men's press, and the market as a whole,
cannot be understood without accounting for the influence of individual intentions, motivations and knowledges, even when these functioned within certain
channels and were themselves socially structured. Whilst economic imperatives
and advertising markets were clear determinants of certain aspects of editorial
tone and the shape of publishing territory as a whole, the conditions of their
determination were themselves dependent on particular cultural languages,
discourses and knowledges. Indeed, my research strongly supports Nixon's
(1996) assertion that we must move beyond crude notions of economic determination and cultural autonomy in order to adequately conceptualize relations
between the economic and the cultural. Instead, we need to think of the relationship between cultural and economic practices as mutually dependent, and to
continue to analyse empirically the discursive nature of commercial production.
In doing so – and to restate the book's main argument – where my work adds to
that of Nixon is in demonstrating that, in the imbrication of the cultural and the
economic in the magazine industry and in connecting – or 'lighting up' – the
cultural circuit, it was editors who were axiomatic. This is not to say, then, that
the market was created out of nothing, nor that we need not go beyond the individuals involved in its production in order fully to understand it. Not least,
Brown himself acknowledged that he conveyed rather than invented the cultures
that *loaded* circulated. Nonetheless, it was through such personnel, and the
resources that they actively deployed to interpret and re-present a rather amor-
phous masculine culture, that the market took on the particular characteristics
that it did. That there was nothing abstractly predestined about these characteristics is a critical point.

I have generally referred to editorial expertise as cultural knowledge.
However, one purpose of the book that is consistent with regarding the cultural
and economic as interdependent has been to show that editorial exercises were
never purely creative or 'cultural'. Whilst editors were formally responsible for
creative executions and publishers for commercial performances, in reality,

absolute divisions between creative and commercial operations did not exist. Editors were required to have commercial nous comprised of 'economic' as well as 'cultural' knowledge. At the same time, although some editors had no objectives beyond the maximization of commercial revenues for their employers, others did have personal and professional aims that were creative and ideological. The latter could find themselves in conflict not only with publishing and advertising personnel but also, in effect, with readerships whose preferences could diverge from their own. Editors concerned primarily with maximizing sales rather than advertising incomes were also likely to find their goals compromised if they threatened to stray beyond certain implicit and accepted boundaries. At the same time, the importance of editors' 'special knowledge' (Ferguson 1983) and the ultimate dependence of advertising revenues upon editorial delivery made these boundaries negotiable. The main point here is to suggest that production processes were governed by a more complex interplay of conflicts, constraints and coalitions than has been offered in previous accounts of the magazine industry. Both amongst editorial practitioners and between occupational functions there were observably different techniques, faculties, motivations, aims and responsibilities. Again then, simplistic notions of the unbounded, undifferentiated and rational pursuit of profit are betrayed here. Assertions that 'mass media content ... is designed to attract consumers that are then sold to advertisers as audiences ... What this means practically is that the interests of advertisers will dominate those of consumers when it comes to media content' (Harms and Kellner 1991) do not do full justice to the complexities that I have delineated.

Although my research and that of others (Negus 1992; Nava 1997; Nixon 1997) has begun to distinguish between the origins, vocabularies, priorities and practices of different occupational strata in the cultural industries, it remains a challenge to take such work further. One distinction I made between editorial and publishing practitioners was the considerably greater degree to which the former were required to import personal concerns and interests into professional life. I demonstrated that this blurring of work and leisure boundaries had a number of implications in terms of the meanings attached to work and its material consequences on editorial careers. This seems a particularly ripe area for further study. A key question is how individuals and organizations construct and negotiate the borders of personal and professional life when the two appear progressively more integrated in a growing range of employment sectors (du Gay 1993). There are personal and political ramifications here. On a practical level, the smudging of borders between labour and pleasure may be problematic where employer expectations are unclear. Such difficulties were suggested in 1998 when three *FHM* staff writers left the company after a dispute over their 'laid back' attitude. Phil Thomas stated that 'it's not the fun and games and cocaine fuelled orgies people think it is working at *FHM*, but nonetheless highlighted the more complicated mode of pleasurable enterprise that Emap had always sought to cultivate: 'Staff enjoy themselves because it's the best fun possible but they all work extremely hard' (*Press Gazette*, 23.10.98: 9).

Thomas' comment divulged the double-edged nature of creative work that I observed in Chapter 4. Whilst manifestly highlighting the pleasures of their jobs, many editors also revealed some of the complementary problems. Peter Howarth's quip that 'everyone thinks we're going for drinks with Brad Pitt. But we're not. We're unshaven people who don't see enough daylight' expressed a common complaint (*Guardian*, 3.9.00). When asked what they did in their leisure time, the immediate response of most editorial and publishing personnel was that they didn't have any. In this respect, the use of familial metaphors to describe work colleagues (VerMeulen's 'substitute family'; *loaded*'s charged fraternity) signified the time demanded by some employers, as well as the intimacies that developed from such commitments. For those personnel who did have families, the work-based social life that many employees cherished, and that publishers often encouraged, could be rather unwelcome.

Encouragements to socialize through work could obscure the official parameters of the working day, and there was certainly potential for such outings to become oppressive. Michael VerMeulen was reported to insist on his staff having fun: 'People were dragged from their desks for the Friday night staff party' (*Daily Telegraph*, 30.8.95). Indeed, publishing's ethos of sociable enthusiasm had more serious consequences for certain practitioners, including VerMeulen himself, whose death was partly attributed to his attempt to embody his magazine's lifestyle with all too much commitment. The industry's other high-profile cases were James Brown and Michael Holden, both of whom attributed their problems to the intensity of *loaded*'s working culture. Brown noted a number of environmental features that had contributed to his alcohol and drugs problems: the stress of the job, the magazine's ethos of excess, and an industry culture in which drink and drugs were relatively freely distributed, and it was legitimate to consume large quantities of the former as part of working life. Holden linked the development of his psychosis to the form of compulsive enthusiasm that *loaded* begat, a combination of hedonism and hard work that put tremendous pressures on relationships beyond the magazine for all of its personnel (Southwell 1998: 182–5). Working with Brown on *Jack*, Holden commented to him: 'It'll be interesting to see if you and I can try to do something that isn't pathological and doesn't take over our whole lives' (cited in the *Guardian*, 22.4.02: Media, 8–9). Reconciling these portraits with the terms of carefree fun used in other depictions was not easy.

Brown's definition of the activities he undertook to incite himself into the role of the *GQ* editor as 'indulgences' also appeared a little contrived (particularly when, after leaving the company, he shed much of the public image of the Mayfair flâneur). The reconstructions that some editorial promotions necessitated could equally well be seen as stressful and self-regulatory. McRobbie labels such demands to 'work at' one's abilities 'technologies of the self' (2002: 109; also see du Gay 1996), highlighting the traces of exploitation and exclusion that lie behind new languages of creative self-actualization. Indeed, many of the 'freedoms' that publishers offered their staff had rather ambiguous implications. Cabal chief executive Sally O'Sullivan's declaration that the company's promotion of flexibility and independence was designed to attract employees who were 'self-generating' was thus striking. Other company executives admitted that the industry's image of fun, fluidity and creative fulfilment could obfuscate the reality of 'people working themselves into the ground' for relatively low wages and with little career support or stability (Sawford 1999).

If there is more work to be done on the empirical realities of working life in creative industries, one important area of interest should be the gendered implications of new forms of work and the breakdown of productivist divisions between labour and leisure. As the primary qualities demanded of a growing number of workers become social, cultural and emotional, my research raises the question of how men whose identities are anchored in notions of working-class masculinity will adjust to an occupational landscape that makes such ideals increasingly unrealizable. Roper's (1994) study of post-war 'organisational men' identified the psychic tensions aroused in men who had to authorize themselves in relation to products that already carried highly masculine meanings. Brown and Southwell expressed anxieties that may become more typical. Not only did they have to warrant themselves in relation to objects that held none of the heroic masculine connotations of industrial objects, but they also struggled to license expertise that they felt to be inherently feminized.

The same shifts in employment patterns have been used, both by industry insiders and academic researchers, to help explain growing consumer demand for men's lifestyle publications. Brown's outline of the subcultural entrepreneurs who formed his ideal audience at *GQ* itself marked a perception of an increasing number of men synthesizing work, leisure and pleasure. A greater proportion of men's magazine consumers do more prosaic work in the service economy, an area in which character, clothing and the cultural knowledge distributed through lifestyle publications also matter. Jackson et al. (2001) have suggested that this provision of lifestyle guidance and the notions of 'naturalness' and 'authenticity' constructed around the new lad identity serve to stabilize masculine anxieties that are the consequence of much wider shifts in social relations. In this reading, men's magazines provide 'constructed certitude' for men no longer able to rely on traditional anchors of male identity (Jackson et al. 2001: 128–9; see also MacInnes 1998). This argument certainly echoes certain voices within men's publishing, in particular, a recent (2002) Emap report which identified the breakdown of male roles as fundamental to men's changing attitudes and suggested that *FHM*'s role should be to build the confidence of its readers through more useful and constructive editorial. 'I think of the magazine as a safe haven in a mad and changing world', commented Phil Hilton, now editor of *FHM*'s Reporter section (MediaGuardian.co.uk, 8.4.02). But in adding that 'we don't sit at our desks in the editorial department thinking of male roles in decline', and that the kind of information the magazine provided was not 'how to express your emotional self in the workplace', but, rather, 'how to get tomato ketchup off your trousers', he highlighted the marginal role of macro-research in the process of editorial production and the micro-level at which broad social change was recognized and articulated by editorial producers (MediaGuardian.co.uk, 8.4.02).

Hilton's resistance to taking too seriously notions of masculinity in crisis was typical of an attitude of many editors. Indeed, between them, there was a striking rarity of what might be called 'masculinity projects'. The absence of a popular, critical language of masculinity commensurate with the terms made familiar by second-wave feminism, and the limited appeal of the 'men's movement' (such that it exists), is worth considering here. McRobbie has recalled descriptions by female journalists working on young women's magazines of struggles to inte-grate feminist ideas into mainstream commercial products (1999a: 28), but there was little equivalent in the men's lifestyle sector. Eshun was almost unique in his explicit interest in issues of masculinity and male identity. What is strongly suggested by Brown and Southwell's antipathy to the 'new man', and the ulti-mately controlled self-consciousness exhibited by Howarth and Eshun, is that men's attitudes towards self-scrutiny and issues around masculinity may them-selves be loaded with gendered associations. To be too self-conscious still seems to connote narcissism, femininity or weakness. If this is the case, there is all the more reason to want to understand and engage with the motives, aversions and values of cultural producers in positions of influence.

Without such understandings, the temptation still remains to cast workers in consumer culture and the creative professions as Thatcherite entrepreneurs (Mort 1989; McRobbie 1998, 1999a). However, it is not enough to deduce that left-wing producers turn out radical products without demonstrating the link between originator and outcome. One ambition of this book has been precisely to show how personal values can be translated into cultural forms. It may be that media content is not only accented by the resources, interests and aspirations of pivotal individuals, but also, following Bourdieu and Featherstone, that certain class strata may hegemonize their values and competences in wider society through their positions in circuits of production. It is only through further empirical research into the dynamics of these circuits that such claims about the long-term consequences of the structural composition of the cultural industries can be veri-fied. Likewise, more research is required to test the concept of 'editorship' that this book advocates. Hesmondhalgh (2002) argues that there exists a general pattern within cultural industries whereby 'symbol creators' are granted consid-erable autonomy by their managers, with much looser control exercised on them than on the reproduction and circulation of the goods they conceive. There are cultural reasons (such as traditions of free speech and romantic ideals of creativity) for this arrangement as well as the kinds of economic rationales that I outlined in Chapter 4. But without more in-depth analysis, it should not be assumed that creative personnel elsewhere, and at other moments of market formation, have as much influence as the editors I have charted in this study.

Meanwhile, some caution is still required about what this book's approach can deliver. A focus upon the production conditions and producers of men's maga-zines cannot reveal or account for all of the processes that affect their meanings. I have not sought to examine how these products are consumed and interpreted by their audiences, nor to engage in a formal and systematic deconstruction of their texts. These are crucial areas, but ones that are beyond the scope and ambi-tion of this project. Nonetheless, analyses of these other moments in the cultural circuit can benefit from research on the spheres of production and circulation. There remains a tendency, particularly within journalistic and popular accounts of the media, for textual analysis to be foregrounded at the expense of enquiry into other moments in the passage of cultural forms, as if the interconnections bare no significance. Popular academic analysis may be no less immune to such reductionisms. In Whelehan's *Overloaded: Popular Culture and the Future of Feminism*, a half-paragraph description of a *loaded* feature on actress Helen Mirren and its concentration on her sexual identity as 'middle-aged crumpet' is said to tell us 'everything we need to know about the *loaded* response to women' (Whelehan 2000: 59). The new lad is summarized simply as 'part soccer thug, part lager lout, part arrant sexist … knowingly offensive, particularly in its sexual objectification of women' (Whelehan 2000: 58). It is hard to accept what is, in effect, a dismissal of the value of a greater understanding of the objectives and intentions of *loaded*'s producers. Unintentionally, though, Whelehan makes a strong case for exploring the circumstances of editorial decision-making when she notes that many new lad jokes 'are only funny when set in a context of presumed ideological disapproval' from a presupposed militant feminism (Whelehan 2000: 60). For many men's press practitioners, as I have indicated, the radical feminist and the new man did indeed function as imagined identities against which they defined themselves. *loaded*'s representational regime was clearly conditional on the prior articulation of the new man through the early men's lifestyle press and its (assumed) editorial champions; that is, on a set of developments within the specific institutional context of men's publishing. In this respect, it is also worth repeating Nixon's observation that the new man's failure to elaborate an adequately heterosexual male identity made it all the more likely that established sexual scripts would resurface (Nixon 1996: 206). It is for such reasons that, to more fully comprehend the identities delineated in the men's magazine market, the personal and professional ambitions of its practitioners merit investigation.

Even if textual analysis showed that magazine codings were degrading to women, it would be false logic to assume that their editors were themselves sexist. Equally, that men like Brown and Southwell were by no means the unreconstructed lads for which some commentators took them tells us nothing in itself about the formal qualities of their representations, and even less about the ultimate meanings attached to them by *loaded*'s consumers. This is not simply because, even in *loaded*'s case, the intentions of editorial producers are always channelled and constrained by other production determinants. It is also because of the inescapable contingencies, or leakages, between authorial intent, textual form and audience interpretation. I noted this indiscipline of meaning in Chapter 5, in relation to the *loaded* tour. It was this 'living hell' that most clearly revealed to the *loaded* team the lack of control they ultimately held over what they had considered a progressive cultural intervention. One journalist disclosed this particularly clearly in bemoaning that instead of attracting 'people who were into the writing, who were into the humour, who got the point of it, who understood that it wasn't about hating women', what they came across one night was 'pure fucking hatred. ... It really was the worst night of my life, meeting those people' (Wilde in Southwell 1998: 234–5). Southwell admitted partial culpability, whilst also protesting that 'The evolution of the "*loaded* lad" is nothing to do with *loaded*' (*Campaign*, 4.12.98: 19). Martin Deeson likewise complained that 'the whole Lad thing ... very quickly became confused not with blokes being honest and respecting women – which is what I thought it was about – but about football violence' (in Southwell, 1998: 106).

It was certainly true that *loaded* was cited as the cause of some phenomena for which its originators could not reasonably be held accountable. Amongst other things, lad mags were reproached for a decline in sperm bank donations (Brown 1999a) and identified as the reason for the decline of the soft-porn sector – a decline that had much more to do with competition from satellite media and the internet (*Campaign*, 4.7.97: 9). As I suggested in the introduction, the media attention given to the men's press amounted to a minor moral panic. However, there was also a strong element of disingenuousness in the refusal of some publishing personnel to accept any responsibility for the representations that they provided whenever the charges carried negative intimations. This was particularly evident when editors and publishers were all too keen to take credit for those influences that could be regarded as positive, from improving men's sexual technique and physical health to navigating them through an otherwise confusing world of consumer goods. None doubted, for example, the power of their title to shift very large numbers of recommended products from shop shelves. Individual items are not, of course, comparable with broad cultural ideologies, yet the terms according to which responsibility was either denied or embraced were nonetheless conspicuous. Moreover, whilst one of the most common discursive mantras through which censures were repelled was the argument that magazines merely mirrored the social worlds beyond them, this study suggests that this reflection is less than perfect, and that cultures beyond the industry are only ever viewed through certain eyeglasses for which editors cannot simply disavow responsibility.

Appendix

Research Background, Process and Methods

I was fairly unaware of men's lifestyle magazines until 1994, my second year of university, when *loaded* began to appear in the student rooms of some of my friends. I was intrigued by this magazine, which covered many of my personal interests – football, music, comedy, popular culture – but in a tone with which I was often uncomfortable. By the time I was a graduate student, in 1997, men's magazines were everywhere, and my interest in them had some academic pretensions. Originally, my fixation was on what they 'said' about contemporary masculinity, that is, what they could reveal about shifts in men's values and attitudes. It was editors who, both as first-hand observers of the market's development, and as key agents in its construction, I thought would be able to tell me; and I had far more enthusiasm for interviewing them than I did for interrogating readers, or carrying out textual analysis.

The personal and intellectual dimensions of this initial preference were somewhat interconnected. Its demonstration of the active nature of media consumption notwithstanding, I had often been unconvinced that audience-based research could establish the insights it strove to deliver. Jackson et al.'s (2001) recent study bolsters these suspicions that the research scale and level of methodological sophistication needed for such work to be insightful and fully credible are daunting. It is unsurprising to be told that men's magazine readers 'make sense' of these publications with 'considerable ambivalence' (Stevenson et al. 2000: 190). Jackson et al.'s (2001: 74–108) analysis of the magazines' stylistic and narrative constructions is much more persuasive. Drawing heavily on Ulrich Beck's notion of 'constructed certitude', they argue that laddish discourses within the magazines function to shore up contemporary anxieties around masculinity – in relation to employment and physical health, for example – by offering a script that appears 'honest', 'authentic' and unambiguous. My aim was not to attempt this kind of analysis, which moves ambitiously from sociological and psychoanalytic theory to textual interpretation. Instead, it was the intermediate sphere between broad social change and its cultural inscription, a sphere that it seemed senseless to bypass, that I sought to investigate. That this book provides little detailed analysis of the magazines as textual and visual commodities, and no attempt to gauge consumer interpretations, is thus partly a matter of filling in some gaps. It is also consistent with my intellectual training, which has not included any schooling in semiotic or textual scrutiny. Inevitably also, it relates to practical limitations of time and resources.

Once I started the PhD research on which this book is based, and as I came to recognize the uses and limitations of interviewing magazine producers, the research focus narrowed somewhat. I was certainly too optimistic about what men's magazine personnel would be able to tell me about *why* the market had expanded, and soon found that industry professionals were no better informed about the wider determinants of its development than external commentators. That their expertise resided not in intensive and reliable social research, but in intuitive, implicit and often highly personal knowledge, was a striking early discovery, and it was these informal assumptions, motivations and cultural repertoires – tacit and explicit, personal and professional – that became the key objects of enquiry.

I had initially approached editorial and publishing personnel in 1998, at first through letters, and then, with much more success, via email: a medium whose informality, immediacy and directness made it hugely practical for such purposes. My eventual response rate of around 80 per cent was requisite as well as gratifying, for I was dependent on a discrete set of professionals for whom there were no substitute data sources. The most disappointing gap in my research sample was the editor of *FHM*, who ignored a number of interview requests, and whose participation in the study would have been extremely generative.

Preparation for the interviews involved thinking about a number of aspects of self-presentation and approach. In an industry that was highly sensitive to appearances, what I wore was bound to be significant. I chose to dress neutrally, in clothes that were on the smart side of casual, hoping to convey something between professionalism and informality. A related concern was how I, as a university representative, would be received in a field whose populist grounding might entail a suspicion of academic thinking (Gamson 1995; see also Bourdieu 1984). Although candid about my research interests, I was reluctant to appear 'over-intellectual'. As it transpired, many editors were, indeed, resistant to analysis, both of themselves and, as Jackson et al. (2001: 55) also report, of the significance of their products.[1]

A counterbalance to the impulse to downplay my academic grounding was my need to probe interviewees beyond the answers they were used to giving to the journalists with whom most of them habitually dealt. Advertising and editorial personnel presented themselves in highly stylized ways in their dealings with the trade press and national media, and, although these modes of self-presentation were relevant to my research, I also hoped to bypass some of their more rehearsed dimensions. Accordingly, I sought to reiterate before each interview that my interest was academic rather than journalistic, and opened with questions – about the skills required for the job and the role of research in decision-making

– that I hoped would emphasize this distinction. Meanwhile, whilst I tried to display the insider knowledge I had picked up about the market through the trade press, I did not want to appear a 'knowing insider' who had swallowed publishing's self-image and was prepared to play its games according to the comfortable conventions of industry reportage. Knowledge gleaned from the trade press also allowed me to tailor certain questions to fit individual interviewees, who were often visibly flattered by these personal customizations.

These were, as a group, powerful and socially successful people, not the vulnerable subordinates of much sociological research. Given the interview skills of my participants, I doubted that they would inadvertently reveal things that they or their companies would regret. I took for granted their confidence to decline questions, and did not want to arouse unwarranted suspicions by running through a lengthy explanation of the interview contract. Instead, it was at the end of each interview that I requested permission to quote. Tacit in such consent was an understanding that, since individual identities and specific events were relevant to the research, anonymity was not an appropriate guarantee. I am confident that this remained an ethical procedure, as well as a practical one. Meanwhile, in taking care to represent my research participants fairly and in ways that will not compromise their professional standing, I have been aware of my own vulnerability as well as theirs: vulnerability to the criticisms and corrections that they could easily, and noisily, make were they to feel slighted or misrepresented. Media insiders are also the readers most likely to identify factual inaccuracies in this book and some of those most capable of challenging its arguments.

A lack of systematized documentation makes media industry research a challenging endeavour. Commercial publishing lacks even the basic records and archives that the Advertising Association and History of Advertising Trust provide for their industry. Reliance on trade publications such as *Press Gazette*, *Media Week*, *Marketing* and *Campaign* comes with its own perils. As Frank Mort observes, any of these journals 'reveals a world-view quite as expansive as that encountered in *The Lancet* or the *British Medical Journal*' (1996: 9); such discursive regimes can blind the researcher to their own assumptions. Certainly, after several months of trawling through a decade's worth of publishing's self-representations, I had absorbed much of its sense of its own glamour and creativity, not least in the tone of breathless exhilaration that, for a short while, marked my writing. At the same time, the magazines themselves, several of which I was receiving on monthly subscription, had lost any appeal that they had initially held. It is now very rare that I buy one.

With the exception of one interview conducted in a café, all face-to-face interviews took place in private offices or empty meeting rooms within the buildings of publishing companies. Interview lengths ranged from half an hour to over two hours, more often than not exceeding the time originally allocated. A typical interview would be introduced with a number of questions about the interviewee's job, including their career route, their typical day, the skills and character required for their position, the main people they dealt with, and their relationships with other key practitioners on their magazine and senior company executives. Issues of freedom, constraint and commercial and artistic ambition were explicitly raised here, and participants were asked to comment on the ethos of their company. The second section of the interview was designed to elicit data about the informal and formal knowledges used in magazine launches, the ongoing production of magazine content, and the conception of readerships. It was at this stage that participants tended to talk in specific terms about their magazines, and the questions that followed built on this by enquiring into the title's history, 'typical reader', market position, distinctive qualities, and appeal to readers and advertisers. The views of participants on the role and influence of their magazine on people's lives, on wider culture and on other media areas were also solicited here.

The fourth part of the interview schedule covered the growth of the men's magazine market over the last fifteen years, and the institutional, cultural, social and economic context in which its development had taken place. Interviewees were invited to discuss changes in their magazine over the last few years, the reasons for these changes and what the future might hold for their magazine and the men's press as a whole. The final section of the interview then included questions on background, education, ambitions and lifestyle, with informants asked openly about their personal and professional goals and the influence of their backgrounds on their work. 'Masculinity' itself was rarely raised in any explicit way, but its terms imprinted the transcriptions in almost every area: in descriptions of expertise, ambition, educational background and company cultures, in comments about market developments and senior executives, and in the verbal transactions that took place with co-workers and secretaries. The difference between James Brown's energetic and inclusive banter, and Stephen Quinn's genteel governance was, in this respect, instructive.

As new research questions came to mind, and details called for clarification, I requested follow-up interviews from almost all my original sample. Only a handful were granted, and some were conducted by telephone, but these were some of the most useful of all the interviews I carried out. Cut loose from the constraints I had imposed upon myself through a rather rigid interview protocol, I was able to react more intuitively to responses on an expanded range of issues. My growing confidence was reflected in new techniques of quoting interviewees back to themselves, picking up on inconsistencies, and asking them to clarify earlier comments, strategies that seemed to elicit more relaxed and dialogic exchanges. By the time of my last few interviews, I was noticeably less naïve and unchallenging than I had been in early encounters.

Appendix

As a young man within the lifestyle demographic targeted by and working upon many of their titles, the influence of my own identity on these interactions merits some consideration. Two kinds of interview seemed to run most smoothly: those with male senior executives of an older generation, and those with certain younger, male editorial practitioners. In the former, I recognize much of what Roper describes of his experience interviewing 'organization men' in the late stages of their careers, whereby his interviewees positioned him as a younger version of themselves, transferring onto him 'fantasies of youthful omnipotence' (1994: 38). As I asked my older informants to recall their career developments, the world of magazines was often contrasted with more subdued professional cultures such as my own, and they both justified and wrote off their academic weaknesses. My own expertise was not, however, derided. Instead, I was encouraged to convert my talents to the glamorous and rewarding field of publishing, where the openings that had presented themselves to them would, likewise, reward me. In exchanges that had distinctly paternal qualities, these men took pleasure in granting me praise or small material gifts (an *Esquire* money clip; pre-release copies of magazines). On more than one occasion, I felt that I was being covertly offered a route into the profession – a job, were I to want one. In luxurious offices in the heart of London, and seduced by such vocabularies of creativity and opportunity, I found such offers mildly, although only briefly, enticing. Like Roper (1994: 39), I was often left with a heightened sense of my own prospects.

With a number of younger personnel, it was peer identification that seemed to lubricate exchange. In such situations, I was undoubtedly flattered to be engaged with as an equal by successful and influential editors, some of whom had quasi-celebrity status. James Brown was a warm and responsive interviewee, whose engagement with my questions made me feel like a skilful and incisive inquisitor. Peter Howarth's interest in the research (where I was studying, whom I would try to publish with) bolstered my view of its worth. Research guides often mention that participants may be grateful that someone has an interest in them, but they rarely discuss how the attentions of the informant may nourish the vanities of the researcher. I was struck by how much pleasure I took in being 'let in' on the 'realities' of an occupational role, drawing out private philosophies on the industry, being told that I had just asked a 'good question', and simply being addressed by name – and I would be surprised if these somewhat laughable satisfactions did not resonate with other researchers. I have endeavoured to ensure that the analysis has not been biased by the personal preferences that I developed for certain magazines and interviewees, or the antipathy I felt towards one editor who treated me with considerable disdain.

My efforts to wean participants from well-practised responses were not always successful. Some were especially accustomed to being questioned about the representation of women in their titles, and having to defend their publications against charges of immaturity and triviality. I was offered almost identical and defensive explanations by several *loaded* staff of its level of female nudity; I was told the same story at three different magazines about an article on testicular cancer that saved a reader's life after he checked himself according to its instructions; and, on several occasions, I recognized, from trade press articles that I had already digested, what were seemingly spontaneous quips. In a close-knit industry such as magazine publishing, it was not surprising to find such 'discursive mantras', nor were they unrevealing. What was harder to gauge was whether they were genuine expressions of personal and professional discourse that might inform production practices, or merely strategies for dealing with commonplace and challenging questions.

A related complication was that interviewees were both the objects of study and the sources of inside information. Some statements about the mechanics of the industry, the development of the market and the aims of individual magazines could be interpreted both as 'factual data' and in terms of what they revealed about the personnel who uttered them. When an office is described as a 'pigsty' or a rival is labelled a 'middle-class liberal', how does one distinguish the actual from the metaphorical? Likewise, editors were prone to amplifying the spontaneous, creative aspects of their work over the routine and bureaucratic – though I am less sceptical about the deceptiveness of this than Jackson et al. (2001). There were difficulties also in the analytical distinction I needed to make between the identities of magazines and those of their editors in order to explore how the former were influenced by the predispositions of the latter. Given after the establishment of magazines, interviews were, to some degree, 'retrospective constructions' (Roper, pers. comm.), in which some editors sought self-consciously to conflate their personalities with those of their titles. Such strategies, as I suggest, served to enhance claims of editorial authority and the 'authenticity' of the editorial voice. As such then, autobiographical narratives were mediated products, and were often reflexively cultivated to emphasize seamless synthesis between personal and product identity. In this respect, to identify without ambiguity the traits, interests and ideologies that pre-existed and piloted the fashioning of a magazine, was by no means straightforward.

Despite these problems, I do wish to defend the distinctions I have made. Through the weighing up of evidence, the drawing out of repeated themes, the exposure of inconsistencies and ambivalences, and the thorough and repeated interrogation of multiple data sources, it was possible to extract from interviews those values and dispositions that could legitimately be considered pre-formed, stable and independent of the magazine at issue. It was striking, for example, that, in writing for the *Daily Telegraph* (18.6.99: 28) on Prince Edward and Sophie Rhys-Jones' wedding (i.e. an article not designed to publicize *loaded*),

Tim Southwell raised his comprehensive school education, and contrasted his 'real world of hard knocks and tough surprises' with the aristocratic comforts of 'ponies and a gold credit card': themes that surfaced repeatedly in his other testimonies.

There is no set method here, and there are judgement calls to be made, judgements that are especially difficult when statements about magazines appear to be metaphors of the self as much as declarations of commercial intent. But interviewees also tend to reveal more of themselves than they realize, in ways that they do not always recognize. Calculated self-presentations may be undermined by less guarded revelations, slippages and narratives. Thus, James Brown's attempts to ventriloquize himself into the *GQ* identity were exposed by his own accounts of the self-consciousness of his incitements ('To understand the magazine you've *got to* live the magazine, so I wander around Mayfair ... I *make sure* my sports car is valeted ...' (*Press Gazette*, 11.12.98: 15; my italics) – and, after leaving the magazine, by further admissions that his adaptations had been strained.

Interviews were transcribed in full and coded using WinMax software, the latter process proving particularly useful for my analysis of launch procedures, advertising pressures, and occupational roles. Secondary sources and additional research methods also helped the analysis enormously. As well as making considerable use of trade magazines, I drew upon a number of newspaper profiles to help make sense of the backgrounds, aspirations and identifications of many of my protagonists. Further triangulation was provided through a questionnaire distributed in September 1999 to 120 advertising and editorial personnel within the men's press, including all of the original interview participants. The questionnaire covered areas such as age, marital status, background, education, parental occupations, voting preferences, and attitudes on class, family, gender relations, politics and fashion. Respondents were asked to chart their career pathways and to list some of their personal tastes, lifestyle preferences and influences. Most questions were taken from established studies such as the British Social Attitudes Survey and the British Household Panel Survey. Forty-nine questionnaires were returned.

Pleased though I was with the level of access I gained to key figures in the industry, there was much about the daily production conditions, professional ideologies and values of these practitioners that I was unable fully to ascertain. Such data might best be gathered through ethnographic approaches, though these have proved difficult to employ in media industries, where public images are fiercely guarded and there may be considerable resistance to being studied. I hope, nonetheless, that such studies are pursued by future researchers within the field.

Note

1. A friend of a friend who worked for Emap initially assured me that there was 'nothing to say' about men's magazines. On a later date he kindly agreed to talk to me informally about *FHM*, for almost two hours.

Bibliography

Research Participants

For the purpose of clarity, I have cited the unpublished interviews I conducted for this book using normal referencing procedures, although without page references. Below, I list research participants, the year(s) of interview, job positions at this time and some additional information where appropriate. I have also included unpublished public papers given by publishing practitioners cited in the book.

Boon, Ralph (1999) publisher, *Men's Health*
Brown, James (1999a, 1999b) editor, *GQ* (former editor, *loaded*)
Brown, John (1998) chairman, John Brown Publishing
Colbert, Paul (1999) editor, *ZM*
Coleridge, Nicholas (1999) managing director, Conde Nast, interview with Kamal Ahmed, Total Publishing Conference, London, 7–8 July 1999
Eshun, Ekow (1998, 1999) editor, *Arena*
Fuller, Eric (1998) publishing director, *Maxim*
Geller, Simon (1999) editor, *Men's Health*
Hepworth, David (1998) editorial director, Emap Consumer Magazines
Hernu, Piers (1998) editor, *Front*
Hilton, Phil (1998) special projects, IPC (subsequently editor, *Later*)
Hilton, Phil (1999) 'The launch of *later*', paper given at the Total Publishing Conference, London, 7–8 July 1999.
Howarth, Peter (1998, 1999, 2000) editor, *Esquire*
Hudson, Gill (1998) editorial director, *Maxim*
Hughes, Chris (1998) publishing director, *Esquire*
Keers, Paul (1999) managing director, Axon Contract Publishing (launch editor, *GQ*)
Lewis, Alan (1998; 1999) editor-in-chief, IPC
Long, Tony (1998) publisher, *Men's Health*
McIlheney, Barry (1998) managing director, Emap Metro
McQuillan, Neil (1998) publishing director, *ZM*

Maillard, Chris (1998) editor, *Maxim*

Mansfield, Terry (1999a) managing director, The National Magazine Company

Mansfield, Terry (1999b) Interview with Roy Greenslade, Total Publishing Conference, London, 7–8 July 1999.

Newbold, Steve (1998) commercial director, Emap Metro

Pettett, Adrian (1999) publisher, *loaded*

Quinn, Stephen (1999) publisher, *Vogue* (formerly launch publisher, *GQ*)

Read, Gary (1998) assistant research director, Condé Nast

Sawford, Bruce (1999) licensing director, Dennis Publishing

Simpson, Paul (1998) editor, *Focus*

Sopp, Rod (1998) advertising director, Wagadon

Soutar, Mike (1997) 'Turning *FHM* around', paper given at the Total Publishing Conference, London, 2–3 July 1997.

Stitt, Alex (1998) publishing director, *Focus*

Southwell, Tim (1999) editor, *loaded*

Sutcliffe, Andy (1998) managing director, Cabal Communications

Tame, Robert (1998) publishing director, *loaded*

Thomas, Philip (1998) executive publishing director, *FHM*

Tiffin, Simon (1999) editor, *GQ Active*

Warwick, Samantha (1998) managing editor, *Men's Health*

Unpublished Works

Bancroft, A. (1998) 'The model of a man: Masculinity and body image in men's lifestyle magazines', paper given at the British Association for the Advancement of Science conference, 10–11 September 1998, University of Cardiff.

Benwell, B. (2001) 'Ironic discourse: Evasive masculinity in British men's lifestyle magazines', work in progress.

Glucksmann, M. (1998) 'Retailing and shopworkers: Filling the gap between production and consumption', paper presented to the Work, Employment and Society conference, 14–16 September 1998, University of Cambridge.

McFall, E.R. (2000) 'Who were the old cultural intermediaries?: An historical review of advertising producers', paper presented at the Third International Crossroads Conference in Cultural Studies, 21–25 July 2000, Birmingham University.

Osgerby, B. (2000) '"Bachelors in paradise": Masculinity, lifestyle and men's magazines in post-war America', paper presented at the Third International Crossroads Conference in Cultural Studies. 21–25 July 2000, Birmingham University.

Vallance, C. (1997) Worthington: 'Putting a brand back on trend', paper given for the Creative Planning Awards. Downloaded from <http://www.warc.com/fulltext/apg/10276.htm.>

Published Works and Articles

Anderson, N. (1961/1998) *Work and Leisure*, London: Routledge and Kegan Paul.

Ang, I. (1991) *Desperately Seeking the Audience*, London: Routledge.

Ballaster, R., Beetham, M., Frazer, E. and Hebron, S. (1991) *Women's Worlds: Ideology, Femininity and the Woman's Magazine,* London: Macmillan.

Benwell, B. (ed.) (2003) *Masculinity and Men's Lifestyle Magazines*, Oxford: Blackwell/ Sociological Review Monographs.

Best, S. and Kellner, D. (1991) *Postmodern Theory: Critical Interrogations*, London: Macmillan.

Bourdieu, P. (1984) *Distinction: A Social Critique of the Judgement of Taste* (translated by Richard Nice), London: Routledge.

Bourdieu, P. (1993) *The Field of Cultural Production: Essays on Art and Literature*, Cambridge: Polity Press.

Boyd-Barrett, O. (1970) 'Journalism recruitment and training: Problems in professionalisation' in J. Tunstall (ed.) *Media Sociology*, London: Constable.

Brannon, R. (1976) 'The male sex role – and what it's done for us lately' in R. Brannon and D. David (eds) *The Forty-Nine Per cent Majority: The Male Sex Role*, Reading MA: Addison-Wesley.

Buckingham, D. (1987) *Public Secrets: Eastenders and its Audience*, London: BFI.

Carrigan, T., Connell, R. and Lee, J. (1985) 'Towards a new sociology of masculinity', *Theory and Society*, 14(5), 551–604.

Chapman, R. (1988) 'The great pretender: Variations on the new man theme' in R. Chapman and J. Rutherford (eds) *Male Order: Unwrapping Masculinity*, London: Lawrence and Wishart.

Chapman, R. and Rutherford, J. (eds) (1988) *Male Order: Unwrapping Masculinity*, London: Lawrence and Wishart.

Chippendale, P. and Horrie, C. (1990) *Stick it up your Punter! The Uncut Story of the Sun Newspaper*, London: Heinemann.

Clarke, J. and Critcher, C. (1985) *The Devil makes Work: Leisure in Capitalist Britain*, London: Macmillan.

Cockburn, C. (1983) *Brothers: Male Dominance and Technological Change*, London: Pluto.

Collinson, D. and Hearn, J. (1996) '"Men" at "work": multiple masculinities/ multiple workplaces' in M. Mac an Ghaill (ed.) *Understanding Masculinities*, Buckingham: Open University Press.

Conekin, B. (2000) 'Fashioning the playboy: Messages of style and masculinity in the pages of Playboy magazine, 1953–1963', *Fashion Theory*, 4 (4), 447–66.

Connell, R.W. (1987) *Gender and Power*, Cambridge: Polity Press.

Connell, R.W. (1995) *Masculinities*, Cambridge: Polity Press.

Crane, D. (1992) *The Production of Culture: Media and the Urban Arts*, London: Sage.

Crane, D. (ed.) (1994) *The Sociology of Culture: Emerging Theoretical Perspectives*, Oxford: Blackwell.

Curran, J. and Seaton, J. (1997) *Power without Responsibility: The Press and Broadcasting in Britain*, London: Routledge.

Davies, B. and Harré, R. (1990) 'Positioning: The discursive production of selves', *Journal for the Theory of Social Behaviour*, 20 (1), 43–63.

Dawson, G. (1991) 'The blond bedouin: Lawrence of Arabia, imperial adventure and the imagining of English-British masculinity' in M. Roper and J. Tosh (eds) *Manful Assertions: Masculinity in Britain since 1800*, London: Routledge.

De Lauretis, T. (1987) *Technologies of Gender: Essays on Theory, Film and Fiction*, Bloomington: Indiana University Press.

du Gay, P. (1993) '"Numbers and souls": Retailing and the de-differentiation of economy and culture', *British Journal of Sociology*, 44 (4), 563–87.

du Gay, P. (1996) *Consumption and Identity at Work*, London: Sage.

du Gay, P. (ed.) (1997) *Production of Culture/ Cultures of Production*, London: Sage.

du Gay, P., Hall, S., Jones, L., Mackay, H. and Negus, K. (1997) *Doing Cultural Studies: The Story of the Sony Walkman*, London: Sage.

du Gay, P. and Pryke, M. (2002) (eds) *Cultural Economy*, London: Sage.

Dyer, R. (1983) 'Don't look now', *Screen*, 24 (6), 61–73.

Edwards, T. (1997) *Men in the Mirror: Men's Fashion, Masculinity and Consumer Society*, London: Cassell.

Ehrenreich, B. (1983) *The Hearts of Men: American Dreams and the Flight from Commitment*, New York: Doubleday.

Ehrenreich, B. (1989) 'A feminist's view of the new man' in M. Kimmel and M.A. Messner (eds) *Men's Lives*, London: Macmillan.

Elliott, P. (1977) 'Media organisations and occupations: An overview' in J. Curran, M. Gurevitch and J. Woollacott *Mass Communication and Society*, London: Edward Arnold.

Ettema, J. and Whitney, D.C. (1994) *Audiencemaking: How the Media Create the Audience*, London: Sage.

Featherstone, M. (1991) *Consumer Culture and Postmodernism*, London: Sage.

Feldman, D. and Stedman Jones, G. (eds) (1989) *Metropolis: London Histories and Representations since 1800*, London: Routledge.

Ferguson, M. (1983) *Forever Feminine*, London: Heinemann.

Ferguson, M. and Golding, P. (eds) (1997) *Cultural Studies in Question*, London: Sage.

Fine, B. and Leopold, E. (1993) *The World of Consumption*, London: Routledge.

Frazer, E. (1987) 'Teenage girls reading *Jackie*', *Media, Culture and Society*, 9, 407–25.

Frith, S. and Savage, J. (1993) 'Pearls and swine: The intellectuals and the mass media', *New Left Review*, 198, March/April.

Gamson, J. (1995) 'Stopping the spin and becoming a prop: Fieldwork on Hollywood elites' in R. Hertz and J. Imber (eds) *Studying Elites using Qualitative Methods*, London: Sage.

Gans, H.J. (1972) 'The famine in American mass communications research', *American Journal of Sociology*, 77 (4), 697–705.

Garnham, N. (1979) 'Contribution to a political economy of mass-communication', *Media, Culture and Society*, 1, 123–46

Garnham, N. (1980) 'The economics of the US motion picture industry', report by the Division of Cultural Action of the European Commission 1980, in N. Garnham (1990) *Capitalism and Communication: Global Culture and the Economics of Information*, London: Sage.

Garnham, N. (1987) 'Concepts of culture: Public policy and the cultural industries, *Cultural Studies*, 1 (1), 23–39.

Garnham, N. (1990) *Capitalism and Communication: Global Culture and the Economics of Information*, London: Sage.

Giddens, A. (1991) *Modernity and Self-Identity*, Cambridge Polity Press.

Gitlin, T. (1983) *Inside Prime Time*, London: Rotledge.

Gitlin, T. (1991) 'Movies of the week' in C. Mukerji and M. Schudson (eds) *Rethinking Popular Culture: Contemporary Perspectives in Cultural Studies*, Berkeley: University of California Press.

Glennie, P. and Thrift, N. (1993) 'Modern consumption', *Society and Space*, 11, 603–6.

Goffman, E. (1979) *Gender Advertisements*, London: Macmillan.

Golding, P. and Murdock, G. (1991) 'Culture, communications, and political economy' in J. Curran and M. Gurevitch (ed.) *Mass Media and Society*, London: Edward Arnold.

Hall, S. (1980) 'Encoding/decoding' in S. Hall, D. Hobson, A. Lowe and P. Willis (eds) *Culture, Media, Language*, London: Hutchinson.

Hall, S. (1997) 'The work of representation' in S. Hall (eds) *Representation: Cultural Studies and Signifying Practices*, London: Sage/Open University.

Hall, S. and Jacques, M. (eds) (1989) *New Times*, London: Lawrence and Wishart.

Bibliography

Harms, J. and Kellner D. (1991) 'Towards a critical theory of advertising', *Critical Perspectives in Social Theory*, 11, 41–67. Originally downloaded from <www.uta.edu/english/dab/illuminations/kell6.html.>

Henriques, J., Hollway, W., Urwin, C., Venn, C. and Walkerdine, V. (1984) *Changing the Subject*, London: Methuen.

Hermes, J. (1995) *Reading Women's Magazines*, Cambridge: Polity Press.

Hesmondhalgh, D. (2002) *The Cultural Industries*, London: Sage.

Hirsch, P. (1972) 'Processing fads and fashions: An organisation-set analysis of cultural industry systems', *American Journal of Sociology*, 77, 639–59.

Hochschild, A.R. (1983) *The Managed Heart: Commercialisation of Human Feeling*, Berkeley: University of California Press.

Hollway, W. (1984) 'Gender difference and the production of subjectivity' in J. Henriques, W. Hollway, C. Urwin, C. Venn and V. Walkerdine (eds) *Changing the Subject Psychology, Social Regulation and Subjectivity*, London: Methuen.

Howarth, P. (ed.) (1997) *Fatherhood: An Anthology of New Writing*, London: Indigo.

Hutton, P.H. (1988) 'Foucault, Freud, and the technologies of the self' in L. Martin, H. Gutman and P. Hutton (eds) *Technologies of the self: A seminar with Michel Foucault*, London: Tavistock.

Jackson, P. (2000) 'Introduction: Consumption, audiences and commercial culture' in P. Jackson, M. Lowe, D. Miller and F. Mort (eds) *Commercial Cultures: Ecomomies, Practices, Spaces*, Oxford: Berg.

Jackson, P., Lowe, M., Miller, D. and Mort, F. (eds) (2000) *Commercial Cultures: Ecomomies, Practices, Spaces*, Oxford: Berg.

Jackson, P., Stevenson, N. and Brooks, K. (2001) *Making Sense of Men's Magazines*, Cambridge: Polity Press.

Jackson, S. (1996) 'Ignorance is bliss: When you are Just Seventeen', *Trouble and Strife*, 33, 50–60.

Jefferson, T. (1994) 'Theorising masculine subjectivity' in T. Newburn and E.A. Stanko (eds) *Just Boys Doing Business? Men, Masculinities and Crime*, London: Routledge.

Johnson, R. (1986) 'The story so far: and for the transformations' in D. Punter (ed.) *Introduction to Contemporary Cultural Studies*, London: Longman.

Katz, A. (1999) *Leading Lads*, East Molesey: Young Voice.

Keat, R., Whiteley, N. and Abercrombie, N. (eds) (1994) *The Authority of the Consumer,* London: Routledge.

Kershaw, A. (1991) 'How new man became new lad', *The Independent on Sunday* (14.4.1991).

Lamont, M. (1992) *Money, Morals and Manners*, Chicago: University of Chicago Press.

Lash, S. and Urry, R. (1987) *The End of Organised Capitalism*, Cambridge: Polity Press.

Lash, S. and Urry, R. (1994) *Economies of Signs and Space*, London: Sage.

Lien, M. (2000) 'Imagined cuisines: "Nation" and "market" as organising structures in Norwegian food marketing' in P. Jackson, M. Lowe, D. Miller and F. Mort (eds) *Commercial Cultures: Ecomomies, Practices, Spaces*, Oxford: Berg.

Lury, A. (1994) 'Advertising: Moving beyond the stereotypes' in R. Keat, N. Whiteley and N. Abercrombie (eds) *The Authority of the Consumer*, London: Routledge.

Lury, C. (1996) *Consumer Culture*, Cambridge: Polity Press.

MacInnes, J. (1998) *The End of Masculinity*, Buckingham: Open University Press

MacKenzie, J. (1987) 'The imperial pioneer and hunter and the British masculine stereotype in late Victorian and Edwardian times', in J.A. Mangan and J. Walvin (eds) *Manliness and Morality: Middle-Class Masculinity in Britain and America, 1800–1940*, Manchester: Manchester University Press.

McGuigan, J. (1992) *Cultural Populism*, London: Routledge.

McLuhan, M. and Fiore, Q. (1967) *The Medium is the Message*, London: Lane.

McNay, L. (1992) *Foucault and Feminism: Gender, Power and the Self*, Cambridge: Polity Press.

McRobbie, A. (1978) '"Jackie": An ideology of adolescent femininity', University of Birmingham, Centre for Contemporary Cultural Studies.

McRobbie, A. (ed.) (1994) *Postmodernism and Popular Culture*, London: Routledge.

McRobbie, A. (1998) *British Fashion Design: Rag Trade or Image Industry?* London: Routledge.

McRobbie, A. (1999a) *In the Culture Society: Art, Fashion and Popular Music*, London: Routledge

McRobbie, A. (1999b) '*More!* New sexualities in girls' and women's magazines', in A. McRobbie *In the Culture Society: Art, Fashion and Popular Music*, London: Routledge. Originally published in J. Curran, D. Morley and V. Walkerdine (eds) (1996) *Cultural Studies and Communications*, London: Edward Arnold.

McRobbie, A. (2002) 'From Holloway to Hollywood: Happiness at work in the new cultural economy?', in P. du Gay and M. Pryke (eds) *Cultural Economy*, London: Sage.

Marx, K. and Engels, F. (1938) *The German Ideology*, London: Lawrence and Wishart.

Miller, D. (ed.) (1995) *Acknowledging Consumption: A Review of New Studies*, London: Routledge.

Mintel (1998) *Men's Lifestyle Magazines*, Mintel Intelligence.

Mort, F. (1988) 'Boy's own? Masculinity, style and popular culture' in R. Chapman and J. Rutherford (eds) *Male Order: Unwrapping Masculinity*, London: Lawrence and Wishart.

Mort, F. (1989) 'The politics of consumption' in S. Hall and M. Jacques (eds) *New Times*, London: Lawrence and Wishart.

Mort, F. (1996) *Cultures of Consumption: Masculinities and Social Space in Late Twentieth-Century Britain*, London: Routledge.

Munt, I. (1994) 'The "Other" postmodern tourism: Culture, travel and the new middle-classes', *Theory, Culture and Society*, 11, 101–23.

Murdock, G. (1982) 'Large corporations and the control of the communications industries' in M. Gurevitch, T. Bennett, J. Curran and J. Woollacott (eds) *Culture, Society and the Media*: Routledge.

Murdock, G. (1997) 'Cultural studies at the crossroads?' in A. McRobbie (ed.) *Back to Reality? Social Experience and Cultural Studies*, Manchester: Manchester University Press.

Murdock, G. and Golding, P. (1977) 'Capitalism, communication and class relations' in J. Curran, M. Gurevitch and J. Woollacott (eds) *Mass Communication and Society,* London: Edward Arnold.

Nava, M. (1997) 'Framing advertising: Cultural analysis and the incrimination of visual texts' in M. Nava, A. Blake, I. MacRury and B. Richards (eds) *Buy this Book: Studies in Advertising and Consumption* London: Routledge.

Neale, S. (1983) 'Masculinity as spectacle', *Screen*, 24 (6), 2–16.

Negus, K. (1992) *Producing Pop: Culture and Conflict in the Popular Music Industry*, London: Edward Arnold.

Negus, K. (2002) 'Identities and industries: The cultural formation of aesthetic economies' in P. du Gay and M. Pryke (eds) *Cultural Economy*, London: Sage.

Nixon, S. (1992) 'Have you got the look? Masculinities and shopping spectacle' in R. Shields (ed.) *Lifestyle Shopping: The Subject of Consumption*, London: Routledge.

Nixon, S. (1993) 'Looking for the Holy Grail: publishing and advertising strategies and contemporary men's magazines', *Cultural Studies*, 7 (3), 466–92.

Nixon, S. (1996) *Hard Looks: Masculinities, Spectatorship and Contemporary Consumption*, London: UCL Press.

Nixon, S. (1997) 'Circulating culture' in P. du Gay (ed.) *Production of Culture/ Cultures of Production*, London: Sage.

Nixon, S. (2001) 'Resignifying masculinity: From "new man" to "new lad" in D. Morley and K. Robins (eds) *British Cultural Studies*, Oxford: Oxford University Press.

Nixon, S. (2003) *Advertising Cultures: Gender, Commerce, Creativity*, London: Sage.

O'Hagan, S. (1991) 'Here comes the new lad! The unreconstructed man', *Arena*, (Spring-Summer 1991).

Osgerby, B. (2001) *Playboys in Paradise: Masculinity, Youth and Leisure-style in Modern America*, Oxford: Berg.

Peterson, R.A. (1976) 'The production of culture: A prolegomenon', *American Behavioural Scientist*, 19 (6), 669–84.

Peterson, R.A. (1994) 'Measured markets and unknown audiences: Case studies from the production and consumption of music' in J. Ettema and D.C. Whitney (eds) *Audiencemaking: How the Media Create the Audience*, London: Sage.

Peterson, R.A. and Berger, D. (1975) 'Cycles in symbol production: The case of popular music', *American Sociological Review*, 40, 158–73.

Peterson, R.A. and Simkus, A. (1992) 'How musical tastes mark occupational status groups' in M. Lamont and M. Fournier (eds) *Cultivating Differences*, Chicago: University of Chicago Press.

Piore, M.J. and Sabel, C.F. (1984) *The Second Industrial Divide*, New York: Basic Books.

Pumphrey, M. (1989) 'Why do cowboys wear hats in the bath? Style politics for the older man', *Critical Quarterly*, 31 (3), 78–100.

Radway, J. (1988) 'Reception study: Ethnography and the problems of dispersed audiences and nomadic subjects', *Cultural Studies*, 2 (3), 359–76.

Robb, J. (1999) *The Nineties: What the f**k was that all about?*, London: Ebury Press.

Roper, M. (1994) *Masculinity and the British Organisational Man since 1945*, Oxford: Oxford University Press.

Rutherford, J. (1988) 'Who's that man?' in R. Chapman and J. Rutherford (eds) *Male Order Unwrapping Masculinity*, London: Lawrence and Wishart.

Ryan, J. and Peterson, R. (1982) 'The product image: The fate of creativity in country music songwriting' in J. Ettema and D. Whitney (eds) *Individuals in Mass Media Organizations: Creativity and Constraint*. London. Sage.

Savage, M., Barlow, J., Dickens, P. and Fielding, T. (1992) *Property, Bureaucracy and Culture: Middle-Class Formation in Contemporary Britain*, London: Routledge.

Schlesinger, P. (1978) *Putting Reality Together*, London: Constable.

Schudson, M. (1991) 'The sociology of news production revisited' in J. Curran and M. Gurevitch (eds) *Mass Media and Society*, London: Edward Arnold.

Segal, L. (1990) *Slow Motion: Changing Men, Changing Masculinities*, London: Virago.

Simpson, M. (1994) *Male Impersonators: Men Performing Masculinity*, London: Routledge.

Slater, D. (2002) 'Capturing markets from the economists' in P. du Gay and M. Pryke (eds) *Cultural Economy*, London: Sage.

Southwell, T. (1998) *Getting Away With It: The Inside Story of Loaded*, London: Ebury Press.

Spencer, N. (1992) 'Menswear in the 1980s: Revolt into conformity' in J. Ash and E. Wilson (eds) *Chic Thrills: A Fashion Reader*, London: Pandora.

Stevenson, N., Jackson, P. and Brooks, K. (2000) 'Ambivalence in men's magazines' in P. Jackson, M. Lowe, D. Miller and F. Mort (eds) *Commercial Cultures: Ecomomies, Practices, Spaces*, Oxford: Berg.

Thompson, J.B. (1988) 'Mass communication and modern culture: Contribution to a critical theory of ideology', *Sociology*, 22 (3), 360–79.

Thornton, S. (1995) *Club Cultures: Music, Media and Subcultural Capital*, Cambridge: Polity Press.

Tolson, A. (1977) *The Limits of Masculinity*, London: Tavistock.

Tuchman, G., Daniels, A.K. and Benet, J. (eds) (1978) *Hearth and Home: Images of Women in the Mass Media*, Oxford: Oxford University Press.

Tunstall, J. (1971) *Journalists at Work*, London: Constable

Tunstall, J. (1996) *Newspaper Power: The New National Press in Britain*, Oxford: Clarendon Press.

Turner, G. (1990*) British Cultural Studies: An Introduction*, London: Unwin Hyman.

Turow, J. (1991) 'A mass communication perspective on entertainment industries' in J. Curran and M. Gurevitch (eds) (1991) *Mass Media and Society*, London: Edward Arnold.

Wernick, A. (1987) 'From voyeur to narcissist: Imaging men in contemporary advertising' in M. Kaufman (ed.) *Beyond Patriarchy: Essays by Men on Pleasure, Power and Change*, Oxford: Oxford University Press.

Whelehan, I. (2000) *Overloaded: Popular Culture and the Future of Feminism*, London: The Women's Press Ltd.

White, D.M. (1950) 'The "gate keeper": a case study in the selection of news', *Journalism Quarterly*, 27 (Fall), 383–90.

Willis, P. (1977) *Learning to Labour: How Working-class Kids Get Working-class Jobs*, Farnborough: Saxon House.

Winship, J. (1980) *Woman Becomes an 'Individual' – Femininity and Consumption in Women's Magazines 1954–1969*, Women's Series: SP No. 65, Birmingham Centre for Contemporary Cultural Studies.

Winship, J. (1983) '"Options – for the way you want to live now", or a magazine for superwoman', *Theory, Culture and Society*, 1 (3), 44–65.

Winship, J. (1987) *Inside Women's Magazines*, London: Pandora.

Wolfe, T. and Johnson, E.W. (1975) *The New Journalism*, London: Picador.

Wynne, D. (1998) *Leisure, Lifestyle and the New Middle-class: A Case Study*, London: Routledge.

Index